$4.50

THE THEOLOGY OF
WOLFHART PANNENBERG

THE THEOLOGY
OF
WOLFHART PANNENBERG

E. FRANK TUPPER

Postscript by Wolfhart Pannenberg

SCM PRESS LTD
BLOOMSBURY STREET LONDON

334 01636 3
First British edition 1974
published by SCM Press Ltd, 56 Bloomsbury Street, London
© The Westminster Press 1973
Type set in The United States of America
and printed in Great Britain by
Fletcher & Son Ltd, Norwich

CONTENTS

Part Two

PANNENBERG'S THEOLOGICAL PROGRAM

Part Three

PROBLEMS AND PROSPECTS

ABBREVIATIONS

AC   Wolfhart Pannenberg, *The Apostles' Creed: In the Light of Today's Questions,* tr. by Margaret Kohl (The Westminster Press, 1972).

BQiT   Wolfhart Pannenberg, *Basic Questions in Theology: Collected Essays,* tr. by George H. Kehm (Fortress Press, Vol. I, 1970; Vol. II, 1971).

IGaHF Wolfhart Pannenberg, *The Idea of God and Human Freedom,* tr. by R. A. Wilson (The Westminster Press, 1973).

JGaM   Wolfhart Pannenberg, *Jesus—God and Man,* tr. by Lewis L. Wilkins and Duane A. Priebe (The Westminster Press, 1968).

OaG   Wolfhart Pannenberg *et al., Offenbarung als Geschichte* [Revelation as History] (Göttingen: Vandenhoeck & Ruprecht, 1961; 2d ed., 1963).

RaH   Wolfhart Pannenberg *et al., Revelation as History,* tr. by David Granskou (The Macmillan Company, 1968).

TaH   James M. Robinson and John B. Cobb, Jr., eds., *Theology as History,* New Frontiers in Theology, Vol. III (Harper & Row, Publishers, Inc., 1967).

TaKoG Wolfhart Pannenberg, *Theology and the Kingdom of God,* ed. by Richard John Neuhaus (The Westminster Press, 1969).

WIM   Wolfhart Pannenberg, *What Is Man? Contemporary Anthropology in Theological Perspective,* tr. by Duane A. Priebe (Fortress Press, 1970).

11

BRITISH PUBLISHERS

of books cited in the footnotes and bibliography

Campenhausen, Hans Freiherr von, *Tradition and Life in the Church*, Collins 1968

Cullmann, Oscar, *Salvation in History*, SCM Press 1967

Evans, C. F., *Resurrection and the New Testament*, SCM Press 1970

Ferré, Frederick, *Language, Logic and God*, Eyre and Spottiswoode 1962

Fuller, R. H., *The Formation of the Resurrection Narratives*, SPCK 1972

Harvey, Van A., *The Historian and the Believer*, SCM Press 1967

Koch, Klaus, *The Rediscovery of Apocalyptic*, SCM Press 1972

Macquarrie, John, *Principles of Christian Theology*, SCM Press 1967

Moltmann, Jürgen, *Theology of Hope*, SCM Press 1967

Moule, C. F. D. (ed.), *The Significance of the Message of the Resurrection for Faith in Jesus Christ*, SCM Press 1968

Ogden, Schubert M., *The Reality of God*, SCM Press 1967

Pannenberg, Wolfhart, *The Apostles Creed*, SCM Press 1972
  Basic Questions in Theology, Vol. 1, SCM Press 1970
  Basic Questions in Theology, Vol. 2, SCM Press 1971
  Basic Questions in Theology, Vol. 3, SCM Press 1973
    (published in the USA under the title *The Idea of God and Human Freedom*, Westminster Press)
  Jesus: God and Man, SCM Press 1968

Perrin, Norman, *The Kingdom of God in the Teaching of Jesus*, SCM Press 1963

Rad, G. von, *Old Testament Theology* (Vols 1 and 2), Oliver and Boyd 1962, 1965

Tödt, Heinz, *The Son of Man in the Synoptic Tradition*, SCM Press 1965

Weiss, Johannes, *Jesus' Proclamation of the Kingdom of God*, SCM Press 1971

PREFACE

THE INNOVATIVE THEOLOGY of Wolfhart Pannenberg attracted my attention in 1966, when I began graduate study in Christian theology. Attention turned to interest and interest to enthusiasm as I discovered in Pannenberg's theology the comprehensive theological perspective I had been struggling to apprehend and to articulate. Since Pannenberg had only discussed specific theological themes in his numerous writings but had not published a systematic theology, I determined in 1968 that a systematic exposition of Pannenberg's theology was needed in order to facilitate an understanding of and an intelligent response to his new theological program. Thus from mid-1968 until late 1971 I devoted most of my energies to an analysis and critical assessment of Pannenberg's theology in fulfillment of doctoral dissertation requirements of the Southern Baptist Theological Seminary in Louisville, Kentucky. The present essay represents a thorough rewriting and reduction of the original dissertation, but the purpose remains the same—to produce a lucid and comprehensive exposition of the theoretical dimensions of Pannenberg's theology and to engage in the debate surrounding it on the basis of that systematic exposition.

Certain features of this book require explanation relative to the 1971 dissertation. First, while I have diligently attempted to interpret Pannenberg's theology fairly and faithfully, the systematic construction is not Pannenberg's own pattern of systematization—a structural limitation of which I am constantly aware. Second, the scope of this study had to be limited to the theoretical dimensions of Pannenberg's dogmatic theology. This limitation precluded an examination of his increasing attention to issues involving church life and Christian

13

ethics, and, in addition, permitted only an elementary analysis of his critical appropriation of Hegel's philosophy. Third, the expansive documentation that characterized the dissertation has been sharply reduced, especially with respect to comparative interpretations of crucial issues; nevertheless, basic alternatives to Pannenberg's approach are suggested in the representative criticisms of Part Three. Finally, whereas most of the dissertation research necessarily involved the study of Pannenberg's published writings in the original German, I have usually employed standard English translations in this book. Consistency and precision have occasionally required my own translation, but the English page references are then specified in brackets. In the case of *Offenbarung als Geschichte*, I have translated all citations and referred the reader to its published English translation, *Revelation as History*, exclusively through brackets.

Although I am entirely responsible for the contents of this analysis of Pannenberg's theology, I want to record my appreciation to several people who contributed significantly to my theological education and its culmination in this essay. Professor W. Boyd Hunt of Southwestern Baptist Theological Seminary, my first teacher of theology, taught me the importance of openness and provisionality when theologizing from a Biblical perspective. Again, I want to thank the faculty of the Southern Baptist Theological Seminary for accepting the original dissertation in partial fulfillment of the requirements for the doctor of theology degree, especially my graduate committee for the assistance and guidance they provided: Professors Eric C. Rust, David L. Mueller, William E. Hull, and James Leo Garrett.

I gladly acknowledge a special academic and personal indebtedness to Professor Wolfhart Pannenberg, who provided invaluable assistance during my year's study and research at the University of Munich in 1968–1969. He subsequently read the bulk of the original manuscript and strengthened it through many constructive suggestions. I am grateful for his generous help, though any blemishes that remain are my responsibility. Needless to say, I am delighted at his positive, thoughtful response to my work.

Words cannot adequately express my appreciation to Professor Dale Moody of Southern Baptist Theological Seminary. He personally guided my graduate studies and the writing of my dissertation with vigorous interest and considerable patience. Not only has he taught me more than anyone else, he has encouraged me to pursue my own theological synthesis, sometimes in contrast to his own theologizing;

nevertheless, his ecumenical spirit and wide-ranging scholarly insights have decisively shaped my theological perspective.

The original dissertation was affectionately dedicated to my friend and fellow churchman, Dr. Lawrence P. Emberton of Edmonton, Kentucky, whose stimulating insights have contributed significantly to my conception of theology in the life of the church. I dedicate this book to my wife, Betty, who has shared the agony and the ecstasy of my theological pilgrimage, and without whose encouragement and support this essay could not have been written.

E. F. T.

Part One

PROLEGOMENA
TO PANNENBERG'S THEOLOGY

I

THE TASK OF CONTEMPORARY SYSTEMATIC THEOLOGY

THE YEAR 1959 signaled the end of the theological epoch that had literally dominated Protestant theology since the publication of Barth's *Römerbrief* in 1919, namely, "the theology of the Word of God." In 1959—placing himself squarely in opposition to the reigning theologies of the day—Wolfhart Pannenberg proposed in his essay "Redemptive Event and History" a bold new "eschatological theology of history," affirming:

> History is the most comprehensive horizon of Christian theology. All theological questions and answers are meaningful only within the framework of the history which God has with humanity, and through humanity with his whole creation—a history directed toward a future still hidden from the world but already revealed in Jesus Christ. The presupposition [of history] for Christian theology must be defended today on two sides within theology itself: on the one side, against the existential theology of Bultmann and Gogarten, which dissolves history into the historicness of existence; on the other side, against the thesis that the actual content of faith is suprahistorical, a conception which was developed by Martin Kähler in the tradition of salvation history . . . and which is still living today especially in the form of Barth's interpretation of the incarnation as "prehistory." [1]

[1] "Heilsgeschehen und Geschichte," *Grundfragen systematischer Theologie* (Göttingen: Vandenhoeck & Ruprecht, 1967), p. 22 ["Redemptive Event and History," *BQiT* I, p. 15].

With these words Pannenberg formally launched a new and influential theological movement subsequently identified according to its different spokesmen and divergent emphases as "theology of hope," "theology of history," "theology of the future," "theology of the Kingdom of God," and "eschatological theology." In spite of the diversity which these indices reflect, however, the fact remains that Pannenberg's compelling new thrust initiated the breakthrough to the future in the 1960's.

The import of Pannenberg's position in 1959 accentuated the primacy of "real history" for understanding the promissory Biblical traditions and for formulating Christian theology. Yet the centrality of the conception of promise and fulfillment as well as the prominence of apocalypticism in the emerging theology indicated a conception of history decisively stamped by eschatology: Pannenberg's reconception of revelation and history was predicated upon the reactivation of the future tense in eschatology. Hence, the new direction was more than a *return* to history, it was a decisive *turn* toward an eschatological theology of history. To be sure, many factors converged in the late 1950's to effect the theological "turn to the future," but Pannenberg's innovative projection constitutes the first and primary stimulus toward contemporary "eschatological theology."[2]

Pannenberg advances a conception of Christian theology that accentuates the horizon of eschatology but that roots in the realities of history. However, he does not arbitrarily project an eschatological theology of history but carefully, even painstakingly, constructs a theology oriented to the post-Enlightenment situation on the one side, yet anchored in the promissory history of the Biblical traditions on the other. The rationale for Pannenberg's developing theological program reflects his estimate of the problematic task of theology today, which is "to take the responsibility for speaking about God in critical thought."[3] Since the Enlightenment critique of the authority of traditions greatly intensifies the problem of religious belief, theology must strive to justify the trustworthiness of the claims of the Christian

---

[2] The author's independently conceived judgment has been confirmed by Carl E. Braaten, "The New Theology of the Future," in *The Futurist Option*, by Carl E. Braaten and R. W. Jenson (Paulist/Newman Press, 1970), p. 11; and, with specific reference to apocalypticism, by Klaus Koch, *The Rediscovery of Apocalyptic*, Studies in Biblical Theology, 2d ser., No. 22, tr. by Margaret Kohl (Alec R. Allenson, Inc., 1972). Koch says: "With Pannenberg the renaissance of apocalyptic in post-war theology begins" (p. 101).

[3] "Response to the Discussion," *TaH*, p. 241.

kerygma whereon faith lives. Hence, theological knowledge, the goal of theological research, makes its contribution to faith when it convincingly provides reasons for the decision of faith. Pannenberg argues that theology has always performed this fundamental task:

> Therefore theology has to deal with the presupposition of faith, with the truth and reliability (already presupposed in the act of faith) of the "object" on which faith depends. Of course it can do this only in a provisional way. The truth or untruth of faith is not decided primarily in the act of faith; rather this decision depends on faith's object, which contains the promise in which faith trusts, and which is also the object of theological knowledge. . . . Therefore it is the business of theological knowledge to confirm the truth which is presupposed for faith and on which it trusts.[4]

Yet Pannenberg defines the task of theology that speaks responsibly of God as universal in scope: "A theology that remains conscious of the intellectual obligation that goes along with the use of the word 'God' will try in every possible way to relate all truth, and therefore not least of all the knowledge of the extra-theological sciences, to the God of the Bible, and to attain a new understanding of everything by viewing it in the light of this God." [5] However, the goal of theology is not primarily to persuade the "modern world" of the truth of Christian faith but Christians themselves, who require confidence in the reliability of the Christian message. Although there will always be a "world" that does not consider the claims of Christian faith convincing, Pannenberg insists that "the question is whether the Christians themselves can be validly convinced of the universal validity of this message—and can also convince, to be sure not 'the modern world,' but indeed individual thinking persons." [6]

THE CONTOURS OF PANNENBERG'S PILGRIMAGE

Wolfhart Pannenberg was born in 1928 in Stettin, Germany (now Poland).[7] While baptized into the church, he was not reared as a

[4] *Ibid.*, p. 271.
[5] "The Crisis of the Scripture Principle," *BQiT* I, pp. 1-2.
[6] Letter cited by James M. Robinson, "Revelation as Word and History," *TaH*, p. 89.
[7] Cf. Richard John Neuhaus' biographical portrait, "Wolfhart Pannenberg: Profile of a Theologian," *TaKoG*, pp. 9-50.

devout Lutheran; instead, he spent his youth largely outside the sphere of Christian influence among people who sought fulfillment in life quite apart from God. As the son of a loyal civil servant, he participated patriotically as a teen-ager in the efforts to defend Germany during the last, desperate days of the Third Reich. After World War II, Pannenberg began university studies in Berlin, then moved in 1948 to Göttingen for instruction in philosophy under Nicolai Hartmann. Yet these postwar days meant more to young Wolfhart Pannenberg than simply the continuation of his formal education, for these university days of serious philosophical reflection marked a decidedly intellectual movement to Christian affirmation.

In 1950 Pannenberg traveled to Basel to study with philosopher Karl Jaspers and theologian Karl Barth. While strongly influenced by Barth, Pannenberg reacted against him at several crucial, interrelated points. Unlike Barth, Pannenberg was compelled to affirm: (1) Systematic theology must be rigorously committed to and essentially informed by a critical, historical study of the Bible. (2) Avoiding an authoritarian posture, the church must subject its theology to the canons of rationality operative in the larger human community: The gospel must be grounded in public evidence instead of supernaturalism or a subjective decision of faith. (3) To relate itself positively to the whole of reality, Christian theology must regain its universality through extensive dialogue with general, nontheological thought. Though the impact of Barth upon Pannenberg should not be minimized, these non-Barthian affirmations provided him with a different frame of reference for his subsequent theological maturation.

Turning in 1951 toward the historical disciplines associated with the University of Heidelberg, Pannenberg entered one of the most formative stages of his intellectual pilgrimage. During the seven years he spent at Heidelberg several factors converged and decisively influenced the shape of his theological program.

Probably the most important aspect of Pannenberg's experience at Heidelberg was his participation in a discussion group of graduate students which crystallized into "the working circle" that advanced a unique "theological conception of history." The formation of the interdisciplinary group was essentially a response to the impasse that characterized modern theology at the end of World War II—an impasse reflected in the chasm between Bultmann's critical interpretation of the New Testament and Barth's theological exposition of church dogmatics. Meeting once a week to discuss issues involving the whole theological enterprise, the students comprising the circle—Rolf Rendtorff (Old Testament), Klaus Koch (Old Testament), Ulrich Wilckens (New Testament), Dietrich Rössler (New Testament), Wolfhart Pannenberg (Systematic Theology)[8]—sought to forge an integrated theological program informed by the various insights of the several theological disciplines. Later Martin Elze (Church History) and Trutz Rendtorff (Church and Society) joined the group. Encouraged by their Heidelberg professors, namely, Hans von Campenhausen, Gerhard von Rad, and Günther Bornkamm, the circle eventually broke free of Barth and Bultmann and began considering new answers to the old question of "faith and history." The group wrestled periodically with the role of apocalypticism in the development of the Biblical traditions. A conception of "revelation as history" suggesting a distinct theological program gradually emerged. Finally, the circle published its unique interpretation of revelation in an interdisciplinary collection of essays appropriately entitled *Revelation as History* (first German ed., 1961),[9] the first supplementary volume of *Kerygma und Dogma*. Though Pannenberg credited Rolf Rendtorff with the "initial impulse" toward the concept of God revealing himself indirectly through historical events,[10] unfortunately and contrary to his wishes, "the working circle" was identified in subsequent theological debate as "the Pannenberg circle," because, as systematician, he provided the overall synthesis for the exegetical and historical work of the others. While other publications might have been expected, this symposium on revelation—the group's first and only joint publication—has come to represent the circle's project in team theology as nothing else. Indeed, the circle continued to convene regularly for several years, but "the theological circle originally of Heidelberg" is not so close-knit today as it was in the 1950's and early 1960's. Pannenberg reports that the circle ceased meeting regularly in 1969, largely because

[8] Although Pannenberg joined the group shortly after its inception, it originated with the four students engaged in Biblical studies, of whom Robert Wilken says: "All four were interested in exegetical-historical questions, all were followers of Bultmann, and all were more or less shaped by problems in hermeneutics" ("Who Is Wolfhart Pannenberg?" *Dialog*, Vol. IV [1965], p. 140).

[9] Pannenberg *et al.*, *Revelation as History*, tr. by David Granskou (The Macmillan Company, 1968). A translation of *Offenbarung als Geschichte* (Göttingen: Vandenhoeck & Ruprecht, 1961).

[10] "Nachwort zur zweiten Auflage," *OaG*, p. 132, n. 1. Pannenberg also repudiated primacy within the circle in his negative response to Lothar Steiger, who had designated the program of the circle as Pannenberg's "personal system."

of differences of opinion about the historicity and fundamental significance of Jesus' resurrection—differences that eliminated the basis for continuing teamwork.

The influence of the theology faculty constituted yet another significant dimension of Pannenberg's experience at the University of Heidelberg. Hans von Campenhausen exerted creative impact upon Pannenberg and "the working circle" through his 1947 rectoral address, "Augustine and the Fall of Rome," wherein he called for an interdisciplinary theological interpretation of history that would present Jesus' life and destiny as the all-embracing center of world history. In addition, von Campenhausen's affirmation of the importance of the historical event of Jesus' resurrection for Christian theology positively affected the position of the circle.[11] Furthermore, the work of Old Testament scholar Gerhard von Rad decisively influenced the members of "the working circle." Interpreting Israel's history as "the history of the transmission of traditions," von Rad provided the circle with the methodological insight for overcoming the cleft between a kerygmatic and a historical-critical reconstruction of Israel's history, i.e., the general theological distinction between "inner" and "outer" history. Consequently, von Rad's conception of history as the process of the transmission of traditions has proven integral to Pannenberg's understanding of the unity of historical event and its meaning.[12]

Again, New Testament scholar Günther Bornkamm impressed "the working circle" with his early criticism of Bultmann[13] and with his post-Bultmannian concern for relating the kerygma to the historical Jesus. Moving beyond Bornkamm, however, Pannenberg interpreted "the history of Jesus" to include the resurrection and found in Jesus' history the ground and criterion for the church's kerygma. Finally,

[11] Hans von Campenhausen, Tradition and Life in the Church: Essays and Lectures in Church History, tr. by A. V. Littledale (Fortress Press, 1968), pp. 201–216 and pp. 42–89. James M. Robinson, "Revelation as Word and History," TaH, pp. 7–10, 25, accurately portrays "the working circle" as fulfilling the vision of von Campenhausen.

[12] Gerhard von Rad, Old Testament Theology, 2 vols., tr. by D. M. G. Stalker (Harper & Row, Publishers, Inc., 1962–1966). Cf. Pannenberg, "Kerygma and History," BQiT I, pp. 81–95.

[13] Günther Bornkamm, "Myth and Gospel," in Kerygma and History: A Symposium on the Theology of Rudolf Bultmann, tr. and ed. by Carl E. Braaten and Roy A. Harrisville (Abingdon Press, 1962), p. 192. Cf. Pannenberg, "Redemptive Event and History," BQiT I, p. 24. James M. Robinson reports in "Revelation as Word and History," TaH, p. 22, n. 66, that Bornkamm has expressed reservations concerning his previous formulation of Bultmann's position and has questioned specifically the use Pannenberg made of it.

Pannenberg is indebted to the confessional Lutheran theologian Edmund Schlink. Not only did Schlink provide Pannenberg with the concept of the doxological structure of language about God,[14] he offered Pannenberg an example of the ecumenical posture the Christian theologian should assume amid the divisions of the contemporary Christian church.

Pannenberg completed his doctor's degree under the supervision of Schlink in 1953 with a dissertation published in 1954, *Die Prädestinationslehre des Duns Skotus*, and he passed his *Habilitation* in 1955 with *Analogie und Offenbarung*, a critical examination of the role of analogy in the knowledge of God from early Greek philosophy to Thomas Aquinas. Pannenberg's academic investment and expertise in pre-Reformation theology, especially patristics and scholasticism, lie behind his continuing critical involvement with several concerns typical of premodern theology, namely, the role of analogy in speaking of God, the problem of predestination and human freedom, and the universality of Christian theology. Appointed *Privatdozent* in systematic theology at the University of Heidelberg in 1955, Pannenberg lectured for the next three years on the history of theology in the nineteenth century, engaging in constructive "debate" with pivotal thinkers of the past—Schleiermacher and Ritschl, Hegel and Troeltsch. Moving behind dialectical theology in the attempt to produce a new theological synthesis, Pannenberg entered still another notable phase of his Heidelberg experience: he became increasingly conscious of and impressed by the massive intellectual achievement of Hegel.[15] Although he recognized the limitations of Hegel's philosophy, Pannenberg saw that Hegel's understanding of truth as history and its corollary of universal history (not incompatible with the universalism of apocalypticism) offered the Christian theologian a unique opportunity for interpreting the Biblical faith. Therefore, a critical dialogue with the giants of nineteenth-century theology, especially Hegel, became one of Pannenberg's central concerns as he sought to forge a reconception of Christian theology.

In 1958 Pannenberg left Heidelberg to accept an invitation to the church seminary at Wuppertal as professor of systematic theology.

---

[14] Edmund Schlink, *The Coming Christ and the Coming Church*, tr. by J. H. Neilson *et al.* (Edinburgh: Oliver and Boyd, Ltd., 1967), pp. 16–84. Cf. esp. Pannenberg, "Analogy and Doxology," *BQiT* I, pp. 211–238.

[15] Cf. "What Is Truth?" *BQiT* II, pp. 21–26; "The Significance of Christianity in the Philosophy of Hegel," *IGaHF*, pp. 144–177.

During the three years he taught at Wuppertal he published the essay "Redemptive Event and History" and developed the substance of both his anthropology and Christology. Moreover, Jürgen Moltmann joined the faculty there, giving Pannenberg the opportunity for dialogue with a theologian of similar interests. However, unlike Moltmann, Pannenberg had not been influenced by the Marxist philosophy of Ernst Bloch. He read Bloch's massive *Das Prinzip Hoffnung* only after completing the initial draft of *Jesus—God and Man;* consequently, Pannenberg should not be indiscriminately lumped with Moltmann as "a theologian of hope" stimulated by the futuristic philosophy of Ernst Bloch. Rather than an "influence" upon Pannenberg, Bloch's philosophy of hope represented a provocative "confluence" with Pannenberg's own eschatological vision of universal history.[16]

Moving to the University of Mainz as systematician in 1961, Pannenberg became a pivotal figure in German theological debate as the editor of the controversial symposium *Revelation as History.* Additional publications followed: *What Is Man?* (first German ed., 1962);[17] *Jesus—God and Man* (first German ed., 1964);[18] *Basic Questions in Theology* (German ed., 1967).[19] Though he declined an invitation to Heidelberg as the first occupant of a chair in philosophy of religion, Pannenberg subsequently accepted the post of professor of systematic theology at the University of Munich in 1968. His publications have continued: *Theology and the Kingdom of God* (1969); *Reformation zwischen gestern und morgen* (1969); *Erwägungen zu einer Theologie der Natur* (1970); *Thesen zur Theologie der Kirche* (1970); "The Later Dimensions of Myth in Biblical and Christian Tradition" (Ger-

---

[16] The tendency to identify Bloch as Pannenberg's philosophical conversation partner derives in part from the latter's praise of Bloch in "The God of Hope" (1965): "Perhaps Christian theology will one day have to thank Ernst Bloch's philosophy of hope for giving it the courage to recover in the full sense its central category of eschatology. . . . He has recovered the biblical tradition's eschatological mode of thought as a theme for philosophical reflection and also for Christian theology" (*BQiT* II, pp. 237–238).

[17] Pannenberg, *What Is Man? Contemporary Anthropology in Theological Perspective,* tr. by Duane A. Priebe (Fortress Press, 1970). A translation of *Was ist der Mensch? Die Anthropologie der Gegenwart im Lichte der Theologie* (Göttingen: Vandenhoeck & Ruprecht, 1962; 2d ed., 1964).

[18] Pannenberg, *Jesus—God and Man,* tr. by Lewis L. Wilkins and Duane A. Priebe (The Westminster Press, 1968). A translation of *Grundzüge der Christologie* (Gütersloh: Gütersloher Verlagshaus Gerd Mohn, 1964).

[19] Pannenberg, *Basic Questions in Theology: Collected Essays,* 2 vols., tr. by George H. Kehm (Fortress Press, 1970–1971). A translation of *Grundfragen systematischer Theologie* (Göttingen: Vandenhoeck & Ruprecht, 1967).

man ed., 1971); *The Idea of God and Human Freedom* (German ed., 1972);[20] *The Apostles' Creed: In the Light of Today's Questions* (1972); plus numerous other articles and essays. In addition, he has promised a volume on the "Theology of Reason," presently in lecture form.

The emergence of Pannenberg as a reputable Continental theologian worthy of serious consideration did not go unnoticed in America. The University of Chicago invited him to teach as guest professor during the spring of 1963. Pannenberg accepted the Chicago summons and similar invitations from Harvard University and the School of Theology at Claremont in 1966–1967. Moreover, during these extended visits he lectured widely in other theological schools around the United States. Pannenberg's impact upon American theologians began to materialize in the latter half of the 1960's, perhaps most conspicuously in the writings of Carl E. Braaten.[21] But the most important affirmation of Pannenberg's significance for the American scene was the selection of his theology as the subject for Volume III of the series New Frontiers in Theology. This symposium, *Theology as History* (1967), effected a sometimes engaging (but somewhat disappointing) dialogue between Pannenberg and the American contributors. The conversation has been more recently advanced by the translation of Pannenberg's most important works and the publication of several essays in English on pertinent theological themes. Pannenberg himself continues to demonstrate unusual openness to American theological trends and to respond positively to the insights of his American critics.

THE CHALLENGE OF ATHEISM

Since Christian theology cannot remain aloof from the assumptions of its own epoch, Pannenberg considers mandatory a critical and convincing response to the challenge of secular atheism in the modern period. Though atheism itself is not new, the scope and the form of contemporary atheism reflect the peculiarities of modern Western

---

[20] Pannenberg, *The Idea of God and Human Freedom* (including the essay "The Later Dimensions of Myth in Biblical and Christian Tradition"), tr. by R. A. Wilson (The Westminster Press, 1973). This is a translation of *Gottesgedanke und menschliche Freiheit* (Göttingen: Vandenhoeck & Ruprecht, 1972) and of "Späthorizonte des Mythos in biblischer und christlicher Überlieferung" from *Terror und Spiel: Probleme der Mythenrezeption* (Munich: Wilhelm Fink Verlag, 1971), pp. 473–525.

[21] Cf. Carl E. Braaten, *The Future of God: The Revolutionary Dynamics of Hope* (Harper & Row, Publishers, Inc., 1969).

thought. Hence, Pannenberg delineates three types of modern atheism, analyzes other theological responses to them, and indicates the issues that yet require solution.

The Atheism of the Science of Religion

The presupposition of contemporary atheism roots in the mechanistic world picture of classical physics, which eliminated the necessity of a "creator" to explain the origin and existence of the universe. However, the establishment of an atheistic metaphysic demanded more than the *possibility* of understanding the world and human existence in themselves; in addition, it required the *demonstration* "that there is no truth in religious assertions about the existence of divine beings." [22] The significance of Feuerbach emerges here, for prior to Feuerbach atheism appeared only as an alternative assertion. But through his genetic theory of religion he provided the "proof" of atheism, showing that the idea of God is the product of the imagination of man. Thus the atheism of Feuerbach's science of religion is the first complete form of atheism, i.e., the first self-contained atheistic metaphysic.

Pannenberg specifies two central elements in Feuerbach's theory of religion: the infinity of the essence of man and the Hegelian concept of estrangement. The infinity of man is expressed in reason, will, and love—powers that drive the individual beyond himself toward the realization of the infinite essence of man in one's own life. However, since man is conscious of himself, a distinction between the ego and the object of consciousness emerges. Aware of his own finitude, Feuerbach argued, man interprets the infinite essence of which he is conscious as another essence, as "God." This illusion issues from the individual's interpretation of the limitations of his own finitude as limitations of humanity itself; hence, alienated from his own human essence, man projects his infinite essence as superhuman, as God. Though Feuerbach modified his position somewhat, these fundamental elements endured as the crux of his atheistic metaphysic.

Christian theology pursued two paths in the attempt to counter Feuerbach's critique of religion. As representative of the first, Karl Barth accepted Feuerbach's critique but insisted that it applied only to man's religions and not to revelatory Christian faith. Rather than beginning at the anthropological starting point of the nineteenth

22 "Types of Atheism and Their Theological Significance," *BQiT* II, p. 185.

century, Pannenberg observes, Barth proclaimed a radical shift, "the restoration of the irreversibility of the relationship with God, which always had to be conceived as proceeding from above to below, from God to man." [23] Yet Pannenberg argues that such a response to Feuerbach is inadequate and evasive.

> Theology has to learn that after Feuerbach it can no longer mouth the word "God" without offering any explanation; that it can no longer speak as if the meaning of this word were self-evident; that it cannot pursue theology "from above," as Barth says, if it does not want to fall into the hopeless and, what is more, self-inflicted isolation of a higher glossolalia, and lead the whole church into this blind alley.[24]

Ernst Troeltsch represents the alternative response to Feuerbach, for he sought to refute Feuerbach's analysis of religion and religious experience. Utilizing religious psychology, Troeltsch perceived a "deeper core" in the religious concepts of God, which roots in a nonarbitrary *original datum of consciousness*. Troeltsch finally realized the inadequacy of religious psychology to substantiate the truth of religious experiences, and he recognized the necessity of constructing a philosophical anthropology as a foundation for such experiences. Unfortunately, however, he conceived the transcendental foundation of religious experience in a theory of "religious *a priori*." Conversely, Pannenberg suggests, if theology were to use Hegelian concepts as Feuerbach himself did, perhaps it could surpass Feuerbach's critique by relating the concept of God to a more penetrating understanding of man.

The Atheism of Freedom

The depth of Feuerbach's atheism contains an understanding of man as the being who absolutely has power over himself—an anthropology that motivates another form of atheism, the atheism of human freedom. Friedrich Nietzsche expounded its basic characteristic in terms of the will to power, namely, the rejection of the religious reduction of man and the elevation of his consciousness of power. Pannenberg analyzes the conceptual transition thusly: "Here, atheism has

---

[23] *Ibid.*, p. 189.
[24] *Ibid.*, pp. 189–190.

developed from a matter of mere enlightenment—as in Feuerbach—into a matter of the will, of self-affirmation." [25]

Theology cannot easily dismiss Nietzsche's atheism, Pannenberg argues, for it was the logical consequence of the tendency of the modern metaphysics of subjectivity. Just as post-Cartesian metaphysics had related all truth to the self-certainty of the subject, Nietzsche oriented all truth to the value judgment of the subjective will. Hence, God could only appear as value, which is the intrinsic root of Nietzsche's atheism. But Pannenberg reasons: "God as the *highest value* is already a posit [*Setzung*] of the human will, and a departure from the deity of God." [26] The strength of Nietzsche's position emerges over against the contemporaneous neo-Kantian theology of the Ritschlian school, which understood God as the postulate of the practical reason and the divinity of Christ as religious value judgment: Both Ritschlian theology and Nietzsche's atheism were founded upon the common presupposition that religious statements are subjective judgments of the valuating will, but they clashed in the consequences of man's self-affirmation—Ritschl decided for God and Nietzsche against God.

The similarity of the valuation of the will between Nietzsche and the Ritschlian school explains Barth's interest in Nietzsche as he struggled with his Ritschlian heritage. Yet Pannenberg argues that a retreat into supernaturalism is not the solution, for supernaturalistic talk of God ultimately depends on the subjective decision of faith. Observing a line running from Tholuck's union of pietistic supernaturalism and Kantianism through Ritschl and Herrmann on the one side, Kähler on the other, to Barth and Bultmann, Pannenberg perceives the common denominator to be the "practical" necessity—or, in modern terms, the "decision" of faith—which motivates a leap into supernatural truth. But he contends: "Nietzsche cannot be overcome along such lines, however, because wherever faith as decision is constitutive for the truth of its contents, one has not yet departed from the basis of Nietzsche's position, his metaphysic of the will." [27] This position can be surpassed only by a more radical inquiry into being (as Heidegger observes). Theology, therefore, must formulate its conception of God in relation to the philosophical question of being, taking account of the subjectivity of modern man, his sovereignty over nature, and his self-transcendence.

[25] *Ibid.*, p. 193.
[26] *Ibid.*, p. 194.
[27] *Ibid.*, p. 195.

31

The Atheism of Empty Transcendence

The impossibility of a revival of the old premodern God-world-metaphysic illuminates a third type of contemporary atheism, that is, "the *hiddenness of God* or the emergence of transcendence as the cultural-historical destiny of the modern period." [28] The hiddenness of God—the inaccessibility of God for human thought and judgment—has two roots. The *Biblical* root accentuates God's hiddenness in the freedom of his activity over against the norms of human foresight, and the *Neoplatonic* root emphasizes the incomprehensibility of the world-ground which lies beyond the phenomenal world of appearances. To be sure, the hiddenness or inaccessibility of God is not synonymous with atheism. In the modern metaphysics of subjectivity, however, for which the structure of cosmological thought has disintegrated, the experience of God's hiddenness has been intensified. When all the contents of consciousness are bound to the finitude of consciousness, not only is the infinity of God incomprehensible, but the deity of the infinite becomes completely inconceivable. The radical consequences of the reduction of all contents of consciousness to finite subjectivity emerged in Fichte's atheistic controversy, for he demonstrated that self-consciousness experienced finitely could not be ascribed to the infinite. Pannenberg believes Fichte's declaration to mark the end of theism and its concept of God as infinite, self-conscious person.

The reduction of all contents of consciousness to man's subjectivity meant the dissolution of God and religion to mythical projections, to the self-representations of man. Hence, religious conceptions have been continually described in categories similar to Feuerbach's, namely, as the expression of human experience and activity. Whether or not the religious activity of man has presuppositions other than those Feuerbach described has become the crucial question. Though Heidegger has attempted to conceive existence from the horizon of being that human existence presupposes, he is unable to identify this being as "God." The interpenetration of being and nothingness in Heidegger's thought seems more commensurate with "empty transcendence," which one finds in Jaspers and Bloch. But the question of God that human existence raises remains unanswered. If such an open position is designated atheism, Pannenberg concludes, it represents a very different kind, for the triumphant note is absent. Yet the question of

[28] *Ibid.*, p. 196.

God remains open, because a return to a theistic world view is not possible. Early dialectical theology approached this position with its emphasis upon God's nonobjectifiability—a situation that motivated Bultmann to formulate theological statements only as statements of man in relation to God, and Barth to deepen God's nonobjectifiability through the concepts of crisis and the theology of the cross. Yet the problem of the nonobjectification of God urgently poses the question of any speaking of God, of the possibility of any revelation of God. Hence, Pannenberg observes:

> Bultmann retreated into existentialist interpretation, although at a decisive point he still continued to speak in a quasi-mythological way of "God's act." Barth, however, effected a leap into the biblical supranaturalism of *Church Dogmatics*. Nevertheless, the problem of the early dialectical theology still remains. *Theology can meet the atheism of* "empty transcendence," for which the theistic world of thought is no longer negotiable, *only if it thinks through in all its consequences the biblically grounded idea of the hiddenness of God* as hiddenness even in his revelation.[29]

Ultimately, when modern atheism affirms simultaneously transcendence and the emptiness of transcendence, it calls itself into question, revealing its negation as essentially the rejection of the traditional concept of God. What God might be beyond the traditional concept remains an open question. Though theological controversy with atheism in the sphere of anthropology cannot get beyond the explication of this question, man's encounter with the transcendent as personal remains the subject of the history of religions and, finally, of revelation.

The Crisis of Theology

The responses of theology to modern forms of atheism intimate the crisis within theology itself, i.e., the crisis of the self-understanding of Christian theology. The crisis is multidimensional—involving simultaneously questions of methodology and identity. Pannenberg addresses himself to the crisis in relation to the history of modern theology.

[29] *Ibid.*, p. 199.

The Crisis of Authority

While neo-orthodoxy has its theological antecedent in the Reformation, Pannenberg believes theology must be essentially post-Enlightenment. Indeed, the post-Enlightenment era remains the consequence of the Reformation, albeit unintended, but the modern period is distinguishable from the Reformation era.[30] Specifically, Pannenberg argues, prior to the Enlightenment Christian theology was a revelatory theology anchored in the supernatural authority of the Bible, the divinely inspired "Word of God." Though the neo-orthodox theology of the twentieth century did not seek the Word of God primarily in the Bible, it sought to maintain the authority of the "Word." Hence, Pannenberg observes:

> [The "Word"] was found rather in the event of Christian proclamation, in the kerygma (Bultmann), or else in Jesus' history, also interpreted as the "Word" of God, which as revelation is the origin both of the word of the Bible and the word of proclamation (Barth). *In both cases the authoritarian character of the appeal to revelation remained untouched.* But for men who live in the sphere in which the Enlightenment becomes effective, authoritarian claims are no longer acceptable, in intellectual as little as in political life. All authoritarian claims are on principle subject to the suspicion that they clothe human thoughts and institutions with the splendor of divine majesty. Thus they are defenseless against the reproach of interchanging the divine and the human, and to the accusation of absolutizing what in truth is finite in content, with the result of subjugating all other men to those who represent this authority.[31]

While man's coming of age on the basis of the Enlightenment does not make all religion and talk of God superfluous, those forms of religion which depend essentially upon authoritarian claims of revelation and exempt themselves from critical inquiry appear increasingly incredible. Pannenberg indicates that he finally "turned away from the 'theology of the Word of God' in its present-day forms," because

---

[30] Pannenberg, *Reformation zwischen gestern und morgen* (Gütersloh: Gütersloher Verlagshaus Gerd Mohn, 1969), pp. 13–18, contends that the modern concept of "the self-determination of man" attained central significance in the Enlightenment over against its subservience to the authority of Scripture in the Reformation.

[31] "Response to the Discussion," *TaH*, p. 226. Italics added.

he saw in it "only the modern expression of such an authoritarian theology of revelation." [32] To be sure, authoritarian forms of tradition occupy a significant place in the Old and New Testaments, but documents from any historical period characterized by authoritarian social and political structures could hardly appear differently. Such authoritarian motifs stamped the Christian tradition beyond Biblical times throughout the history of the Christian church—in the medieval understanding of episcopacy and the papacy, in the positivism of the Reformation's *sola scriptura,* and in the neo-orthodox characterization of faith as "obedience." Conversely, the legacy of the Enlightenment champions the freedom of the human spirit beyond all "established" traditions, ultimately, as the demand of liberating Christian faith.

Though the Biblical texts often reflect authoritarian features, Pannenberg thinks the basic ingredients in the Biblical experience of God are independent of such restrictive elements. Hence, the initial requirement of the interpreter of the Biblical tradition is not to demythologize but to remove the authoritarian forms of the premodern Christian tradition. Pannenberg argues: "Only after such *depositivization* would it be possible to determine the extent to which a 'demythologization' would still be necessary, or whether the latter would not already be accomplished in the over-all task of the former." [33]

The crucial question that the Enlightenment critique of religious traditions thrusts upon theology is the question of the revelation of God and, finally, of the reality of God himself. The question of revelation formulated within the sphere of the Enlightenment cannot be answered by an appeal to an established authority, i.e., to a supposedly "self-evident" tradition, but only by a manifestation of divine reality which convinces man's matured understanding and judgment. Yet the test of critical reason does not automatically disqualify the revelatory traditions of the Old and New Testaments, for the Biblical writings, as they understand themselves, actually seem to emerge from the self-manifestation of divine reality. Pannenberg declares:

> Such self-manifestation . . . may have been much more fundamental for the Israelite and Christian bearers of tradition than all the authoritarian features of their thought and of

[32] *Ibid.,* p. 227.
[33] *Ibid.,* p. 228. Cf. esp. Pannenberg, "The Later Dimensions of Myth in Biblical and Christian Tradition," *IGaHF,* pp. 1–79.

their ways of handing down tradition. Indeed, the self-manifestation of divine reality *in a preauthoritarian* sense was a
central *theme* of Israelite and early Christian thought.[34]

While all categories of divine manifestation are of interest to the
history of religions, modern philosophy of religion and systematic
theology seek a self-manifestation of divine reality that is able to
convince post-Enlightenment man as the deity's self-confirmation of
his reality. Pannenberg contends: "Against all the deities *claimed* by
the religions, the doubt is directed whether they can also be regarded
by us as God, as the power over everything." [35] Hence, the question of
revelation is the question of those experiences that permit an individual to trust "everything" to a specific deity claimed by others;
correspondingly, it is the question of whether it is possible to "conceive" a deity alleged to be the power over everything. Unlike those
limited forms of divine manifestation which were convincing to their
immediate recipients in the past, e.g., epiphanies, modern man requires the self-confirmation of God through his action as the power
over everything. Therefore, the contemporary problem of revelation
seeks a convincing self-manifestation of God, a revelation that is by
definition universal. Such a revelation would not depend upon an
authoritarian tradition but would be susceptible to and could be
appropriated by the critical understanding of modern man.

The Crisis of Scripture

The crisis of authority presupposes another crisis, sometimes disputed, that confronts Christian theology—namely, the crisis of Scripture.
Pannenberg declares: "The dissolution of the traditional doctrine of
Scripture constitutes a crisis at the very foundation of modern Protestant theology." [36] The point of departure for the transformation and
fragmentation of Protestant theology accomplished through the influence of historical consciousness can be found in the relationship of
the "Scripture principle" to historical-critical exegesis.

Luther and the other Reformers shared the conviction that Holy
Scripture is the ultimate criterion of doctrine. Though the Reforma-
tion churches demonstrate considerable diversity, Pannenberg notes:
"The decisive common denominator was the conviction of the Re-

[34]"Response to the Discussion," *TaH,* p. 230. Italics added.
[35] *Ibid.,* pp. 231–232.
[36] "The Crisis of the Scripture Principle," *BQiT* I, p. 4.

formers that the Word of God himself, his Law and his promise, is to
be found in the Bible." [37] Luther and the Protestant dogmaticians
were able to understand the Bible as the authoritative Word of God
because they accepted the ancient doctrine of the inspiration of Scripture, which "meant that the Holy Spirit—hence, God himself—is the
actual author of the Biblical writings." [38] Indeed, Luther usually referred inspiration and thus the authority of Scripture to its "essential
content," namely, the person and history of Jesus Christ. Thus, while
affirming divine inspiration, he criticized specific statements and entire
books by reference to Christ. Yet Luther's appeal to the Bible as God's
Word remained established in the conviction of the divine inspiration
of its words.

Since the Enlightenment, however, weighty difficulties have appeared that preclude the understanding of the Bible itself as the inspired Word of God. A perception of the human character of the
Biblical writings has emerged with increasing clarity and intensity.
It is "much more intense than can be united even with the free form of
the doctrine of inspiration." [39] Not only words and formulations but
also the concepts themselves were shown to be human concepts chosen
by the Biblical authors themselves; consequently, the differences in
the Biblical writings and the influence of the conceptualizations of
its environment have rendered the concept of the divine inspiration
of the Bible as such untenable. Pannenberg judges this fundamental
change that the Enlightenment produced beyond the Reformation to
mean that *"for us the Scriptures can no longer be an authority basically
antecedent to Jesus himself."* [40]

The modern view of the relation between theology and Scripture
differs from that of Luther and the Reformers in two respects. First,
whereas Luther identified the literal meaning of Scripture with its
historical content, historical-critical exegesis demonstrates that the
New Testament portrayal of the history of Jesus cannot, without
qualification, be regarded as identical with the actual course of events.
Second, though Luther could identify his own doctrine with the content of the Scriptures, it has become impossible to overlook the his-

---

[37] "Wort," *Theologie für Nichttheologen,* ed. by Hans Jürgen Schultz (Gütersloh:
Gütersloher Verlagshaus Gerd Mohn, 1969), Vol. III, p. 108.
[38] *Ibid.*
[39] *Ibid.,* p. 109.
[40] Pannenberg, "Schriftautorität und Lehrautorität," in *Mainzer Universitätsgespräche* (Sommersemester, 1962), p. 8.

torical distance between any conceivable contemporary theology and the situation of primitive Christianity. These two interrelated aspects of the modern crisis of Scripture derive from the same methodological principle basic to the Reformation, namely, the interpretation of the texts according to the author's intention and the understanding of their original recipients.

Since the essential content of Scripture, namely, the person and history of Jesus Christ, could not be found *in* the texts but only *behind* them, the theological problem arose as to which of these constitutes the critical norm for theology: the Biblical texts themselves or the history of Jesus they contain. The issue has been debated repeatedly in Protestant theology, but recently theology has maintained the importance of going behind the texts to the history of Jesus on the one side and the necessity to remember the connection between the historical Jesus and the primitive Christian kerygma on the other. Though the inner logic that unites the apostolic witness to Jesus is difficult to grasp and to affirm, Pannenberg contends:

> Only the resurrection of Jesus, conceived in the framework of the cultural situation of primitive Christianity, renders intelligible the early history of Christian faith up to the confessions of Jesus' true divinity. If the resurrection of Jesus cannot be considered to be a historical event, then the historical aspect of the primitive Christian message and its different forms, both of which have crystallized into the New Testament, fall hopelessly apart.[41]

If the church's confession of Christ is not to appear arbitrary or simply a subjective interpretation, the historical gulf between the text and the event reported and the hermeneutical distance between the interpreter's present and the text must be resolved—specifically with reference to Jesus' history, including his resurrection. The crisis of Scripture cannot be resolved through a so-called "Biblical theology," for the difference between the modern period of the exegete and the intellectual world of primitive Christianity excludes a theology materially identical with the thoughts of Paul or John. Furthermore, a theology of the Word of God or "Reformation theology" is similarly inadequate, for the relationship of the Word to the Biblical words is

---

[41] "The Crisis of the Scripture Principle," *BQiT* I, p. 8.

thoroughly problematic and cannot withstand the Enlightenment critique of the doctrine of inspiration. So Pannenberg insists that the solution to the crisis of Scripture can be found only in history—the historical events that the Biblical texts report and the historical process wherein they communicate their universal significance. Yet a historical solution to the crisis of theology also confronts obstacles, specifically, the disengagement of the kerygma from history.

The Crisis of History

Though the modern crisis of history did not envelop contemporary Christian theology until the ascendancy of dialectical theology, Pannenberg considers the earlier work of Martin Kähler the most important root of kerygmatic theology. Kähler's famous dictum, *"The real Christ is the Christ who is preached,"* reflects the theme of kerygma theology, especially its antihistorical position against the life-of-Jesus research of the nineteenth century.[42] Though Kähler himself identified the Christ of faith with the truly historic Jesus, the impetus of his thought reflected in the kerygmatic theology of Rudolf Bultmann sharply illuminates his fundamental tendency to depreciate real history.

Kerygmatic theology accentuated the witness character of the Biblical writings against two other related ways of approaching historical materials: (1) against the quest for general truths, and (2) against the conception of historical research that excluded any reference to God. Kerygmatic theology saw itself over against this particular, time-bound form of historical thinking and developed itself in contrast to it. Since the reigning historiography (as defined by Troeltsch and others) bypassed the intention of the Biblical texts to witness to the acts of God (most evident in the nineteenth-century life-of-Jesus research), Kähler and, subsequently, kerygmatic theology strongly protested. Pannenberg speaks positively of the protest, noting:

> Where [the Biblical writings] are read as merely documents
> of secular events and human religiosity, their genuine content,
> which is precisely their witness to the deeds of God, remains
> untapped. Kerygma theology, in discovering this, was per-

---

[42] Martin Kähler, *The So-called Historical Jesus and the Historic, Biblical Christ,* ed. and tr. by Carl E. Braaten (Fortress Press, 1964), p. 66. Cited in Pannenberg, "Kerygma and History," *BQiT* I, pp. 81 ff.

fectly correct over against the historical practice and methodology of its time.[43]

However, instead of reformulating the historical-critical method, the developing kerygmatic theology largely ignored the historical basis of the Biblical witness. The Biblical proclamation was isolated from history, and it increasingly appeared as unfounded assertion. Whether or not the events reported actually occurred—the presupposition for the claim of the Biblical witness upon modern man—was an inquiry vigorously rejected by kerygmatic theology. Indeed, the inquiry itself was branded as a sign of unbelief!

The loss of history had not already occurred in Kähler, for he maintained the event as the foundation of faith. Nevertheless, Kähler asserted that the reports of the *historical fact* are accompanied by supplementary testimonies of *revelatory value* available only to faith. Pannenberg contends that the whole problem is already contained in the distinction between "revelatory value" and the "historical fact," the former added to the latter. Either the meaning of an event is inherent in it, or, if Kähler's distinction is valid, the possibility emerges that the "revelatory value" can stand alone, disinterested in its historical reference. Subsequent to Kähler, the autonomy of the kerygma over against its historical correlate eventuated under the influence of form-critical investigation of the New Testament, especially in the theology of Bultmann. The history of Jesus was eclipsed as interest was taken in the kerygmatic formulation of primitive Christianity in order to ascertain the interpretation of human existence contained therein, but the historical basis of the kerygma itself remained an open question. The important thing was not the "what" but only the "that" which produced the Easter faith.

New Testament research could isolate the kerygma from its historical basis in Jesus' resurrection because the latter appeared inaccessible to current historical research, outside the contemporaneous understanding of reality; hence, the resurrection was designated an "eschatological" in contrast to a "historical" event. Conversely, the action of God in Old Testament history cannot be eliminated from the testimonies of Israel's faith. Thus, Old Testament studies show tendencies that counteract the depreciation of history in kerygmatic theology (insofar as Jesus and primitive Christianity are to be understood in connection with Israel's promissory history). Pannenberg judges Ger-

[43] *Ibid.*, p. 85.

hard von Rad's *Old Testament Theology* most significant "for a genuine corrective . . . of the one-sidedness of kerygma theology," though perhaps more in von Rad's execution of his method than in his programmatic formulation.[44]

The starting point for von Rad's entire exposition is the perception that Israel's faith is fundamentally established in a "theology of history."[45] While aware of the tension between the historical-critical picture of Israel's history and the Old Testament understanding of it as salvation history, von Rad states that Israel's confessional history and not the historian's critical reconstruction is the proper object of Old Testament theology. Against his critics, von Rad argues that historical-critical knowledge of Israel's history is presupposed when he attempts to understand the origin and transformations of Israel's traditions within their actual historical situation. However, he refuses to abandon the historical witness of Israel to the activity of God in favor of the historical-critical picture of Hebraic history. Instead, von Rad unites critical and confessional history in a conception of the historical process as "the history of the transmission of traditions."

Not only does von Rad transcend the impasse between "outer" and "inner" history, he also avoids the nonhistorical harmonizations of the older supernatural conceptions of salvation history while magnificently maintaining the theological substance of Israel's salvation history on the one side and the diversity of intentions and perspectives of the various Old Testament witnesses on the other. Sketching Israel's traditions as distinctive contemporizations and actualizations of the salvation events by successive generations, von Rad consistently uses the historical-critical method to show how each new generation represented and actualized the kerygma to disclose its validity and effectiveness within changing historical situations. Though von Rad does not make this entire process of the transmission of traditions the object of comprehensive reflection, Pannenberg contends that the aspects for perceiving the unity of Israel's history beyond the multiplicity of its traditions are already provided in his detailed exposition:

> That which links the different witnesses together is to be found precisely in the process of the history of the transmission of traditions, insofar as each of them in their different situations refers back to a few foundational traditions, and

[44] *Ibid.*, p. 88.
[45] Cf. Gerhard von Rad, *Old Testament Theology*, Vol. I, p. 106.

these in turn coalesce in a meaningful way in the process of their actualization.[46]

Indeed, a decisive shift occurs in the prophetic movement, which anticipates the redemptive action of God in the future; however, the shift itself coheres with the older traditions, which were transmitted as the saving deeds of God and as the fulfillment of earlier promises.

Moving from the Old Testament to the New, Pannenberg suggests that the New Testament problems of the early Christian transmission of traditions, including the history of Jesus, could be effectively treated with a differentiation similar to von Rad's treatment of the Old Testament traditions: "In this way one would overcome in principle a kerygma theology isolated from history and oriented to a point-like saving event abstracted from the tradition-determined form in which it is portrayed." [47] The unitary conception of the history of the transmission of traditions, which is the deeper concept of history generally, finally poses the question of describing an event historically as an act of God. Since events were described as acts of God in Israel's history of traditions, Pannenberg questions von Rad's "especially cautious" attitude about the appropriateness of historical statements and suggests the *possibility* of the historian speaking of a deed of God in a specific event.[48] Pannenberg believes that the full significance of von Rad's history-of-traditions method emerges only when it modifies the conception of history and historiography almost universally accepted since the time of Troeltsch. Therefore, over against a kerygmatic or ethical [49] solution to the crisis within Christian theology, Pannenberg

---

[46] "Kerygma and History," *BQiT* I, p. 92.

[47] *Ibid.*, p. 93.

[48] *Ibid.*, pp. 93–95, n. 20.

[49] As an alternative to a conception of revelatory history, Protestant theology has often retreated to an ethical grounding of faith. Pannenberg, "Die Krise des Ethischen und die Theologie," *Theologische Literaturzeitung*, Vol. LXXXVII (1962), cols. 7–16, addresses himself to the problem in relation to the theological influence of Wilhelm Herrmann, especially upon Ernst Fuchs and Gerhard Ebeling. Pannenberg, however, rejects the ethical solution to the crisis of theology. Since the pattern of ethical action is not self-evident, the basic contours of ethical behavior can emerge only from a specific understanding of the whole of reality. Thus Pannenberg argues that theology cannot demonstrate the truth of its content through ethics: "Rather the reality of God and of his revelation must already be firmly established for itself, if it should somehow have ethical relevance, although the ethical confirmation of its proponent can react upon the general judgment about the truth of the message. The Christian ethical consciousness already presupposes the truth of the Christian message" (col. 14). Therefore, he concludes: "The question of the reality of God and of his revelation must be posed for itself, pre-

proposes a reexamination of history and the historical method—a suggestion that orients the solution of the crisis of theology to the horizon of revelatory history.

The Crisis of Eschatology

The crisis of history implies another fundamental crisis for a theology anchored in the Biblical traditions—the crisis of eschatology. From Kant to Ritschl theologians considered the Kingdom of God an ethical goal to be achieved by men, but Johannes Weiss[50] shattered the ethical interpretation of God's Kingdom with the discovery of Jesus' imminent eschatological expectation of the coming Kingdom of God—the expectation of the immediately impending end of the world and God's transformation of the entire cosmos. However, Pannenberg notes, "Theology today has yet to digest this radical change from the ethical to the eschatological understanding of the Kingdom of God." [51] While Weiss and Schweitzer began to regard the eschatological Jesus with a sense of estrangement, dialectical theology simply disregarded Jesus' message of the Kingdom as an expectation of a concrete temporal future. Eschatology became a timeless slogan, because Jesus' expectation of the imminent end of history proved an embarrassing illusion. Pannenberg observes:

> The rediscovery . . . of Jesus' eschatological understanding of reality had such a shocking effect upon the satiated feeling for life at the beginning of the twentieth century that it was hardly possible to face the utter strangeness of this Jesus except by presumptuous excisions and artificial reinterpretations. These novel interpretations are still alive today in the efforts to rob the eschatology of Jesus of its relation to time and to convert his passion for God's future into the presence of eternity in the momentary now.[52]

Thus Pannenberg rejects the different interpretative reductions of Jesus' eschatology as theologically and exegetically inadequate. Against

---

cisely in the interest of ethics. Only when the truth of God and of his revelation is established firmly for itself can one lead a life appropriate to it" (col. 16). Cf. "Christian Theology and Philosophical Criticism," *IGaHF*, pp. 118 ff.

[50] Cf. Johannes Weiss, *Jesus' Proclamation of the Kingdom of God*, tr. and ed. by Richard Hyde Hiers and David Larrimore Holland (Fortress Press, 1971).

[51] "Theology and the Kingdom of God," *TaKoG*, p. 52.

[52] "The God of Hope," *BQiT* II, p. 237.

the elimination of Jesus' temporal-historical expectation of the coming Kingdom for the sake of existential openness to the future, Pannenberg insists: "Without the conviction of the temporal imminence of the transformation of the world with the coming of the Kingdom of God, that openness toward the future which is so characteristic of Jesus' message would never have arisen." [53] Furthermore, Pannenberg argues, the abstraction of the sayings about the presence of the Kingdom from the whole of Jesus' message grievously distorts his proclamation of the present impact of God's coming rule. Similarly, the interweaving of present and future in Jesus' message does not justify the salvation history schema wherein the Kingdom of God essentially begins in Jesus' presence and only remains to be fulfilled in the future; rather, the starting point of Jesus' message in Jewish eschatological hope for the coming Kingdom of God requires a reversal of the relationship of present and future, acknowledging the priority of the future.

Against all de-eschatologized theology, Pannenberg declares: "This resounding motif of Jesus' message—the imminent Kingdom of God —must be recovered as a key to the whole of Christian theology." [54] Two factors prompt Pannenberg's call for a theological reassessment of Jesus' eschatological expectation. First, because the whole of Jesus' proclamation, including his message of God's love, has its basis in his imminent expectation of God's Kingdom, "there is not a single word and not a single thought that [Jesus] uttered which remains what it was on his lips once we take away this horizon of imminent expectation." [55] Second, if the message of Jesus' resurrection could be established historically, an anticipatory fulfillment of his eschatological expectation could be affirmed (which would maintain the relationship of Christian faith to Jesus himself). Acknowledging the demands of eschatology at each stage of his theologizing,[56] therefore, Pannenberg affirms the constitutive significance of eschatology for defining the task of theology today:

> The insights obtained by Johannes Weiss and Albert Schweitzer into the eschatological determinant of the message of Jesus and of early Christian faith signify a great task for

---

[53] *JGaM*, p. 242.
[54] "Theology and the Kingdom of God," *TaKoG*, p. 53.
[55] *AC*, p. 52.
[56] Cf. Pannenberg, "Foreword," *BQiT* I, pp. xv–xvi.

theological thought—a task which demands a thorough reshaping of our whole understanding of reality. Furthermore, the validity of this understanding must be decided on the basis of the key problems of ontology, epistemology, anthropology, and the philosophy of history.[57]

[57] "Vorwort," *Grundfragen systematischer Theologie*, p. 6, n. 2 [adapted].

II

THE TEXTURE OF PANNENBERG'S THEOLOGICAL METHOD

T HOUGH PANNENBERG has not delineated the structure of his theological method systematically, he has addressed himself repeatedly to methodological problems. The definition of the task of theology implies a complementary methodological solution; consequently, the explication of Pannenberg's understanding of the task of contemporary theology contains definite methodological impulses already distinguishable. Since an adequate theological method must cohere with one's conception of the task of theology, Pannenberg's description of the theological enterprise is quite instructive for a comprehension of his methodology:

> Systematic theology always takes place within the tension between two tendencies. On the one hand, it is concerned about the faithfulness of theology itself . . . to its origin, the revelation of God in Jesus Christ as this is attested in Scripture. On the other hand, however, the task of theology goes beyond its special theme and includes all truth whatever. This universality of theology is unavoidably bound up with the fact that it speaks of God. The word "God" is used meaningfully only if one means by it the power that determines everything that exists. . . . It belongs to the task of theology to understand all being [alles Seienden] in relation to God, so that without God they simply could not be understood. That is what constitutes theology's universality.[1]

[1] "The Crisis of the Scripture Principle," *BQiT* I, p. 1.

Pannenberg's conception of the theological enterprise is characterized by the tension between historical revelation and the whole of reality. Correspondingly, the methodology that he employs in the construction of a contemporary systematic theology reflects the interpenetration of particularity and universality. While a delimitation of the *components* of Pannenberg's theological method might seem appropriate, such a project would be untimely, for he has published neither a systematic theology, which would indicate the precise structure of his methodology, nor his epistemological lectures on the "Theology of Reason." Nevertheless, the questions of "how" he does theology and "why" he comprehends a theological theme in a particular way are answerable, at least in part. Hence, an examination of Pannenberg's treatment of foundational theological issues should highlight the *texture* of his distinctive theological method.

THEOLOGY AS HISTORY

In formulating an eschatological theology, in contrast to Moltmann, Pannenberg does not begin with the category of the future but with a concern for wholeness, with the question of the truth of the whole.[2] Since the Enlightenment the question of truth has been presented to Christian faith with constantly increasing poignancy—as the question of its power to encompass the whole of reality and to claim all knowledge as evidence for the truth of the Christian message, as the question of its ability to disclose the unity of the whole of reality. Pannenberg contends: "Thus, the question regarding the truth of the Christian faith is not concerned with a particular truth of one kind or another but with truth itself, which in essence can only be one." [3] Whether or not the Christian faith is the truth that gathers everything together into a coherent whole cannot be answered by the mere assertion that Jesus Christ is the truth but only with reference to the whole of reality. If Christian proclamation were to surrender its consideration of the totality of reality, it would forfeit its claim to speak plainly of *the* truth. Hence, theology must ask about the one truth when it reflects upon the truth of the Christian message.

[2] "A Theological Conversation with Wolfhart Pannenberg," *Dialog*, Vol. XI (1972), p. 287.

[3] "What Is Truth?" *BQiT* II, p. 1.

Contrasting Conceptions of Truth

The Western understanding of truth has two roots, the Greek and the Hebrew; moreover, the different views of truth denote divergent conceptions of reality. In the Hebrew concept (unlike the Greek) truth is not a timeless, once-for-all state of affairs, but continually happens. As Hans von Soden argued, for the Hebrews truth is "reality seen as history." Truth does not lie hidden in the core of things, but *"truth is that which will show itself in the future."* [4] The Greek concept of truth, however, lacks the historical character of the Hebraic: Truth is always the same within itself, that which is hidden behind changing appearances. Though the Greek and Hebrew understandings of truth have common characteristics, namely, that truth is dependable and durable, the truth of the God of Israel did not disclose itself fully to reflective perception but only to trust in God's faithfulness, trust based on his trustworthiness previously shown in his historical action. Thus Israel's perception that God is stable and reliable occurred historically through definite divine manifestations, not through the logical necessity that "what is" is. So Pannenberg reasons: "The truth of God must prove itself anew in the future, and . . . only trust can anticipate it." [5] Therefore, while the Greek understanding of truth could grasp the identity of truth only through a concept defined by unchangeableness, the Hebraic concept of truth integrated the truth which continually happens with ongoing historical change: "True being is thought of not as timeless but instead as historical, and it proves its stability through a history whose future is always open." [6]

Complementary Dimensions of Truth

Pannenberg specifies rather schematically two different aspects of truth: on the one side, the experience and criterion of truth; on the other side, the unity of truth. Whereas the experience of truth was originally conceived in Greek philosophy as the passive reception of the true, a fundamental change occurred through the Biblical, Christian message whereby the experience of truth was understood as the creative act of man, meaning: Subjectivity constitutes the source of

[4] Hans von Soden, *Was ist Wahrheit? Vom geschichtlichen Begriff der Wahrheit,* Marburger akademischen Reden 46 (Marburg, 1927), p. 15. Cited by Pannenberg, "What Is Truth?" *BQiT* II, p. 3. Italics added.
[5] "What Is Truth?" *BQiT* II, p. 8.
[6] *Ibid.,* p. 9.

truth. Yet agreement with nonhuman reality is a problem for this creative subjectivity of man, for the independence of thought from the external world makes it difficult to bridge the gulf between subjective thought and the objective world. Since man represents the image of God, Nicholas of Cusa and later Descartes reasoned that human ideas must be similar to the things God creates: Thus God is the presupposition for true cognition of nonhuman reality. Conversely, Kant presented *theoretical truth* as independent of the presupposition of God, making the agreement of an idea with the universal laws of reason the criterion of its "objective validity." He not only presupposed that the basic structures of reason are established *a priori* in all men, but more importantly, he failed to recognize historicness as the actual root of the spontaneity of reason. Against Kant, Pannenberg argues that the "objective validity" of thought is guaranteed only on the presupposition of a common ground between the human mind and nonhuman reality (a problem that led unavoidably beyond Kant to German idealism): "The agreement of human thought with extra-human reality, and thus its truth, is possible only on the presupposition of God." [7] Thus the modern understanding of truth from the subjectivity of man assumes the presupposition of God. That truth demonstrates itself in relationships and thus has personal character shows that the modern subjectivization of truth is characterized by the Biblical, historically determined concept of truth. Since the truth of human conduct occurs only through its harmony with God's truth, which embraces the whole world, the question of man's experience of truth flows into the question of the unity of truth.

In Greek thought the unity of truth excluded all change from it; correspondingly, the essence of truth was considered unchangeable, without beginning or end. However, since the Enlightenment critique of authoritarian traditions and the Romantic perception of the inseparability of truth from its historically diverse forms, the radical historicness of truth emerged, and also, a critical threat to the unity of truth itself. If the unity of everything real is essential to the truth, then truth cannot simply deal with the present world; on the contrary, the unity of truth must also comprehend other peoples and cultures of distant times who experienced the whole of reality quite differently.

[7] *Ibid.*, p. 18. Cf. *ibid.*, pp. 26–27, esp. where Pannenberg says: "Subjectivity cannot understand itself and its thought as truth without presupposing God as the one origin of everything real. In this regard, the act of adopting this presupposition can only mean having an open question, not an actual knowledge of God" (p. 26).

Thus the historicality of truth shows that every absolutization of a present truth would misconstrue from the outset the historical multiplicity of the figures of truth. Hence, Pannenberg reasons:

In this situation, unity of truth can now only be thought of as the history of truth, meaning in effect that truth itself has a history and that its essence is the process of this history. Historical change itself must be thought of as the essence of truth if its unity is still to be maintained without narrow-mindedly substituting a particular perspective for the whole of truth.[8]

Pannenberg believes that Hegel's philosophy represents the most significant attempt to solve this problem, because he distinctively recognized that the truth is not already available somewhere as a finished product. Hegel conceived truth as history, as process. He perceived that the truth is the whole; consequently, the truth of the whole, the whole truth, becomes visible only at the end, for the preliminary stages are characterized by contradictions. Ultimately, Hegel envisioned the Absolute as the reality that would embrace all contradictions and all preliminary syntheses. Hegel's thesis that the truth of the whole emerges only at the end, Pannenberg judges, converges with the Biblical understanding of truth in two respects:

It does so, firstly, by the fact that the truth as such is understood not as timelessly unchangeable, but as a process that runs its course and maintains itself through change. Secondly, it does so by asserting that the unity of the process, which is full of contradictions while it is under way, will become visible along with the true meaning of every individual moment in it, only from the standpoint of its end. What a thing is, is first decided by its future, by what becomes of it.[9]

However, Pannenberg raises a vigorous protest against Hegel, for the horizon of the future is lost in his thought. In order to conceive of the unity of history—and thus the truth—he had to understand his own position as the end of the history of thought; consequently, he denied the horizon of an open future. The other problems in Hegel's system, such as devaluating the contingency of events and slighting the uniqueness of the particular, stem from this fundamental error.

[8] Ibid., pp. 20-21.
[9] Ibid., p. 22.

Pannenberg contends, nonetheless, that the question of the unity of truth has not been posed with comparable depth since Hegel.

The comparison of Hegel's concept of history with the primitive Christian understanding of history intimates a solution to the modern problem of truth. Though the Biblical tradition affirmed the essence of truth to have a history (here Hegel agreed), it conceived the unity of history in Jesus Christ without eliminating the openness of the future (in contrast to Hegel). The ultimacy of God's revelation in Christ did not preclude the openness of the future, for the Christ event occurred as the prolepsis of the End of history within history. Though the End remains outstanding on the horizon of the future (indeed, it is difficult to say what resurrection really is), it has occurred provisionally in Jesus Christ, making a conception of the unity of history possible without sacrificing its openness. Pannenberg contends:

> Thus, the proleptic character of the destiny of Jesus is the basis for the openness of the future for us, despite the fact that Jesus is the ultimate revelation of the God of Israel as the God of all men. And, conversely, without this proleptic character, the [destiny] of Jesus could not be the ultimate revelation of the deity of God, since the openness of the future belongs constitutively to our reality—against Hegel.[10]

If the understanding of the prolepsis of God's revelation in Jesus is to be effective today, the viability of the apocalyptic expectation of the resurrection for contemporary anthropology and the historicality of the resurrection of Jesus must be established. These hypotheses, if shown to be true, would satisfy the legitimate objections against Hegel and permit a conception of the unity of truth through the ultimate, eschatological revelation of God in the history of Jesus.

THEOLOGY AS PHILOSOPHY

The question of truth impinges upon another dimension of theology, namely, the problematic and controversial relationship of theology and philosophy. Protestant theology does not have a "characteristic" posi-

---

[10] *Ibid.*, p. 25. Translation altered. As George Kehm usually recognizes, *Geschick* should be translated as "destiny" instead of "fate," for it positively connotes resurrection as Jesus' end beyond the disaster of the cross. "Destiny," therefore, coheres with "prolepsis," the anticipation of the *eschaton* in the Christ event.

tion regarding philosophy and its intellectual heritage, but reflects a multiplicity of sharply contrasting positions. The difficulty involves not only the relation of Christian faith to the specific philosophical projections but also the relation of faith to critical thought generally. While the problem includes the question whether or not modern theology will adopt the model of patristic Christianity, which claimed the Greek philosophical heritage for itself, the problem urgently concerns the question whether Christian theology affirms the protest of the Enlightenment against the authoritarian claims of sacred traditions or identifies those positions attacked by enlightened criticism as representative for the Christian faith generally.[11] As a post-Enlightenment theologian grappling with the problem, Pannenberg calls for a new dialogue between theology and philosophy, and he indicates the structure wherein such a dialogue should proceed, giving special attention to the perennial problem of faith and reason.

Theology and Philosophy

The response of Protestant theology to the Enlightenment's tendency toward intellectual emancipation has usually produced definitions of the relationship of theology to philosophy that are more or less dualistic. Insofar as Protestant theology has identified itself with positions of the traditional authority of revelation assailed by the Enlightenment, it has represented its relation to philosophy and a philosophically established doctrine of religion through a variation of contrasts: (1) the sharp antithesis of supernaturalism and rationalism at the end of the eighteenth century; (2) the nineteenth- and twentieth-century theologies of religious experience which maintained a revelatory claim but borrowed conceptually from philosophy to describe the content of religious experiences; and (3) the increasing modern theological concentration upon the problem of ethics, which "restricts the theological relevance of the questions posed by philosophy to the themes of a practical philosophy, to man as ethically constituted, and to the resistance of his disposition to his constitution as an ethical being." [12] Over against these alternatives, Pannenberg conceives the relationship of theology to philosophy from the standpoint of revelation, which, if legitimate, is also determinative. When the revelatory standpoint is recognized and affirmed, the dialogue between

[11] "Christian Theology and Philosophical Criticism," *IGaHF*, pp. 116 f.
[12] *Ibid.*, p. 118.

theology and philosophy does not disintegrate but continues on a new level. Pannenberg indicates the basic structure of such a dialogue.

First, a theology of revelation cannot be reduced to insights that are attained outside the circle of the concrete historical appearances of divine reality—"revelations" in the wider sense of the philosophy of religion. Yet the confirmation of the claim of God's revelation does require the use of the concept of revelation in the plural and in connection with other religions. Hence, Pannenberg contends: "The revelation of God to which the Biblical writings testify . . . cannot be isolated by an act of irrational and arbitrary choice from the sphere of other religions and their claims to be revelations." [13] The question of the truth of the Christian revelation—whether it involves only human religion or the self-manifestation of divine reality in the form of human religion—can only be answered through a comparative analysis of the Biblical and non-Biblical religious traditions, which is impossible without a philosophical theory of religion. Yet theology is not subjected to the authority of philosophy but examines the suitability of the categories and judgments available in religious philosophy, developing alternatives when necessary.

Second, a theology of revelation contains within itself an understanding of revelation and religion, which ultimately includes a philosophy of religion. Thus self-critical theological thinking must deal explicitly with the entire scope of philosophical problems, because a theology of revelation not only makes assertions about man and his situation but also about the world and history.

Third, making statements that contain truth claims concerning various aspects of reality, a genuine theology of revelation cannot honestly evade philosophical interrogation about the meaning of its statements and its use of language. Since theological sentences have the character of assertions—not just a performative function—the criteria for the truth or untruth of such assertions must be specified.

These reflections indicate that theology cannot limit its relationship toward philosophy to the problem of ethics. A theoretical understanding of reality actually precedes any ethical deliberation; consequently, theology cannot circumscribe its dialogue with philosophy but must finally engage in the entire scope of the philosophical inquiry. Though such an enterprise is rare in the modern period, an exception exists in Protestant theology among those theologians motivated by im-

[13] *Ibid.*, p. 120.

pulses from German idealism, namely, Schleiermacher, Troeltsch, and Tillich. However, the comprehensive scope of the theological enterprise was initially forged in the classical epoch of patristic theology, which exemplifies the magnitude of the theological task for the modern period. To be sure, the patristic conception of theology as the "true philosophy" will hardly permit a peaceful, tensionless coexistence between philosophy and theology; nevertheless, when theology restricts its horizon, it tends to deny the universality of its truth.

If theology retreats to a sphere of "revealed truth," it loses the universality that is intrinsic to the concept of God. Pannenberg insists: "Rightly understood, the revelation of God as the revelation of *God* is only borne in mind when all other truth and knowledge is organized around it and appropriated by it." [14] Hence, "Scripture positivism," which was developed in the pre-Reformation era but has become increasingly characteristic of Protestant theology, now endangers the ability of theology to speak credibly of God as the creator and perfecter of all things. Correspondingly, if theology seeks correlation with a specific secular philosophy (such as that of Aristotle) for the sake of acceptable comprehensiveness, it compromises its Christian presuppositions and thereby its universality. Against such compromise, Pannenberg protests: "Either theology is universal, and its thinking corresponds to the one God with whose revelation it is concerned, or else it loses its intellectual integrity." [15] The attempt to delineate spheres for philosophy and theology is inadequate, for philosophy, no less than theology, has to do with the whole of reality. The interpretation of philosophy essentially as the preparation for the truth of revelation unattainable by reason also stumbles. Similarly, philosophy and theology cannot be interpreted as complementary but different perspectives of the one truth, Pannenberg argues, for the question of the coordination of such perspectives in the one truth is decisive: "[Theology] must either be classified and categorized by the philosophy which reflects upon the unity of the truth as a subordinate form of the knowledge of truth, or else it must assert its own right to be considered the 'true' philosophy." [16] Since philosophy and theology lay claim to the whole of reality, the conflict between them is unavoidable. Yet the truth which the controversy involves is one

---

[14] "The Crisis of the Scripture Principle," *BQiT* I, p. 2.
[15] "Christian Theology and Philosophical Criticism," *IGaHF*, p. 128. Cf. "The Crisis of the Scripture Principle," *BQiT* I, p. 13.
[16] "Christian Theology and Philosophical Criticism," *IGaHF*, p. 129.

and the same; consequently, a constructive dialogue should be established within the dispute and the arguments of the one side should be recognized as beneficial for the other.[17]

Faith and Reason

The definition of the problematic relationship of faith and reason constitutes one of the fundamental issues that philosophy has thrust upon theology.[18] Although theology is the accomplishment of thought and may be expected to proceed in a reasonable way, it cannot be dissolved into those structures of thought which have been variously described in Western philosophy as "reason" without damaging the primacy of God and revelation beyond all human conceptuality. Rather, the interrelatedness and cooperation of faith and reason in Christian thought must be initially clarified through the tension that exists between them. Though this relation might well be a "unity of tension" instead of opposition, the difference between faith and reason may not be overlooked. The perfect unity of faith and knowledge is promised only in the *eschaton,* but the attempt to develop a preliminary conception of the unity of faith and reason is especially urgent for contemporary theology, because the tension between them has been aggravated in the modern period into opposition. Indeed, some early church theologians portrayed the relationship of faith and reason as essentially antithetical; however, all used reason and philosophy in the development of theology despite their arguments against it. Hence, Pannenberg observes: "The relative opposition of faith and reason which was occasionally—by no means predominantly—championed in the ancient and medieval churches, was marked by the tension between free, rational insight and obligation to an authoritative norm." [19] The source of the theological prejudice against reason and in favor of a tangible authority can be traced primarily to the premodern understanding of history: Historical knowledge depended entirely upon the credibility and the *authority* of a tradition. Hence, the reference of the Christian message to history and the necessity of the acceptance of the authority of the Biblical tradition were concomitants. Thus Luther did not disparage the affirmation of the truth of history as insignificant, but valued it as a self-understandable presupposition on the basis of the authority of tradition. The con-

[17] Cf. esp. *ibid.,* pp. 129 ff., where Pannenberg discusses the problem of metaphysics.
[18] "Faith and Reason," *BQiT* II, pp. 46 ff.
[19] *Ibid.,* p. 48.

trast between *authority* (which supports faith) and *reason* established the foundation for Luther's statements about the relationship of *faith* and *reason*.

Since the Enlightenment, however, the relationship of reason and the authority of revelation has shifted. Whether or not the Scriptures, the authoritative source of revelation, can be accepted by reason without contradiction is not the issue; instead, whether reason, after it has demonstrated that belief *on the basis of* a traditional authority is irrational, can generally permit some place for Christian faith has become the decisive question. Therefore, the modern denial of the meaningfulness of the Christian faith cannot be effectively answered through a retreat of theology to a traditional authority. With acid clarity Pannenberg writes: "The difference between the modern and the medieval situations consists in the fact that the authority of the Christian tradition (be it of the church and its dogmas, or of Holy Scripture) can scarcely be viewed any longer as unproblematically authoritative." [20] Historical questions cannot be answered in the modern period by appeal to authorities but only through historical-critical inquiry. Hence, the insistence upon an authority that is not generally convincing appears to be coercion, and, as was not the case in the Reformation era, the acceptance of such an authority claim appears to be a *sacrificium intellectus* and a work of man.[21] The understanding of the kerygma, therefore, is materially related to faith, for the obedience of faith to the kerygma would constitute an illusionary self-salvation if it were not motivated by understanding rooted in the truth of the message. The question of the truth of the Christian message cannot be restricted to self-understanding but must also include an understanding of the world. Therefore, the problem of the truth of the kerygma cannot be solved by reference to religious and ethical *experience*, for religious and moral contents are always mediated through theoretical consciousness.

Hence, the task of a rational account of the truth of Christian faith has become quite urgent. Yet the problem of faith's compatibility with critical reason stubbornly resists solution—a solution, at least, that maintains the integrity of faith and reason. Pannenberg suggests that the understanding of reason itself is the key to the solution.[22] When examined closely, "reason" does not represent a uniformly defined norm; correspondingly, the various representations of the re-

[20] *Ibid.*, p. 51.
[21] *Ibid.*, p. 52.
[22] *Ibid.*, p. 54.

lationship of faith and reason presuppose differing conceptions of reason. Therefore, in order to clarify the issue and to formulate a solution, Pannenberg examines and evaluates several conceptions of reason that essentially define the corresponding faith-reason relationship.

First, there is the Aristotelian-Thomistic understanding of reason, of which Luther made use, which distinguishes between the reason and the intellect. Whereas the intellect lives in quiet contemplation of truth, reason moves from conception to conception in order to grasp through discursive thought the one truth which binds all truths together. The intellect does not engage in discursive thought, however, for it perceives intuitively what reason can attain only as the result of its *discursus*. Since man achieves knowledge through sense impressions and not through the immediate comprehension of reality, he requires discursive thought; however, man does immediately possess some general principles that enable him to reason in theoretical knowing. Obviously the activity of reason conceived as the application of aprioristic principles to sense impressions is not open to anything that does not coincide with these principles. Precisely because the content of the Christian faith contained in the Biblical traditions could not be deduced from any aprioristic principles, Luther vigorously repudiated reason itself (though he accepted the illumination of the intellect through the supernatural truths of faith and extolled the reason illuminated by faith). Significantly, Kant's valuation of reason is similar to that of Luther; consequently, Luther's conception of the "knowledge of faith" in opposition to reason as such remains effective today. Pannenberg, however, rejects any conception of an illumination of the aprioristic reason and the relation to faith that it implies.

> The history of the relationship between philosophy and theology clearly shows that this illumination of the reason which Luther had in mind cannot result from an infusion of supernatural principles. The truths of faith imposed as supernatural principles are always felt, by a reason that understands itself as knowing by means of principles, to be nothing but fetters that have to be struck off, and not as the fulfillment of the essence of reason.[23]

---

[23] *Ibid.*, p. 57.

Second, there is the Platonic concept (revived by William Kamlah) of insight through "receptive reason," which stands over against Kantian aprioristic reason. The sudden illumination of receptive reason seems compatible with faith, for it appears open to supernatural revelation; however, Pannenberg rejects it as conceptually inadequate. Whereas the Christian faith is directed toward the future (Heb. 11:1), toward the God who promises and guarantees a lively, open future, the receptive reason is thoroughly Greek, concentrating upon what is instead of what will be. Since the truth itself is eschatological, it cannot be apprehended by a conception of reason oriented to the structures of existence, to what always is. Thus the concept of receptive reason has continually obstructed the historical truth of the promising God. Though not opposed to the concept of insight or illumination as such, Pannenberg protests against a conception of truth and reason that slights the historicness of reality and perception as well as against a definition of reason that obscures its creativity.

Third, there is historical reason. This conception, which is certainly not a theological postulate, designates the historicness of reason, the discovery of which has profoundly transformed the understanding of reason since Kant. Indeed, Kant's conception contained a viable impulse toward historical reason, insofar as the "productive imagination" or "creative fantasy" formed the actual core of his concept of reason, but he failed to acknowledge the creative profuseness of imaginative activity. The discovery of the dynamic movement taking place in reflection, however, revealed that imagination must continually produce ever-new syntheses of thought.

While Hegel did not recognize the unrestricted process of the reflective movement of thought (which produced the breakdown of his system), the historical movement of reason, which continually drives it into the open, was subsequently discovered. Dilthey advanced the understanding of the historical life of reason through an investigation of the category of "meaning." Since each event has significance only in relation to the whole, the end of life—and ultimately the end of history itself—can finally reveal the meaning of the whole—retroactively. Yet man does not stand at the end of history, Dilthey realized, so all assertions of meaning are relativized. Pannenberg, however, draws the opposite conclusion: "Every assertion of meaning rests upon a fore-conception of the final future, in the light of which the true meaning of every individual event first becomes expressible in a valid way." [24] Against Heidegger, Pannenberg contends that the individual human life remains a fragment even in death:

> The fore-conception of a final future which alone yields the true meaning of all individual events must therefore be, on the one hand, something that points beyond the death of the individual, and on the other hand, something that embraces the totality of the human race, indeed, of all reality. Only from such a fore-conception of a final future, and thus of the still unfinished wholeness of reality, is it possible to assign to an individual event or being—be it present or past—its definitive meaning by saying what it is. [25]

The definition of the historical essence of reason moves toward the horizon of eschatology. Not only faith but also reason anticipates the future—faith in trust and creative reason through imaginative fore-conception. *Hence, the eschatological structure of reason permits faith to speak of an eschatological future for the whole of reality without appearing irrational as such.* The relationship of faith to historical reason, therefore, cannot be defined as antithetical, but a difference between faith and reason nonetheless remains. While reason is not restricted to the present (indeed, it anticipates the future), the present is its primary concern; conversely, faith is directed toward the future which constitutes the whole of reality and perfects each individual entity within it. Yet faith reminds reason of its own absolute presupposition by speaking about the eschatological future and its preappearance in the eschatological history of Jesus.

THEOLOGY AS GOD-TALK

Perhaps the fundamental issue in the new dialogue between philosophy and theology concerns the perennial problem of the nature and function of God-talk. Hence, Pannenberg acknowledges: "A crucial, if not *the* most basic question of all theology is the question about the right way to speak of God." [26] The problem of theological lan-

---

[24] *Ibid.*, p. 62.
[25] *Ibid.*
[26] "Analogy and Doxology," *BQiT* I, p. 211. Although Pannenberg developed his conception of analogy in critical conversation with medieval theologians, he is knowledgeable about the issues in the Anglo-Saxon debate over religious language. He considers the work of Frederick P. Ferré, *Language, Logic and God* (Harper & Row, Publishers, Inc., 1961), a classic analysis of the controversy, but poses the penetrating question to Ferré: "What are 'metaphysical facts'?" (cf. Ferré, pp. 159 ff.).

guage is especially urgent for Pannenberg. Disavowing a special status for Christian speaking of God over against that of other religions, he subjects his use of theological language to the general critique of God-talk; consequently, he presents a structural analysis of theological assertions that intimates the path to their legitimation.

Doxology and Analogy

If, as Pannenberg contends, the reality of God appears only indirectly in the world, divine reality, which is not directly experienced, can be spoken of only in an indirect way. The indirectness of speaking-of-God means that man can speak of him only analogically, "only by transferring the meaning of words formed in other contexts." [27] The analogous character of speaking of God is independent of how divine reality is conceived or where such reality is encountered. Pannenberg emphasizes: "The constitutive factor behind the assertion that all speech about God is analogical and involves a transference of meaning is simply the indirectness of the divine disclosure." [28] However, whether analogical descriptions belong to God's being in and of itself, or only to the human perspective, is another question.

The classical theory of analogy, developed by scholasticism in the thirteenth century, said that the reality of God stands in an analogical relation to the world, that an analogy between God and the world actually exists (although the world falls short of the divine archetype—which limits analogy). Conversely, when the Biblical writers speak of God by transferring to him words understood from human life, they portray pictures that usually designate the uniqueness of a specific divine action. However, on the basis of his deeds, statements are also made about God which, from the characteristics of his actions, designate God himself. Though such statements describe God's reality by analogy with human action, the intention of such language is not to define theoretically the being of God through "analogy"; instead, these analogous affirmations are characterized by a "doxological" structure that expresses adoration of God on the basis of his works. Pannenberg declares: "All biblical speech about God, to the extent that its intention is to designate something beyond a particular deed, namely, God himself and what he is from eternity to eternity, is rooted in adoration and is in this sense doxological." [29] The recognition that

[27] "Analogy and Doxology," *BQiT* I, p. 212.
[28] *Ibid.*, p. 213.
[29] *Ibid.*, pp. 215–216.

theological statements about God are rooted in adoration guards the mystery of God against erroneous calculations.

Unlike the attempt to infer the attributes of God from his effects through analogy, which presupposes a commonality between the realm of finitude and the infinite God, the act of adoration includes the sacrifice of the worshiper's "I" as well as the conceptual univocity of his speech. While human words whose meanings are derived from other contexts are employed in the act of adoration, an essential continuity of usage is not presupposed, because the human word is surrendered in its praise to God and loses its everyday meaning, becoming mysterious. To be sure, there is a relationship that justifies the choice of a particular word for the praise of God; but the word used in adoration is released from human disposal and is given to God himself, making it impossible to survey the change of content that occurs or to determine the relationship of the language of praise to the essence of God. "Rather," Pannenberg argues, "the word is sacrificed by the adoration of God, and only the association of the worshipper with God, the experience of further concrete acts of God, serves to show—always in a merely provisional way—what has become of our words in this connection." [30] So Pannenberg interprets the doxological analogy as an analogy of language but not an analogy of being: "Thus, talk about God rooted in adoration does indeed intend to speak about God's eternal reality by analogical transfer of meaning, but it does not intend to accomplish this as an analogue, but rather by opening itself unreservedly to the infinity of God." [31] Since the act of adoration transcends the concept of analogy between God and creation, there is no attempt to comprehend God in concepts but a recognition of God's infinity, of divine transcendence.

Doxology and Kerygma

Pannenberg's rejection of an analogy between statements about God and God himself poses the crucial question of the basis for specific doxological statements that are attributed to God in praise. If there is no essential analogy between human words and God's being, the validity of any specific statement about God requires concrete substantiation. An explanation is necessary to indicate why the equivocation that is introduced in the transfer of human words to the infinite

[30] *Ibid.*, pp. 217–218.
[31] *Ibid.*, p. 218.

God does not represent an arbitrary use of language. Pannenberg believes that the metaphorical use of language requires a foundation in a situation which occasions its usage, a situation which is related to the original, somewhat normal usage of the language employed.

The occasion for doxological speech about God is a definite experience of a divine act. On the basis of his activity God is praised as one who is eternally good, faithful, and righteous. However, since the experience of God and the speech about God occur indirectly, an event as an act of God can also be described without reference to God. To be sure, such a description might be less appropriate or more superficial, eclipsing the depth of an event; nonetheless, such obscuration has become typical today. When one speaks of an act of God in the circumstances of human experience, it appears to be an unnecessary appendix, merely a subjective interpretation of a particular event. Yet this appearance is misleading, for a conception of God-talk as an unnecessary appendage indicates a lack of comprehension of the inner motivation of speech about God. Pannenberg reasons incisively:

> Namely, in the moment in which we grasp, by means of a single event, the totality of the reality in which we live and around which our lives circulate, there we experience a work of God in the individual event. This happens when and to the extent that we are able to think of the unity of all reality and of our own existence only on the basis of a presupposition that transcends everything we find before us or within us, and which we name God or the divine.[32]

The indirectness of speech about God involves (1) the difference between the individual event and the whole of reality experienced therein, and (2) the task of describing the individual experience in relation to the whole of reality, in relation to God as its origin. The depth dimension of an event that is illuminated through its relation to the whole of reality is perceived indirectly; similarly, an indirect language is required to describe its depth dimension as an "act of God"—the language of analogical transference. Therefore, when the safe passage of the Israelites through the Red Sea and the drowning of the Egyptians is understood as an "act of God"—as a personal act— language is used that has nothing to do with the immediate description of the visible circumstances at the Red Sea. Yet personal language

[32] *Ibid.*, p. 229.

is required when the event is related to the divine power that defines its total horizon. Pannenberg insists:

> This power is now thought of as an acting person, analogous to man. And since the event in question, whose improbability made awareness of the operation of this power possible, allowed the Israelites (or proto-Israelites) involved to see salvation coming to them in a situation of dire need, this event thus comes to be understood as a redemptive, merciful act of God.[33]

Though the analogies that express the depth dimension of events are derived from human conduct, such anthropomorphic personification reflects the mysterious, nonmanipulatable character of the power that determines the whole of reality. Since speaking of an act of God as a personal act involves an analogizing transfer that is grounded in a total understanding of reality, such kerygmatic speech partakes of the same structures as doxological speech about God, but it is distinguished by its intention to designate a specific event as an act of God. Correspondingly, the divine action that underlies kerygmatic formulations provides the basis for additional doxological statements about God. The transfer of such descriptive anthropomorphisms to God generally presupposes an understanding of God as personal and specifically requires support in the peculiarity of the particular event experienced as an act of God. "By means of such doxological statements," Pannenberg observes, "Israel built up something like a characterological picture of its God, based on the cumulative experience of how this God had shown himself to be through his dealings with Israel." [34] The tension between the "attributes" of God that emerged in Israel's history preserved the provisionality of all speech about God, a provisionality rooted in the analogizing transfer from worshiping man to the infinite God.

If the provisionality of all statements about God is to escape an absolute impasse, Pannenberg argues, the question of the validity of God-talk must be oriented to the problem of revelation:

> The idea of the revelation of God goes beyond this [provisionality], provided that revelation means an ultimate self-disclosure and thus a self-commitment, a final self-demonstra-

---

[33] *Ibid.*, p. 231.
[34] *Ibid.*, p. 234.

tion of God. When occasion arises for speaking about a self-revelation of God, then and only then is our speech about God, in all its provisionality, nevertheless carried beyond this provisionality "in all its provisionality," because speaking of God as a self-revealing person is itself doxologically fashioned and open to the infinity of the freedom of God.[35]

Thus the ultimacy of the eschatological history of Jesus must finally establish the Christian affirmations concerning the revelation of God in him. Therefrom, Pannenberg reasons: "The metaphorical character of our speech about God, which Jesus also shared when he spoke of God as Father, is at the same time taken up by God himself, insofar as he raised Jesus and gave acknowledgment to him." [36] However, while God has acknowledged the metaphors of devotional speech about him in the Christ event, such analogical language remains provisional, for only the *eschaton* will reveal the full reality of what happened in Jesus' resurrection. Statements about God rooted in the ultimacy of the eschatological history of Jesus still retain a doxological-proleptic structure. Therefore, affirming the doxological structure of all analogical statements about God (instead of analogical correspondence between statements about God and God himself), Pannenberg asserts the priority of the concept of revelation for apprehending knowledge of God.

THEOLOGY AS DOGMATICS

The enterprise of dogmatics is closely related to dogma, which Pannenberg understands as a synonym for the church's confessions. While revelation through Jesus Christ constitutes the criterion of dogma, the distinction between revelation and dogma defines the task of dogmatics, of theology, which is to examine and to establish the agreement of dogmas with revelation.

The Content of Dogmatics

Although the Reformation conception of the task of dogmatics as a summary synopsis of the contents of Scripture tends to oversimplify the relationship of exegesis and dogmatics, it does accentuate the as-

[35] *Ibid.*
[36] *Ibid.*, p. 235.

sociation of dogma with dogmatics and their common dependence upon Scripture. In addition, as synopses of the contents of apostolic preaching expressed in Scripture, dogma and dogmatics obviously cannot add any supplementary content to Scripture but must remain open to critical scrutiny and modification by Scripture. However, the tradition of the church is not subsequently depreciated, for the origin of Scripture is to be understood as the product of a history of the transmission of tradition, as a process of tradition whose responsible bearer is the church. Yet Pannenberg emphasizes:

> But in this whole process of the transmission of Christian tradition, the rise of the New Testament writings and their consolidation into a canon constitutes a fundamental break which structures the whole process insofar as all subsequent tradition of the Christ-event is mediated by this written witness and is accomplished in confrontation with it.[37]

Thus the Scriptures constitute the norm for the post-Biblical confessions of faith and the theological formulations of the church within the ongoing Christian tradition; moreover, the relation between the norm and theological formulations defines the structure of the ongoing tradition.

If all dogmatic statements, as summaries of the content of Scripture, are grounded in and examined by Scripture, the revelation of God must be completely expressed by it, at least with respect to the requirements for man's salvation; correspondingly, the testimony of Scripture must be able to communicate its unitary contents plainly and clearly. Thus, Pannenberg observes, Luther asserted the clarity of the central content of Scripture, distinguishing two dimensions of such clarity:

> On the one hand, there was the inner clarity which was experienced in the heart, made one certain of personal salvation, and was bestowed only by means of the Holy Spirit. The outer clarity, on the other hand, consisted in the unambiguity and uncontrovertibility of the essential content of Scripture whose exposition and defense were charged to the ministry of the word [ministerium verbi].[38]

---

[37] "What Is a Dogmatic Statement?" *BQiT* I, pp. 186–187.
[38] *Ibid.*, pp. 188–189.

While the outer clarity must contain a tendency toward the inner—if the outer Word really bears the Spirit in itself—the crucial question involves the content made visible through the clarity of Scripture. Luther considered only the central content of Scripture, Jesus Christ, transparently intelligible; consequently, he refused to draw a fundamental distinction between historical and dogmatic content. Therefore, Pannenberg concludes:

> The dogmatic significance of the results of historical-exegetical study of Scripture follows immediately from Luther's doctrine of the outer clarity of Scripture, the heart of which is his conviction of its self-evident nature. The dogmatic content of Scripture must be demonstrable by means of historical arguments. This is the true "significance of the critical historical method for church and theology in Protestantism." [39]

Pannenberg believes that Luther's concept of the "outer clarity" of Scripture is similar in direction to the concept that the history of Jesus embraces the revelation of God in itself and can be grasped precisely as history when it is seen in its revelatory particularity. Yet the "outer clarity" of Scripture and the self-contained revelatory history of Jesus are only similar in direction, for Luther was unable to distinguish between the witness of Scripture and the event attested by it—a distinction that is unavoidable for the theologian today. Nonetheless, the concept of the "outer clarity" of Scripture is of fundamental importance for Pannenberg's theological method.[40]

The Norm of Dogmatics

The clarity and unity of Scripture are closely related in Protestantism, for the clarity makes its essential and unitary content accessible. Yet modern historical research, which is rooted in the clarity of Scripture, has led to the dissolution of the traditional concept of the unity of Scripture through the analogy of faith. The progress of the historical-critical investigation of Scripture has shown that a doctrinal unity of the New Testament writings does not exist. Since the loss of the conception of a doctrinal unity of Scripture, two basic possibilities for understanding Scriptural unity have emerged: First, the unity of Scrip-

[39] *Ibid.,* p. 191.
[40] "Redemptive Event and History," *BQiT* I, pp. 61 ff.

ture may be established in a hermeneutical principle which concurs with the spirit of the witnesses. However, a "canon within the canon" (Käsemann) or a "unity of proclamation" (Diem) must finally be constituted in the mind of the interpreter, for it is not evident as an "objective" unity that exists in itself. Second, the unity of Scripture may be rooted in the Christ event witnessed to in the different New Testament writings. Pannenberg observes:

> But in order to accomplish this, the Christ-event must be distinguishable from the process of its—continually differing —proclamation, and from early on the different forms of the primitive Christian witness must give evidence of and be capable of supporting the judgment that they represent the unfolding of the inherent meaning of the Christ-event itself. Thus, what is needed is precisely the historical quest, moving behind the kerygma in its various forms, into the public ministry, death, and resurrection of Jesus himself in order in that way to obtain in the Christ-event itself a standard by means of which to judge the various witnesses to it, even those actually within the New Testament.[41]

The prerequisite for such a conception hinges upon the capacity to distinguish the history of Jesus from the kerygma on the one side and the inherent meaning of the event in its original historical context on the other. Pannenberg considers this "historical" alternative the only possibility for illuminating the content of Scripture as a unity that is above the different forms of the primitive Christian kerygma and that thereby constitutes its norm. Such an approach is continuous with Luther's concept of the outer clarity of Scripture wherein Jesus Christ is its actual content—a content that emerges through the outer clarity of Scripture conceived as the historical investigation of the Bible. Though this content appears different in the modern period, a depth dimension of the process of traditions is now visible wherein the Christ event is distinguishable from the several New Testament witnesses. Thus the contemporary theologian distinguishes between the historical sense and the literal sense of the Scriptures as different dimensions of exegesis; consequently, Pannenberg reasons:

> Therefore, the dogmatician has not only to deal with exegetical statements that bring out the original meaning of

⁴¹ "What Is a Dogmatic Statement?" *BQiT* I, pp. 195–196.

the different writings, but also, beyond this and above all, with historical statements (in the broadest sense of the term) about the history of Jesus himself and the process of its transmission in tradition and interpretation in primitive Christianity.[42]

Exactly this historical understanding of the primitive Christian process of tradition brings dogmatics to the position—much more differentiated and methodologically clearer than in the Reformation era—wherein Jesus Christ is the discernible criterion of the New Testament writings. As the ultimate criterion of Scripture, therefore, Jesus the Christ is the norm of all dogmatic formulations.

The Universality of Dogmatics

Unlike historical affirmations, dogmatic statements do not usually attempt to explain the particularity of historical events; rather, they attempt to formulate the universal meaning of the historically unique for the whole of reality and for man's consciousness of truth. The historian inquires into the specific individuality of an occurrence through an imaginative sketch of the whole—a conception confirmed or modified in the light of concrete historical research. The dogmatician, however, asks how a universal context of meaning emerges from a specific historical event, the history of Jesus. Yet the universal significance and the specific individuality of the Christ event are so interwoven that inquiry continually moves from one to the other.

The universality of dogmatic statements about Jesus' meaning presupposes that the entirety of the history of Jesus is comprehended as the action of God. Since statements about God relate to the totality of reality and imply an understanding of this whole, statements about Jesus which speak about God's activity and revelation in him correspond to an understanding of reality as a history effected by God—i.e., to the Biblical-Israelite view of reality. Thus the universal meaning of the history of Jesus is grounded in its eschatological character, wherein the goal and thus the origin of all things is revealed in him, especially in his resurrection destiny. Pannenberg affirms: "There the God of the Old Testament reveals himself as the true God, as the origin and Lord over all men and all things." [43] Therefore, through the eschatological key of the Christ event, dogmatics unfolds the universal significance of this particular historical event in relation to the

[42] *Ibid.*, p. 197.
[43] *Ibid.*, p. 200.

whole of reality and speaks thereby of the activity of God in the history of Jesus. Yet the time-conditionedness of theological statements is not obscured by their universality. Since any understanding of reality is only approximate and constantly changes, dogmatics must participate in such change, confirming the deity of God revealed in Jesus in relation to the experience of reality of every successive historical present.

The Provisionality of Dogmatics

The transmission of the tradition of the history of Jesus, which is presupposed in confession, is the task of doctrine, of dogmatics. So Pannenberg says: "Dogmatic teaching lives in the tradition and itself has the task of passing on that which has been transmitted in the tradition." [44] Since the transmission is united with personal advocacy for the truth of the traditions, the witness to the truth of the tradition is possible only in conjunction with reflection upon the context of its initiation and with a testing of its claim to truth. Indeed, such testing focuses upon the Christ event and its inherent meaning, but the approach to the Christ event is always shaped by the tradition wherein one lives. Though the significance of a new situation and the creative power of the imagination must not be minimized, questions and hypotheses regarding the history of Jesus are defined through the life of the inquirer within his tradition. The testing of these questions and hypotheses of tradition include: (1) the primitive Christian tradition of Jesus, which is interrogated as a historical source; (2) the ideas and conceptions about Jesus arising in different traditions, which are to be tested by the existing indices of the history of Jesus; and (3) the verification of the truth of the Jesus tradition in the light of the changing experience of reality wherein the tradition asserts a universal and, hence, a binding claim.

Dogmatics must continually accomplish a new and contemporary explication of the universal meaning of the transmitted tradition, because the historic expressions of the universal truth of the Christ event are conditioned by time and culture. While the universality of dogmatic statements demands the preservation of the unity of tradition, such continuity does not mean the irreformability of a doctrinal concept once considered valid. The unity of tradition is not destroyed through different dogmatic formulations or through the criticism of earlier dogmatic formulations; on the contrary, the unity of the tradi-

44 *Ibid.*, p. 206.

tion is established in the common relation of different theologians of different epochs to the norm of the Christ event. The history of Jesus in its unity with the eschatological future produces the unity of tradition, just as it establishes the unity of Scripture.

The provisionality of dogmatics roots in the doxological and proleptic structure of all theological statements. Pannenberg says: "The statements used in confession of Christ have a doxological character insofar as they speak, on the basis of the Christ-event, of God himself in his eternal essence [Wesen] and of the eternal deity of Jesus Christ." [45] Since doxological adoration requires the sacrifice of finite language and conception to the infinity of the Biblical God, Pannenberg accentuates the radicality of the mystery, the incomprehensibility, the transcendence of the God revealed in Christ beyond all human understanding and power to conceptualize. Furthermore, Pannenberg emphasizes the limitation imposed by the proleptic element in dogmatic statements, which means they depend entirely upon the anticipation of the *eschaton:* "The foundation of the whole history of the transmission of tradition in primitive Christianity is, in fact, a vision of the Easter event which telescopes it together with the eschatological event of the end of the world and resurrection of the dead which is still outstanding for us." [46] Though theological statements are guided by the pre-happening of the *eschaton* in Jesus' history, these dogmatic formulations always retain the infinite tension between the "already" and the "not yet," they contain the fundamental limitation that derives from this tension. Reflecting upon the provisionality of all theological statements, which is imposed by their doxological-proleptic structure, Pannenberg concludes that Christian theology necessarily embraces a plurality of doctrinal formulations[47] and that dogmatic options assume the form of "engaging hypotheses." [48]

[45] *Ibid.,* p. 202.
[46] *Ibid.,* p. 204.
[47] Cf. Pannenberg, "The Working of the Spirit in the Creation and in the People of God," in Pannenberg *et al., Spirit, Faith, and Church* (The Westminster Press, 1970), pp. 25–30.
[48] Cf. Pannenberg, "Nachwort," in *Geschichte, Offenbarung, Glaube* by Ignace Berten (Munich: Claudius Verlag, 1970), pp. 140–141; and "What Is Truth?" *BQiT* II, p. 16, n. 37.

THEOLOGY AS ANTHROPOLOGY

Since theology involves man's encounter with the manifestion(s) of God, Pannenberg considers the understanding of man constitutive for the approach to theology: "The single legitimate point of departure of theological cognition lies in the historical situation wherein man is met by the revelatory action of God." [49] Hence, the problem of revelation, of God's revelatory disclosure, impinges upon and immediately presupposes an anthropology, or more precisely, a theological anthropology. Thus the concurrence of the emergence of Pannenberg's revelatory theology and the publication of *What Is Man? Contemporary Anthropology in Theological Perspective* (first German ed., 1962) is not coincidental; on the contrary, Pannenberg attempts to integrate the understanding of man in the several anthropological disciplines in the light of the Biblical portrait of man.

The Openness of Man

Instead of being a microcosm of the world, man has emerged as a decision-making individual who uses the world for his own transforming activity. Though the existential definition of man is too abstract, man is really free to make decisions that transcend every given regulation of his existence, a distinctive freedom of "openness to the world." [50] Such a descriptive image of man is pregnant with anthropological implications. When "openness to the world" is related to the distinction between man and animals, it signifies that man *has* a world, while each species of animal is *limited* to a fixed environment. Unlike other animals, man is open to innumerable experiences and possibilities beyond his environment. Since man's drives are not directed unambiguously from the time of his birth, they are stamped distinctively by choice and habit, education and custom. Lacking clearly defined instincts that circumscribe his vision, man uniquely experiences the realities and opportunities of the world reflectively and mysteriously.

In addition, modern man is confronted by the experience that he is always able to ask beyond every horizon open to him. Thus "openness to the world" propels man completely into the "open" beyond

---

[49] "Christliche Glaube und menschliche Freiheit," *Kerygma und Dogma*, Vol. IV (1958), pp. 274–275.
[50] *WIM*, p. 3.

every experience, situation, and picture of the world. As man seeks
his destiny in openness, he cannot find complete satisfaction in either
his technology or his culture. The ensuing restlessness constitutes one
root of all religious life, which ultimately defines "openness to the
world" as "openness to God." So Pannenberg reasons:

> Man's chronic need, his infinite dependence, presupposes
> something outside himself that is beyond every experience of
> the world. Man does not simply respond to the pressure of
> his surplus of drives by creating for his longing and awe an
> imaginary object beyond every possible thing in the world.
> Rather, in his infinite dependence he presupposes with every
> breath he takes a corresponding, infinite, never ending, other-
> worldly being before whom he stands, even if he does not
> know what to call it.[51]

Human language has the word "God" for this entity upon which man
is dependent in his infinite striving. Hence, the crux of man's openness to the world is his infinite dependence on something or someone
which is beyond him. Though these observations neither identify the
object of man's dependence as God nor constitute a theory of a
religious a priori, they do suggest man's openness to the revelation of
divine reality.

Man's openness to the world, which ultimately includes his openness to God, directs him back into the world to attain dominion over
it as God's responsible representative. Since worldly control requires
the ability to communicate and, eventually, to think abstractly, man
spins a network of words and relations between words in order to
integrate the diversity of the external world as well as to conceptualize
in the inner world of silent consciousness. The creative development
of language enables man to project a broad mental overview that goes
beyond the particular present moment, and to grasp things in their
broader interconnections. Such language is prerequisite for the formation of an artificial world of culture, including a spiritual culture of
diverse imaginative creations that involve man's infinite destiny—
open to, yet beyond the world. To explain the creative achievements
of man linguistically and culturally, Pannenberg accentuates the relationship of imagination to human freedom and creativity: "In hu-

[51] Ibid., p. 11. Cf. ibid., p. 13, where Pannenberg says: "What the environment is
for animals, God is for man. God is the goal in which alone his striving can find
rest and his destiny be fulfilled."

man behavior, to the extent that it is creative, imagination occupies the key position that instinct holds in animals." [52] Man constantly discovers new forms, structures, and configurations in things that previously appeared unrelated through the creative power of imagination; consequently, the synthesis of diverse elements into a general concept is an act of imagination. Such imaginative constructs not only provide access to empirical knowledge (subsequently confirmed through testing) but, as the arts indicate, also serve for conceiving man's infinite destiny. Yet the power of imagination, man's most creative ability, also contains a passive element, because imagination does not function logically but through a loose series of inspirations whereby the imaginative man is more recipient than producer. These inspirations probably issue from man's infinite openness, which ultimately means that the Biblical God-who-acts also produces new things in man's contemplative nature.

Furthermore, man's openness to the world includes dependence upon the world and the reality that transcends it. Thus man must trust, abandoning himself to the faithfulness of the object of trust; nevertheless, trust is not blind risk, for man trusts what has shown itself to be trustworthy. Though it is not guaranteed that trust will be justified, trust risks itself on an expectant future, depending upon the reliability of another beyond man's knowledge and thereby beyond his control. Hence, trust is person-oriented, for in contrast to the transparency of things men are in principle mysterious. Similarly, the origin of the whole of reality is beyond the comprehension and control of man; consequently, man's relationship to the reality beyond him also requires a continuing relationship of trust. Pannenberg comments incisively:

> The origin of everything real is essentially infinite. So our questioning after that upon which we know ourselves to be dependent is also infinite, insofar as this questioning again moves beyond every answer and nowhere comes to rest. We seek the unity of everything real in order to become certain of the unity of our existence.[53]

The Egocentricity of Man

Since man cannot get beyond the infinite and control it, he can only trust the infinite origin and personal depth of everything. Man,

---

[53] *Ibid.*, p. 23. Italics added.
[53] *Ibid.*, p. 28.

however, seeks security through control instead of fulfillment through trust. Striving to avoid the risk of trust by control, man subsequently trusts finite things and himself instead of the infinite God. Hence, while defining man's openness to the world essentially as openness to God, Pannenberg does not posit a naïve, "optimistic" view of historical man. Precisely because man makes himself the assertive center of the world through his egocentricity, Pannenberg observes, man fails to live in constant movement beyond himself in openness: "Thus, a man not only has a tendency to break out into the open, but he also has a tendency toward a certain self-enclosement." [54]

The tension between self-centeredness and openness is characteristic of all organic existence. However, while other animals unite the opposing poles of tenacious independence and environmental involvement instinctively within themselves, man lacks the instinctive certainty of his environment, experiencing the tension of self-centeredness and openness as contradiction. Destined to openness but driven to self-assertion, man experiences an irresolvable tension which continually leads to conflict and threatens to blind him to his destiny. Man himself cannot solve the conflict between openness to the world and the egocentricity of the self, because he is unable to embrace and unify the whole of reality, including the contingencies of nature and history, through the universal extension of his own ego.

Since the conflict between self-centeredness and openness can be united into a meaningful whole only from outside the ego, man's quest for unity finally becomes the question of transcendence, of the One in whom the unity of reality has its basis. Pannenberg contends: "By warranting the unity of the world as the Creator, the one God also warrants salvation, that is, the wholeness of [man's] existence in the world, which surmounts the conflict between selfhood and openness to the world." [55] Asking the question of God, therefore, man seeks his destiny beyond the world, yet remains related to the world. However, because man lacks a direct relation to the infinite (which would enable man to control God), he perverts his relation to God through the worship of images of finite creatures. This throws the ego back upon itself. Unable to live in openness to God's truth, man traps himself in the conflict between openness and selfhood. So Pannenberg says reflectively:

Man remains imprisoned in his selfhood. He secures him-

self through what has been attained, or he insists on his plans.
In any case, to the extent that he is able, he fits what is new
into what was already in his mind. In this way not only does
he readily damage his destiny to be open to the world; he
also closes himself off from the God who summons him to his
destiny. The selfhood that is closed up within itself is sin.[56]

Like Augustine, Pannenberg identifies the core of sinful self-centeredness as self-love, the elevation of the ego as the final purpose toward
which everything else is related (which defines sin essentially as a
structural instead of a moral phenomenon). Since man's selfhood is
extensively associated with his organic structure, it is difficult to understand the identification of the ego with sin. But Pannenberg insists:
"In and of itself, selfhood is not sin, any more than control over the
world—with which the ego asserts itself and prevails—is sin; . . .
however, it is sin insofar as it falls into conflict with man's infinite
destiny." [57] That happens because the ego adheres to itself instead of
integrating itself into the higher unity of life—beyond the individual
and the community to the origin of the whole of reality. Therefore,
the sin of egocentricity, seemingly unavoidable, belongs to man's
givenness.

The Hope of Man

Since he cannot be satisfied with his strivings in the present, man
hopes and plans for the future, but the future itself brings the new
and the unexpected. Hence, every imaginative calculation that eventuates from man's hope is also surpassed by hope. The ultimate question of hope is the question of life beyond death, for all hope appears
foolish if death is really the end. Pannenberg puts it bluntly: "Whether
or not hope is a meaningful attitude in life at all is decided for the
individual in the final analysis in the question of whether there is
anything to be hoped for beyond death." [58] Yet he contends: "It is
inherent to man to hope beyond death, even as it is inherent to man
to know about his death." [59] Just as man's destiny of openness to the
world drives him to think beyond the world to God, so also his
destiny compels him to conceive of a life beyond death. Correspond-

[56] Ibid., p. 63.
[57] Ibid., pp. 64 f.
[58] JGaM, p. 84.
[59] WIM, p. 44.

ingly, Pannenberg reasons: "The God upon whom man is infinitely dependent in his search for his destiny also warrants its fulfillment beyond death." [60] Precisely because man can apprehend his destiny only by thinking of life beyond death, what one decides about the question is not incidental but crucial for the understanding of human existence and for the hope of its fulfillment. Whereas the expectation of a life beyond death has often been conceived as the "immortality of the soul," Pannenberg prefers the more realistic conception of the "resurrection of the dead" (which nonetheless preserves the positive impulses of the idea of immortality). The metaphor of resurrection anticipates a radical transformation, a "new creation" that embraces the community of men and, in some sense, the universe itself; moreover, the image of resurrection acquires concreteness for the Christian through association with the eschatological destiny of Jesus.

In addition to eschatological hope beyond death, the hope of man positively embraces life in the world. As he strives to fulfill his destiny, man seeks a unified existence which ultimately includes a unified humanity, because man's destiny to the unity of the ego with the whole of reality transcends the individual and attains configuration only in community, wherein the bond of conscience and the gift of freedom are established through love. Though one can scarcely overestimate the significance of community for man's humanity, the community never achieves the final shape of human destiny. Separation and suppression continually shatter the wholeness of community, but man cannot relinquish the goal of a perfect community of men with one another, for this goal belongs indispensably to human destiny. Pannenberg perceives an intertwining of the idea of God and that of a just community in the historic hopes of nations and men: "The Israelites also hoped for the complete revelation of their God, which was expected in the future, in the form of a perfect community of justice among men." [61] They expected the eschatological Messiah, who would establish God's Kingdom on earth. Through the presence of the Kingdom in Jesus of Nazareth, the Christian faith affirms that one can anticipate the Kingdom in the present; however, the full reality of God's Kingdom lingers in the future—the ultimate community of mankind in God's life of love.

Finally, the hope of man entails the hope of history, for man him-

[60] Ibid.
[61] Ibid., p. 107. Cf. ibid., pp. 82–136.

self is historical.[62] Not only is a man's life shaped through "historic" decision, it is defined by the context of events, which includes his decisions and everything that happens to him. The individuality of a man is decisively defined through the course of his life, for a chain of contingencies really shapes the concrete content of each single life. The goal of man's unique path in life is the fulfillment of his destiny for God; correspondingly, the individuality of man seeks integration into community and, finally, into the whole of humanity. Since history is the reality wherein man lives, the unity of humanity in world history cannot eventuate from its beginning but only from its end, where past, present, and future are embraced as a single history. Thus the hope of *man* for the fulfillment of human destiny is an eschatological hope for history. However, if the openness of man—which expresses itself as hope for the future—is to be more than an illusion, it requires a foundation outside man himself. Therefore, the question of hope, the question of the fulfillment of human destiny, encounters the question of God.

[62] *Ibid.,* pp. 137 ff.

Part Two

PANNENBERG'S
THEOLOGICAL PROGRAM

III

REVELATION
AS HISTORY

KEENLY AWARE of the difficulties inherent in God-talk for a post-Enlightenment age, Pannenberg presents an interpretation of revelation open to thoughtful discussion and susceptible to critical examination. Since Christian faith is founded upon historical revelation, he reasons, its claims must be subjected to and substantiated by historical investigation: The believer must honestly submit the truth claims of the Christian faith to reasoned historical judgments determined by rigorous historical research. Precisely at this point Pannenberg represents a radical departure from neo-orthodoxy—specifically, from the supposedly incongruous theologies of Barth and Bultmann. Of them Pannenberg surprisingly says:

> Both theological positions, that of pure historicness and that of the suprahistorical ground of faith, have a common extratheological motive. Their common starting point is to be seen in the fact that historical-critical research as the scientific verification of events did not seem to leave any room for redemptive events: Therefore, the theology of salvation history fled into a harbor supposedly safe from the historical-critical flood tide, the harbor of a suprahistory, or, with Barth, of pre-history. For the same reason the theology of existence withdrew from the meaningless and salvationless "objective" course of history to the experience of the significance of history in the "historicness" of the individual. Therefore, the historical rootedness of redemptive event must be asserted today in debate with the theology of existence, with the

theology of salvation history, and with the methodological principles of historical-critical research.[1]

Affirming the historicity of revelatory events against existentialist and salvation-history theology on the one hand and against a doctrinaire historiography on the other, Pannenberg constructs a unique conception of "revelation as history." Revelation is conceived in relation to the comprehensive whole of reality, as a temporal process of history that is not complete but open to the future—yet a future already anticipated in the history and destiny of Jesus. To give systematic form to the historicality of revelation perceived in the Biblical traditions by "the working circle," Pannenberg proposes his celebrated "Dogmatic Theses on the Doctrine of Revelation," a *tour de force* of remarkable logical power:[2]

1. The self-revelation of God, according to the Biblical witnesses, did not take place directly, after the fashion of a theophany, but indirectly, through God's historical acts.

2. Revelation happens, not at the beginning, but at the end of revelatory history.

3. In contrast to special manifestations of deity, the historical revelation is open to anyone who has eyes to see. It has universal character.

4. The universal revelation of the deity of God is not yet realized in Israel's history, but was realized first in the destiny of Jesus of Nazareth, insofar as the end of all events took place beforehand in what happened to him.

5. The deity of Israel's God is revealed by the Christ event, not as an isolated occurrence but only insofar as it is an integral part of God's history with Israel.

6. The universality of the eschatological self-demonstration of God in the destiny of Jesus comes to expression in the development of non-Jewish concepts of revelation in the Gentile Christian churches.

7. The "word" is related to revelation as prediction, instruction, and report.

These pregnant theses essentially contain Pannenberg's understanding of revelation. To clarify the interpretation of revelation that he

---

[1] "Heilsgeschehen und Geschichte," *Grundfragen systematischer Theologie*, pp. 22–23 ["Redemptive Event and History," *BQiT* I, p. 16].

[2] "Dogmatische Thesen zur Lehre von der Offenbarung," *OaG*, pp. 91–114 [*RaH*, pp. 125–158].

advocates, therefore, the key ideas expressed in and developed from these several theses require summary examination. These key ideas are: the problem of the conceptualization of revelation, the Biblical pattern of God's self-disclosure, Pannenberg's unitary understanding of history, and the logical priority of knowledge to faith.

THE PROBLEM OF CONCEPTUALIZATION

Pannenberg observes that two different but interrelated questions are currently raised under the theme of revelation: *if* God is and *who* God is. Though the frequency of these questions suggests that it has not been definitely decided that all God-talk is illusory, the importance of these questions betrays the widespread uncertainty as to God's existence and identity. In this situation the problem of revelation for the knowledge of God has gained fundamental importance. To be sure, man exists as a question for himself, a question pointing him beyond himself and everything finite; consequently, man exists as "questioning toward God." But the openness of the question does not prove God's existence; it simply constitutes man's openness to the possibility of revelation. Pannenberg puts it directly:

> Indeed, even the claim that by his questioning concerning himself and the meaning of his existence and of everything that has being, man is questioning toward *God,* can, strictly speaking, only be justified if the reality on which man turns out to be dependent in the openness of his questioning meets him personally and hence as "God." [3]

Does God exist? If so, which God? Though not easily answered, if these questions are to be answered by reference to "revelation," the contemporary concept of revelation must be carefully defined and clearly oriented to the actuality of God's revealing activity.

The Implications of "Self-revelation"

While a confusing variety of definitions for "revelation" exists in contemporary dogmatics, Pannenberg emphasizes "a noteworthy consensus" transcending all distinctions and variations: Revelation is not the imparting of supernatural truths about God, but it is "essentially the self-revelation of God." [4] Whereas it was largely the influence

[3] "Response to the Discussion," *TaH*, p. 225.
[4] "Einführung," *OaG*, pp. 7–8 [*RaH*, p. 4].

of Karl Barth which effected this consensus among theologians, it was actually Hegel who first introduced the strict definition of revelation as the self-revelation of the Absolute.[5] Hence, Hegel's philosophy of history and Barth's theology of revelation provide the background for Pannenberg's understanding of the concept of revelation as self-revelation. To define revelation strictly as God's self-revelation, Pannenberg contends, has several important but often neglected implications.

First, though there have been many appearances of God, if revelation is self-revelation, there can only be a single revelation of God, which is unique by definition. When God is ultimately revealed in one event, he cannot "also" be revealed in another, completely different event; otherwise, he has not disclosed himself fully in the one event, but at most partially.[6] Thus Pannenberg restricts the *dogmatic* term "revelation" to God's self-revelation, which denotes disclosure of essence, including therein the demonstration of the divinity of God as the power over everything, because "what we mean by the word 'God' is the power that is powerful over everything that has being." [7] Conversely, Pannenberg usually refers to those appearances of God which do not unveil God's essence as "manifestations." [8] Thereby he emphasizes the *uniqueness* of revelation as self-revelation: a disclosure of God's essence that is final. How then are God's numerous manifestations related to the one self-revelation? Two suggestions seem relevant: (1) Self-revelation presupposes a provisional knowledge of God, which originates with divine manifestations but remains indistinct and inadequate.[9] (2) Prior to God's self-revelation there are partial anticipations of the one revelation of God—manifestations that foresee the disclosure of God's deity over the whole of reality. These provisional anticipations of God's one revelation, however, are to be distinguished from the final (though anticipatory) revelation of God in Jesus Christ.[10]

---

[5] Noting Barth's repeated citations of the Hegelian Philipp Marheineke, Pannenberg, in *JGaM*, p. 127, suggests that "Hegel's concept of revelation may well have been mediated to Barth particularly through Marheineke."

[6] "Einführung," *OaG*, p. 10 [*RaH*, p. 6]; *JGaM*, p. 129.

[7] "Response to the Discussion," *TaH*, p. 232.

[8] "Einführung," *OaG*, p. 12 [*RaH*, p. 9].

[9] "The Revelation of God in Jesus of Nazareth," *TaH*, p. 118.

[10] "Response to the Discussion," *TaH*, pp. 239–240. Pannenberg characterizes single events announcing God's deity in a given situation as partial anticipations of the one revelation; yet these events, e.g., the words of the prophets, do not have the character of revelation in and of themselves, "but at most as the anticipation of the

Second, if revelation is interpreted strictly as self-revelation, the medium of revelation cannot finally be distinguished or separated from God himself. To speak of self-revelation implies that the revealer and the content of the revelation are identical; consequently, the medium through which God reveals himself cannot be something alien to him, for only when the distinction between God and the revealing medium disappears can *self*-revelation occur. To speak of the self-revelation of God in Jesus of Nazareth, therefore, means that Jesus belongs to the essence of God: "The creaturely medium of revelation, the man Jesus Christ, is raised up in his distinction from God, he is received into unity with God himself." [11]

Third, if revelation is actually God's self-disclosure, if the medium of revelation is intrinsic to the revelation itself, the form of revelation cannot simultaneously constitute a veiling. Against Barth, Pannenberg argues that a medium of revelation that inherently reveals *and* conceals God actually contradicts the unity of revelation implied in self-revelation. If God is the Subject revealing and the One revealed, the unity of revelation requires the form of revelation, Jesus Christ, to be adequate to reveal God, which is, "rightly understood," to unveil him.[12] However, while vigorously denying that the form of revelation implies a veiling, Pannenberg emphasizes God's beyondness and incomprehensibleness precisely in the divine self-disclosure.

> The God of Israel is revealed in Jesus' destiny as the hidden God. The hiddenness and transcendence of God, revealed in the crucified Jesus, surpasses the canon of the incomprehensibility of the philosophical conception of God. Indeed one can know that the resurrection of the One crucified is the eschatological self-demonstration of God . . . but no one can comprehend or exhaust what is specifically contained in this self-demonstration of God.[13]

Though there is much that can be said about God's self-disclosure in

---

whole of reality, in the prophetic announcement of final judgment or salvation" (p. 239). Unlike the revelation of God demonstrating his power over everything, "such partial revelation allows the divinity of God to appear only under a finite *aspect* in some one given case" (p. 240). The sharp distinction is between partial, provisional "anticipations of revelation" and the final, though anticipatory, "revelation."

[11] "Einführung," *OaG*, p. 9 [*RaH*, p. 5].

[12] *Ibid.*, p. 11 [*RaH*, pp. 7–9].

[13] "Dogmatische Thesen," *OaG*, p. 105 [*RaH*, pp. 142–143].

Jesus, Pannenberg urges caution, for the inconceivable future that has already happened to Jesus remains outstanding for us. Furthermore, he reasons that "the incomprehensibility of God precisely in his revelation means that the future is still open and full of possibilities for the Christian.' [14] Thus the revelation of God's final intention and essence does not mean that he becomes non-mysterious. Since history continues after the unveiling of God in Jesus Christ, God remains the incomprehensible One who is free to do new things in the open and incalculable future. Moreover, the Christian can hardly imagine what the "resurrection" actually is, much less understand completely what the Christ event says about God! Therefore, Pannenberg argues, what actually limits man's knowledge of God in his self-disclosure is not the form of revelation but the proleptic structure of knowledge itself. "Christian knowledge stands under the sign of the same 'already' and 'not yet' that marks every aspect of the life of Christians between the resurrection and the second coming of Jesus." [15] Pannenberg draws attention to the fact that, from the point of view of our limited human comprehension, the implications of revelation as an eschatological event are inexhaustible. If this is not recognized, one "easily misunderstands what has been said about the knowledge of the self-disclosure of God as a claim to a rational knowledge of everything." [16]

The Illusion of Direct Revelation

To legitimate the contemporary theological definition of "revelation" as God's self-disclosure, Pannenberg necessarily turns to the Biblical traditions, acknowledging:

> The language of the self-revelation of God must somehow be verified by the Biblical witnesses, if it is to be theologically justifiable . . . because the Biblical Scriptures are the fundamental witnesses of the events to which the theology refers when it speaks of revelation.[17]

Pannenberg specifies two different ways of conceiving the Biblical pattern of revelation—"direct revelation" or "indirect revelation."

---

[14] "Wie wird Gott uns offenbar?" *Radius,* 1960, No. 4, p. 7.
[15] "Insight and Faith," *BQiT* II, p. 45.
[16] "Dogmatischen Thesen," *OaG,* p. 105 [*RaH,* p. 143]. Cf. "Nachwort zur zweiten Auflage," *OaG,* p. 144, where Pannenberg indicates that this point should be correlated especially with Thesis 3 on the universality of revelation.
[17] "Einführung," *OaG,* p. 12 [*RaH,* p. 8].

Whereas indirect revelation initially has content other than what is ultimately to be communicated, namely, the unveiling of God's essence, direct revelation would have God himself *immediately* as its content and would thus be analogous to a divine epiphany but in the sense of a complete self-disclosure.[18]

Questioning the actuality of a direct self-revelation, Pannenberg critically surveys the alternatives supposedly confirming it.[19] He notes that the Biblical expressions translated by "to reveal" refer to God's revealing "something" or "someone" but never simply "himself"; consequently, terminological expressions rendered "to reveal" do not correspond to the direct self-revelation of God. Moving beyond the limits of terminology, Pannenberg asks if anything in the Biblical traditions conforms to a direct self-revelation of God, analyzes those instances often so conceived, and subsequently rejects each one. (1) Neither the announcement of Yahweh's name to Israel nor the knowledge of the name Jesus Christ constitutes a direct self-disclosure of God, for the simple knowledge of the name does not imply a full understanding of the being involved in the name. (2) Furthermore, the fundamental importance for Israel and primitive Christianity of the "Word of God" should not obscure the fact that it does not have God directly as its content: both the prophetic word authorized by Yahweh and the apostolic kerygma reporting the Christ event have various functions and specific contents distinct from God himself. (3) Likewise, the declaration of law on Sinai as well as the New Testament proclamation of the gospel fail to qualify as the revelation of God's essence, for the law followed a revealing of Yahweh to Israel and the gospel points back to events constituting God's revelation in Jesus Christ. Instead of a direct self-revelation of God, therefore, Pannenberg's analysis of the Biblical materials implies a concept of indirect self-disclosure.

The Indirectness of Divine Self-disclosure

Unlike direct revelation, indirect revelation does not purport to have God himself immediately as its content; rather, every activity and act of God indirectly expresses something about God, saying he

---

[18] *Ibid.*, pp. 16–17 [*RaH*, pp. 14–15]. "Immediately" as used here does not refer to the *act* of revelation, whether there is a mediator or messenger; but it refers to the *content* of revelation, implying that such content initially coincides with the ultimate intention of the revealer.

[19] "Einführung," *OaG*, pp. 12–16 [*RaH*, pp. 9–13].

is the One who does this or that. Through reflection upon the content
of an occurrence—reflection stimulated by the incident itself or the
anticipation of it—an event points beyond itself to God as its origi-
nator. Although the immediate content of an event is apprehended
"for itself," it subsequently demands consideration from a different
perspective, whereby it is perceived as an act of God. Pannenberg
reasons: "As acts of God, these events cast light back upon God,
communicating something about God himself." [20] Yet, he argues,
single acts within the ongoing course of history do not actually "reveal" God nor does God "reveal himself" in them.

> Each individual event regarded as an act of God illumi-
> nates the being of God, but only fragmentarily. God performs
> many other acts, continually unforeseeable, which in different
> ways refer back to him as their author. So, it seems, no single
> act could possibly reveal him.[21]

Hence, when the self-communication inherent in every act of God
is considered revelatory, there are numerous "revelations"—as many
revelations as there are acts of God in history and nature; or, conversely, there is a single "revelation"—one which encompasses the
totality of divine activity. Since multiple revelations would negate the
strict definition of revelation as self-revelation (a disclosure of essence
that is final), revelation must be understood as comprehending the
entirety of God's activity. If the whole of reality constituting the sphere
of God's action is conceived as history instead of cosmos, a construct
of indirect revelation emerges as a reflex of God's activity in history.
Therefore, while cognizant of the difficulties involved, Pannenberg
suggests a conception of *revelation as history,* by which is meant that
the totality of God's speech and activity, the whole of history effected
by God, shows indirectly who he is.

THE PATTERN OF REVELATION

In order to validate the proposal of God's indirect revelation in
the whole of history, Pannenberg carefully examines the Biblical materials. Moving from the Old Testament to the New, he correlates

[20] *Ibid.,* p. 17 [*RaH,* p. 16].
[21] *Ibid.*

rather incisively the revelatory traditions of ancient Israel with the prolepsis of revelation in Jesus Christ.

The Sphere of Revelation—History

Though the subject of the self-revelation of God is terminologically absent from the Scriptures, Pannenberg considers the "word of demonstration" (*Erweiswort*) of the Old Testament to be directly related to the contemporary conception of revelation as the self-revelation of God.[22] Following the lead of Rolf Rendtorff, he seizes upon the exploratory investigations of Walter Zimmerli into a complex of Old Testament formulas affirming Yahweh's divinity: the "self-presentation formula" (*Selbstvorstellungsformel*), "I am Yahweh"; the "cognition formula" (*Erkenntnisformel*), "and they shall know that I am Yahweh"; and the "word of demonstration," the prophetic word attached to the "cognition formula" predicting God's action in history.[23] The prophet's statement in I Kings 20:28 is a basic example of the "word of demonstration":

> And a man of God came near and said to the king of Israel, "Thus says Yahweh, Because the Syrians have said, Yahweh is a god of the hills but he is not a god of the valleys, [therefore I will give all this great multitude into your hand *and you shall know that (I am Yahweh)*]." [24]

Zimmerli designates this entire pattern of prophetic speech the "word of demonstration." The prophetic "word" affirms that Yahweh will "demonstrate" himself to be God through historical events yet to take place. The issue, as Pannenberg sees it, is to ascertain the essential locus of revelation. Is it the "prophetic word" announcing Yahweh's action or the "historical event" fulfilling the prophet's expectation? This question stimulates a lively form-critical debate between Zimmerli and Rendtorff, hinging upon the age of the shorter "self-presentation formula" and the age of the longer "cognition formula." The earlier formula demands priority and thereby determines the primary locus of revelation as word or event. Indeed, it is

---

[22] *JGaM*, p. 128.
[23] Rolf Rendtorff, *OaG*, pp. 21–41 ["The Concept of Revelation in Ancient Israel," *RaH*, pp. 23–53], builds upon Zimmerli's earlier form-critical work but takes exception to several of his conclusions.
[24] The "word of demonstration" is bracketed, the "cognition formula" is italicized, and the "self-presentation formula" is enclosed in parentheses.

not an either/or issue, for both Zimmerli and Rendtorff insist upon
the unity of word and event; rather, it is a question of how these
categorical terms are to be coordinated, i.e., which category is definitive
for conceiving the unity of the two.[25] Zimmerli argues that the shorter
"self-presentation formula" is the older: God is present in his word
and reveals himself in the proclamation, "I am Yahweh." Conversely,
Rendtorff contends that the "cognition formula" is the older: God
demonstrates himself in historical events in order to produce the
acknowledgment of him as God. When the short "self-presentation
formula" occurs independently, Rendtorff reasons, it represents a
later development, becoming a pregnant summary of Yahweh's claim
of power, a claim that ultimately embraces the entirety of human history.[26] Since Zimmerli locates the earliest instances of the "self-presentation formula" precisely in those texts containing the "cognition formula," Pannenberg, concurring with Rendtorff, considers it far more
probable that the "cognition formula" is the older and hence the
decisive one.[27] Hence, Pannenberg concludes, "the word of demonstration" *embraces* the "self-presentation formula" as Yahweh's claim
of power, it *accentuates* the "cognition formula" as the expectation of
the acknowledgment of Yahweh as God, and, finally, it *anticipates* a
specific event as the public demonstration of Yahweh's power, an event
which openly reveals him as "God." Essentially, therefore, the locus
of revelation is not the word presenting God's name (or claim) but the
event demonstrating God's deity.[28]

Pannenberg's attention to the "word of demonstration," with his
accent upon the moment of demonstrability, is quite significant: (1)
It intimates a promising solution to the contemporary problem of

---

[25] James M. Robinson, "Revelation as Word and History," *TaH*, pp. 42–62, but
esp. pp. 61–62, indicates the essential difference between the two positions: "Rendtorff
has tended to locate the revelation primarily in history, in which the word is
grounded and which in turn confirms the word so that knowledge of God takes
place; or to define history as including the word in the form of the history of
the transmission of traditions; or to see the valid claims of the word met in the
form of an overarching plan of history. Zimmerli has tended to locate the revelation primarily in the (prophetic) word, which calls forth history and recalls history
so that knowledge of God takes place; i.e., the occurrence of the word is itself the
decisive historic event" (p. 62).

[26] Rolf Rendtorff, *OaG*, p. 34 [*RaH*, p. 40].

[27] *JGaM*, p. 128, n. 30.

[28] Yet neither Pannenberg nor Rendtorff desire to eliminate the significance of
the word, only to deny the necessity of the intervention of a prophetic word for an
event to become revelatory. Cf. Pannenberg, "The Revelation of God in Jesus,"
TaH, p. 129.

revelation, i.e., the question "whether an alleged deity is really God," the power over everything. (2) It implies a correspondence between the visibility of revelation to those experiencing it and the accessibility of revelatory events to historical research. These projections reflect Rendtorff's summary analysis of the Old Testament expectation of God's revelation as self-confirmation:

> Therefore, the revelation of Yahweh is not so understood that it is visible only to a specific circle of men or that it requires special presuppositions for its perception. All peoples, "all flesh," the ends of the world, see what happens, and its significance as the self-demonstration of Yahweh is recognizable by them all.[29]

Hence, Pannenberg concludes, the "word of demonstration" portrays the revelation of God's deity through the public demonstration of divine power, which is available to the understanding of man precisely as man.

The Scope of Revelation—Universal History

Pannenberg refers the prophetic "word of demonstration" to the larger context of Israel's history, observing, "the whole of Israelite tradition was convinced that it was the will of Yahweh that his divinity should be made known by his historical acts." [30] Though the more primitive Old Testament traditions relate instances of the appearances of Yahweh in connection with Israel's cult and places of worship, these are suppressed and displaced (beginning with Moses) by the thought that Yahweh is to be revealed in historical events. Initially the exodus from Egypt was understood as the primal act of salvation, the historical proof of Yahweh's deity effecting faithful trust in Israel. But eventually the emphasis upon a single event was replaced by attention to a whole complex of history, the history stretching from God's promise to the patriarchs to its actual fulfillment in Israel's occupation of the land in Palestine (Deut. 4:37–40; 7:7–11). No longer a single event but a whole connected history demonstrates Yahweh's deity; moreover, the expressed purpose of the entire history is to produce the recognition of Yahweh as God, the recognition "that only he is God and has power." [31]

---

[29] Rendtorff, OaG, p. 39 [RaH, p. 46].
[30] "The Revelation of God in Jesus," TaH, p. 119.
[31] Rendtorff, OaG, p. 36 [RaH, p. 43].

Yet the prophets of the exile, experiencing the loss of the land of promise, could no longer accept the events connected with its former occupancy as the ultimate self-vindication of Yahweh; the decisive revelation of Yahweh was removed to the future, when God would manifest his glory to "all flesh" (Isa. 40:5).[32] Subsequently, Jewish apocalyptic conceived the whole history of the world from creation onward as unfolding according to divine plan. Though the deity of Yahweh was at present hidden, the apocalyptists envisioned God's appearance at the end of history—the final revelation of God's glory, the terminal event, which would gather all earlier events into a single history and reveal the significance of each within the whole. Expanding the history that demonstrates God's deity to include the totality of all events, thus transforming "salvation history" into "universal history," apocalypticism presented a conception of world history corresponding to the universality of Israel's God, "who intends to be not only the God of Israel but the God of all men." [33]

Pannenberg attributes Israel's understanding of "revelation in history" to its unique historical consciousness, the presuppositions of which lie in its conception of God. Unlike other peoples of the ancient Orient, who experienced divine reality in a retreat to primal myth, Israel encountered God increasingly in historical change itself. Consequently, Pannenberg observes, Israel acquired a special consciousness of history, originating with and oriented toward God's historical activity. "The certainty that God again and again performs new acts, that he is a 'living God,' forms the basis for Israel's understanding of reality as linear history hastening toward a goal." [34] Furthermore, as

---

[32] Two aspects of the manifestation of God's glory are especially important for Pannenberg's understanding of revelation: (1) Rendtorff, *OaG*, p. 29 [*RaH*, p. 35], identifies the appearance of God's glory with the public accomplishment of divine power whereby the demonstration of power is fundamental to and constitutive for God's being. (2) Pannenberg, *JGaM*, pp. 128–129, identifies the apocalyptic expectation of the glory of God with the self-revelation of God. When these two aspects of the manifestation of God's glory are correlated, the conjunction of the demonstration of divine power with the disclosure of God's essence orients the apocalyptic concept of God's glory to revelation as self-demonstration.

[33] "Dogmatische Thesen," *OaG*, p. 97 [*RaH*, p. 133]. Though the major prophets and the Chronicles had already universalized salvation history *in principle*, the apocalyptists were the first to give systematic expression to universal history. Cf. Dietrich Rössler, *Gesetz und Geschichte: Untersuchungen zur Theologie der jüdischen Apokalyptik und der pharisäischen Orthodoxie*, Wissenschaftliche Monographien zum Alten und Neuen Testament, 3 (Neukirchen: Neukirchen Verlag, 1960), esp. pp. 56–65, 110–111.

[34] "Heilsgeschehen und Geschichte," *Grundfragen systematischer Theologie*, pp. 24–25 ["Redemptive Event and History," *BQiT* I, p. 18].

Israel developed the writing of history, the horizon of its historical consciousness became ever wider, the length of time ever more extensive. Finally, Israel discovered reality as history itself.

> After the genealogies of the Chronicles had already begun history with Adam, Jewish apocalypticism completed the extension of history so that it covered the whole course of the world from Creation to the end. . . .
> Thus Israel not only discovered history as a particular sphere of reality; it finally drew the whole of creation into history. History is reality in its totality.[35]

Since history as a whole is eschatologized, reality as history attains completion only in the End. Hence, indirect revelation, the defined goal of the course of history, cannot occur until all events constituting history have transpired. Only the End of history can reveal Israel's God as God, "the power over everything." The End event terminates the progress of history and gathers all history as God's activity into a coherent whole; consequently, the End alone can illuminate the revelatory significance of each event within the whole of history, whether an event points to man's unfaithfulness or to God's faithful execution of his purpose. However, the accent upon the End does not restrict the scope of revelatory history to the *eschaton* (as though God were not active in history prior to its consummation),[36] for indirect revelation affirms that God reveals himself through the whole of history, which implies that God himself has a history in time.

> Indeed it is not so much the whole course of history but only "the End of history as the revelation of God" which is one with God's essence; but to the extent that the End presupposes the course of history as the perfection of it, history

---

[35] "Redemptive Event and History," *BQiT* I, pp. 20–21. In dialogue with Rudolf Bultmann, Friedrich Baumgärtel, Gerhard von Rad, Karl Löwith, and Wilhelm Kamlah, Pannenberg shows convincingly that Judaism and the New Testament maintain the reality of history discovered by Israel (*ibid.*, pp. 21 ff.). Ultimately he concludes: "The theology of history now appears in principle at least as the legitimate heir of the biblical understanding of reality" (*ibid.*, p. 31).

[36] Pannenberg, in "Response to the Discussion," *TaH*, pp. 250–255, says: "Only because the infinite reality, which as personal can be called God, is present and active in the history of the finite, can one speak of a revelation of God in history." But "it is misleading to say that history reveals God," as if history were "a subject which subsists independently over against God"; rather, "history is constituted by the active presence of the infinite God, and therefore one can only say that God reveals himself in history" (p. 253).

itself belongs essentially to the revelation of God, for history receives its unity from its End.[37]

The Shape of Revelation—Prolepsis

Yet, Pannenberg concedes, in the theological conception of *revelation as history* a major difficulty emerges, namely, the propriety of the church's affirmation that Jesus Christ is the final revelation of God. If the totality of history constitutes God's self-revelation, how can the historical particularity of Jesus of Nazareth, one event within the whole of history, possibly be the final revelation of God? If only the End of history illuminates God's revelation in the whole of history, how can a figure now past constitute God's revelation within the ongoing process of history? Responding to these questions, Pannenberg argues: "But in the destiny of Jesus the End of all history has happened in advance, as prolepsis." [38] Hence, without eliminating the horizon of the open future, it can be said that "Jesus is the anticipated *end* and not the *middle* of history." [39] As the pre-actualization of the End, as the anticipation of the End event binding history into a unitary whole, Jesus of Nazareth is the self-revelation of God. To clarify and to validate such an unusual proposal, Pannenberg develops the conception of the prolepsis of God's revelation in Jesus Christ.

Though Yahweh had established himself as the God of Israel through the events constituting Israel's history, he had not therein demonstrated his deity as the God of all men. So the apocalyptic visionaries anticipated the final manifestation of God's glory at the End of history, which would reveal the universal deity of Yahweh as the one and only God. Since apocalypticism linked the revelation of God's glory at the end with the general resurrection of the dead, the true significance of the single (though unexpected) resurrection of Jesus was comprehensible to the Jew acquainted with apocalyptic hopes. In the resurrection of Jesus the End of history has erupted within history, and God has revealed himself in the destiny of Jesus as "the power over everything." Pannenberg reasons: "Through the resurrection of Jesus the God of Israel is revealed as the God who is powerful

---

[37] "Dogmatische Thesen," *OaG*, p. 97 [*RaH*, p. 133].
[38] *Ibid.*, p. 98 [*RaH*, p. 134]. Cf. above, Chapter II, n. 10; and below, n. 79 of this chapter.
[39] "Redemptive Event and History," *BQiT* I, p. 24. Italics added.

over all events, because the One who controls the end of all things is likewise the One powerful over everything." [40] As the inauguration of the End of history, therefore, Jesus' history and destiny constitutes the final revelation of God. To be sure, God remains active in the events of history after Christ (events that actually say something about him as God), but the prolepsis of revelation in the eschatological destiny of Jesus means there will be no distinctively new disclosure of God that will surpass the Christ event.[41] Instead, the history that continues after Christ bears his mark; it is essentially defined and shaped by the proclamation of the "revelation in Christ." Pannenberg insists, however, that it is not simply the history of Jesus that reveals God but Jesus himself, for the event of revelation must not be separated from the being of God. To define God's revelation by the history and destiny of Jesus, therefore, can only mean that Jesus himself belongs to the self-definition of God.

While God did not actually reveal himself in the history of Israel, the revelation of God in Jesus of Nazareth is continuous with (and may not be isolated from) Israel's history and traditions, especially the prophetic and apocalyptic traditions. Actually Jesus was neither a prophet nor an apocalyptist; nevertheless, Jesus' proclamation of the imminence of the Kingdom of God and his claim to be the mediator of the coming salvation—witness the eschatological character of the entirety of Jesus' activity—point to the prophetic-apocalyptic horizon. Pannenberg tenaciously argues: "The activity and destiny of Jesus was distinctively defined by the prophetic-apocalyptic expectation of the End, no matter how much this was transformed by the proclamation of the presence of salvation." [42] The apocalyptic context is, if possible, even more obvious in the early church's message about Jesus' resurrection. "Only in reference to the 'understanding of history' of apocalypticism and its expectation of an end-time resurrection of the dead does the resurrection of Jesus have the significance of the pre-happening of

[40] "Wie wird Gott uns offenbar?" Radius, 1960, No. 4, p. 6. Yet Pannenberg insists: "In the event of Jesus' resurrection not only the power of God but also his love for us is revealed" (p. 7) especially as it illuminates the significance of Jesus' death "for us."

[41] Pannenberg, "Response to the Discussion," TaH, pp. 240–241, qualifies his earlier understanding of the finality of revelation in Jesus Christ as the anticipation of the end of all events and their completion. He states: "Above and beyond this I now see the distinctiveness of the history of Jesus, which establishes its finality as the revelation of God, in the fact that it is itself the event uniting and reconciling all events to the whole."

[42] "Dogmatische Thesen," OaG, p. 107 [RaH, p. 146].

the End." [43] To speak in the language of apocalyptic expectation, therefore: the resurrection of Jesus authenticated his pre-Easter claim and actualized the End of history within history; it was an eschatological event which ultimately identifies Jesus Christ as the final revelation of God. Hence, Pannenberg argues, for a Jew everything hinged upon the question of Jesus' resurrection.

Pannenberg not only emphasizes the importance of Israel's history and traditions for understanding God's revelation in Jesus; he also affirms the legitimacy (but recognizes the limitations) of the theological formulations of the Christ event in the non-Jewish soil of Gentile Christianity. Particularly, gnostic thought appears to have had a significant role in the transition from Jewish to Hellenistic Christianity, and it served effectively to make the God who raised Jesus from the dead intelligible as "God" to the Gentiles. However, the appropriation of gnostic concepts related to revelation can be justified theologically only from the perspective of the historical demonstration of the deity of God in the destiny of Jesus. Pannenberg observes:

> The theology of incarnation, which undoubtedly has one of its roots in the gnostic conception of revelation, cannot be an independent basis of theological thought, but it is to be understood as an interpretation of the historical self-demonstration of God in the destiny of Jesus of Nazareth—in his earthly works, in his cross, and decisively in his resurrection.[44]

Indeed, the concept of incarnation is irreplaceable, for it expresses the development of God's revelation and its achievement in the man Jesus of Nazareth, the movement from the distant majesty of God to his nearness which is revealed for all times in the Christ event. Hence, Pannenberg concludes: "The acknowledgment of the incarnation is a final résumé of the revelatory history of the God of Israel." [45] Yet the concept of incarnation does not constitute the basis for an understanding of revelation; on the contrary, the resurrection of Jesus of Nazareth, the event of revelation, is itself the foundation of the confession of incarnation.

The Significance of Revelation—Grace

The issue confronting contemporary philosophy of religion and systematic theology is to locate, if possible, a manifestation of divine

[43] *Ibid.*
[44] *Ibid.*, p. 111 [*RaH*, p. 151].
[45] *Ibid.*

reality capable of convincing modern man that it constitutes the self-confirmation of God. Correlating Israel's traditions to the modern, post-Enlightenment situation, Pannenberg perceives a direct correspondence between the Old Testament eschatological "word of demonstration"—that is, "Yahweh will prove his divinity, for Israel and for all other peoples, through events which show that the God of Israel is powerful over all things"—and the contemporary problem of revelation, which is,

> whether an alleged deity is really God, i.e., powerful over all things, a matter that can only be demonstrated in the event in which, according to the assertion, he is supposed to be powerful. It can finally be demonstrated only in the totality of all events, insofar as what we mean by the word "God" is the power that is powerful over everything that has being.[46]

Admittedly the *structure* of revelation conceived as self-demonstration magnifies the exercise of God's power as the public confirmation of his deity; however, the content of revelation, how God is God in relation to man, is not necessarily restricted or impaired. Pannenberg insists:

> In Christian theology it can always be a matter only of the power (and therewith the divinity) of *the* God whose essence is revealed through Jesus as love. However, if this love were powerless, then it would not be God; and if it were only one power among others, then it would not be the one God from whom and to whom are all things and who alone in all seriousness can be called God.[47]

Precisely in the eschatological demonstration of power—the raising of the crucified Jesus from the dead—the God whom Jesus proclaimed as "the loving Father" confirms his deity as "the power over everything" and therein reveals himself as the creative power of love.

Furthermore, the logical (but relative) priority of revelation to salvation does not depreciate the importance of the latter. On the contrary, interest in revelation presupposes a concern for salvation, but the perception of revelation, Pannenberg contends, is prerequisite to participation in salvation. Only the knowledge of God's nearness makes salvation possible, for the possibility of community with God

---

[46] "Response to the Discussion," *TaH*, p. 232.
[47] *Ibid.*, p. 232, n. 10.

and therein the fulfillment of human destiny hinges upon the proximity of God to man. Consequently, the prolepsis of God's revelation in the Christ event, God's coming near to man in Jesus, creates a unique opportunity for men to have community with God. If God chose to reveal himself only at the temporal End of history in the judgment of the living and the dead, it would mean damnation to the sinner, for there would be no occasion to respond positively to God's revelation. However, as Jesus himself recognized, the proleptic announcement of the imminent Kingdom offered man "a chance to participate in God's future rather than being overwhelmed by its sudden arrival and being conquered as an adversary of that future." [48] Thus the prolepsis of God's revelatory demonstration, which affords man the exceptional opportunity for repentance and salvation within history, coincides with the revelation of God's grace. Hence, Pannenberg concludes, for the man open to God, revelation in its deepest sense means salvation. Conceptually, therefore, "the salvatory meaning of the revelation of God essentially coheres with its proleptic character." [49]

The Phenomenon of History

If God reveals himself indirectly through the whole of history (but proleptically in the history of Jesus), it is crucial to understand how Pannenberg defines the elusive term "history." Pannenberg's concept of history can be appropriately described under the categories "universal history" [50] (*Universalgeschichte*) and "the history of the transmission of traditions" (*Überlieferungsgeschichte*). The former denotes the binding of history's contingencies into a coherent whole and the latter embraces the intrinsic unity of event and meaning, *Historie* and *Geschichte*.

Universal History

Though it is impossible to survey the whole of reality, it is indispensable to think of reality in its entirety, Pannenberg argues, for each individual entity has its meaning only in relation to the whole

---

[48] "Theology and the Kingdom of God," *TaKoG*, pp. 64–65.

[49] "Dogmatische Thesen," *OaG*, p. 101, n. 14 [*RaH*, pp. 156–157, n. 14].

[50] The centrality of universal history for Pannenberg's program points beyond Hegel's philosophy of history to the constitutive significance of apocalypticism for his "theological conception of history." So also Carl Braaten, "The New Theology of the Future," *The Futurist Option*, p. 14.

to which it belongs. When reality is conceived as history, which means it is open to the future and not yet complete, universal history becomes an inescapable theme of historical work. Each event in history achieves its significance only in relation to other events with which it is interwoven; consequently, the question of the significance of any particular event turns initially on its immediate context but broadens progressively to encompass the whole of history, i.e., universal history, wherein the ultimate consequence and significance of the specific event in question can be evaluated. Therefore, historical thinking—explicitly or implicitly—presupposes a conception of the whole of history, a scheme of universal history.[51]

The recognition that the historian functions with a presupposed outline of the course of history exposes the inadequacy (if not the actual impossibility) of historical positivism. The historian does not collect isolated facts and subsequently reconstruct the event(s) in question; he begins with an imaginatively projected theory of event(s) which research confirms, modifies, or eliminates.[52] Hence, the validity of a particular historical reconstruction depends not only upon specific historical-critical research but also upon the adequacy of the historian's "sketch of the whole," for *it tends to delimit the historian's conception of what could or could not occur in the course of history.* With profound insight Pannenberg reasons:

> Historical statements . . . presuppose a universal horizon of meaning, at least implicitly and in a provisional way. When the historian inquires into the specific individuality of a process, an event, or a figure, he always brings with him a provisional consciousness of reality generally, as well as an approximate idea of the nexus of events in which the occurrence to be clarified belongs. *This determines his consciousness of the possibilities with reference to the special object of his investigation.* We are talking here about the so-called "pre-understanding." The point of departure for historical work is constituted by a spontaneous pre-projection of nexuses of meaning which then are tested against observation of all the available individual details, and confirmed or modified in accord with each of these.[53]

[51] Cf. "Response to the Discussion," *TaH,* pp. 241–244.
[52] "Redemptive Event and History," *BQiT* I, p. 70.
[53] "What Is a Dogmatic Statement?" *BQiT* I, p. 199. Italics added.

Therefore, not only is a conception of universal history a necessary presupposition for the understanding of events in history; the historian's imaginatively projected theory of history influences his judgment and interpretation of reported historical events.

Furthermore, an adequate solution to the problem of revelation—if God is, and if so, which God—demands a conception of universal history. Only in the horizon of universal history can one meaningfully ask whether or not God has revealed himself here or there in history. When the historian examines a limited segment of history, which is usually what he does, the question of God's revelation in history must essentially remain open. To ask the question whether or not God has revealed himself in the Christ event in distinction to all other events in nature and human history obviously requires an overview of the whole of history (for revelation must correspond to the universality of God). Thus, Pannenberg concludes, "Only on the assumption of a universal-historical horizon can there be such an inquiry." [54]

Turning from the whole of universal history to the particularity of events constituting history, Pannenberg argues that the fundamental character of the historical is contingency and individuality. Every historical event is more or less unrepeatable. An adequate concept of history, consequently, must be oriented to the unique and the contingent; correspondingly, the unity of history must be conceived so as not to sacrifice the radical contingency of individual historical events.[55] Therefore, Pannenberg specifically rejects several interpretations of history that minimize historical contingency or suppress history's openness to the future. (1) Though analogy as a methodological principle is crucial to the work of the historian, Troeltsch's exclusive dependence upon known analogies to fix the limits of historical knowledge is unacceptable, for such dependence presupposes the essential similarity of all historical events instead of the genuine uniqueness of the historical.[56] (2) Also, while developmental unities may occur within limited segments of the historical process, each essentially evolutionary or teleological interpretation of history must be repudiated, for the assumption that the future flows from the past denies the contingency of the open future, the incalculable newness of the "not yet." [57] (3) Similarly, all morphological conceptions of

[54] "Redemptive Event and History," *BQiT* I, p. 67.
[55] *Ibid.*, p. 72.
[56] *Ibid.*, pp. 45–46.
[57] *Ibid.*, pp. 42, 72.

historical unity prove inadequate, for the contingency of events is obscured by concentrating upon types.[58] (4) Likewise, Hegel's conception of history must be rejected, for Hegel could understand history as a unity only by identifying his own standpoint as the end of the history of thought, thereby losing historical contingency and the openness of history to the future.[59]

Given the radical contingency of the historical, Pannenberg acknowledges that it is a formidable task—but not an impossibility—to construct a conception of the unity of history without forfeiting its contingency. Initially, Pannenberg suggests, the continuity of history and the contingency of historical events must have a common root. Though some locate this common root in mankind, such a solution proves inaccurate: Man exists only as an individual, not as a *generic* historical process; moreover, the historicness of human existence cannot constitute the unity of history, for man's historicness is itself grounded in the experience of history.[60] Instead, Pannenberg points to a transcendent root of history's unity and contingency: "God, who is the origin of the contingent in the world through the transcendence of his freedom, establishes also the unity of the contingent as history, but in such a way that the contingency of events, which is integral to history, is not excluded." [61]

The continuity of contingent events converging as a unitary whole is itself an expression of the faithfulness of God. When the unity of history is grounded in the faithfulness of the incalculable God, however, the continuity of history cannot flow essentially from the past into the future (i.e., in a manner somewhat comparable to the process of evolution), for the free God produces new events (and realities) in history that simply cannot be anticipated from the past. Hence, the continuity of history must be constantly reestablished. Unforeseen contingent events are retroactively joined to the past, transform it, and thereby restructure history's continuity. Precisely through such *retroactive integration,* which continually reconstitutes the unity of history, the faithfulness of God expresses itself. Pannenberg contends: "Only in this way, as the backward-reaching incorporation of the contingently new into what has been . . . can the primary connection

---

[58] *Ibid.,* pp. 72–73.
[59] "What Is Truth?" *BQiT* II, p. 22.
[60] To be sure, the life of the individual has the form of a historical process; however, it does not represent a *generic* process wherein the unity of history itself can be grounded (Wolfhart Pannenberg, April 6, 1971: personal communication).
[61] "Heilsgeschehen und Geschichte," *Grundfragen systematischer Theologie,* pp. 73–74 ["Redemptive Event and History," *BQiT* I, pp. 74–75].

of history be conceived without losing its contingency." [62] Hence, the continuity of events is actually visible only in retrospect. Pannenberg's conception of retroactive continuity ultimately means that history flows fundamentally from the future into the past, that the future is not basically a product of the past: "The essential nature of the future lies in the unpredictable new thing that is hidden in the womb of the future." [63]

Since only the Biblical conception of God as the creator and sustainer of history permits an understanding of the unity of history that does not sacrifice its contingency, Pannenberg believes that the concept of God should actually be indispensable to the historian. Yet he does not thereby embrace supernaturalism and deny the humanity of history. Instead, Pannenberg contends:

> [God's] will does not occur at the expense of human activity, but precisely through the experience, plans, and deeds of men, despite and in their sinful perversion. By grasping God's works in such indirectness that it seeks the connections between events in concrete, inner-worldly circumstances, without explaining away the novel, more or less analogy-less aspects of the events, theological history writing bears witness to God as the Creator of the world. Proper theological research into history must absorb the truth of the humanistic tendency toward an "immanent" understanding of events. It may not supplant detailed historical investigation by supranaturalistic hypotheses.[64]

Therefore, Pannenberg rejects as equally reprehensible radical humanism and theological supernaturalism. The former neglects the uniqueness of history, avoids the question of God, and limits the mystery of man, while the latter arbitrarily obstructs historical research into immanental conditions and analogies through the assertion of transcendent intervention. Suggesting an open stance on the part of the historian, Pannenberg continues:

> The God who works in the contingency of events and at the same time creates their continuity can at first be only a problem for the historian as he sets about his work. How

[62] "Redemptive Event and History," *BQiT* I, p. 76.
[63] *WIM*, p. 42.
[64] "Redemptive Event and History," *BQiT* I, p. 79.

God works and how he has created the continuity of history
again and again can only be taught by history itself.[65]

Though the question of God is unanswerable and indecisive in wide
areas of historical research, it occasionally becomes unavoidable, especially in the field of the history of religions, for that is the place
where the question of God immediately confronts the historian. In
the context of the history of religions the historian must face the
question of the deity of Israel's God in contrast to the gods of other
religions. While necessarily approaching the problem with the Greek
question of the true form of divine reality, the historian can finally
answer the question of God only with reference to history and historical
research.

Precisely at the point of historical research as a truth-determining
enterprise Pannenberg's universal history distinguishes itself from
salvation history, because the theological conception of universal
history is *in principle historically verifiable*. Its ability to account for
all known findings would constitute the positive criterion of its truth;
moreover, the demonstration that without its specific assertions the
accessible findings are not (or are not fully) explainable would function
as its negative criterion.[66] Although the task of verification extends to
all accessible phenomena, a theology of history does exhibit a selective tendency. It will focus generally upon historical events—specifically upon the more distinctive and unique. Consequently, interest
will concentrate especially upon the eschatological history of Jesus of
Nazareth, for in the destiny of Jesus the End of all history has occurred in advance, as prolepsis. But the anticipatory appearance of
the End of history within history does not mean history itself is
abolished.[67] On the contrary, since the End of history is already present,
an understanding of history as a unitary whole is made possible for the
first time.

Yet Pannenberg urges caution: "Jesus Christ, the end of history,
is not available to us as the principle of a 'Christologically' grounded
total view of world history." [68] The resurrection of Jesus, the inbreak
of the *eschaton*, confronts human understanding as a light that blinds,
as incomprehensible mystery; consequently, one may not use it to

[65] *Ibid.*, p. 76.
[66] *Ibid.*, p. 78.
[67] *Ibid.*, p. 36.
[68] *Ibid.*, p. 37.

calculate the course of history. This does not mean, however, that a theological conception of universal history is impossible. While it is necessary to disavow every comprehensive conception of universal history, it is something quite different if the total view of reality as history is broken open from within. Since the End of history is given in advance in Jesus Christ but precisely therein is deprived of absolute comprehension, Pannenberg concludes:

> We can say what such an outbreak of the incomprehensibility of the eschaton in history means only in the framework of a universal historical understanding of the reality in which this outbreak occurs, just because through it the universal historical scheme itself is forced open.[69]

The selective tendency of a theological conception of history to focus upon the history and destiny of Jesus is curbed, nevertheless, through the universal claim of Israel's God to be the God of all men and through the definitive exercise of God's authority by Jesus. Therefore, Pannenberg judges, it is necessary to discover the connection between the Christ event and all other occurrences in order to apprehend the authenticity of the universality of Israel's God and the truth of his revelation in Jesus Christ.

The History of the Transmission of Traditions

Projecting a conception of revelation *as* history, Pannenberg posits an interpretation of history that must ultimately embrace event and meaning. In his essay "Redemptive Event and History" (first published in 1959) Pannenberg attempted to establish a theological conception of history constituted by the tension between promise and fulfillment. However, the Old Testament schema of the divine Word effecting history and the realization of the Word in historical event proved inadequate, for "as a rule the promises do not enter so literally into fulfillment as one would assume that they would if they were the word of God effecting history." [70] Taking account of the discontinuity between promise and fulfillment, therefore, Pannenberg turned in *Revelation as History* (first German ed., 1961) to the more comprehensive, less schematic conception of "the history of the transmission of traditions."

[69] *Ibid.*, pp. 37–38.
[70] "Response to the Discussion," *TaH*, p. 259. Cf. also "Foreword," *BQiT* I, pp. xvii–xviii.

Pannenberg disavows those conceptions of history which concentrate (exclusively or predominantly) upon the external course of events; instead, he understands history essentially as a process of traditions, for historical events always occur in a traditions context in which and through which they communicate their significance. To clarify the intertwining of *Historie* and *Geschichte* within history, Pannenberg offers a terse but pregnant statement of the dynamics and implications of the history of the transmission of traditions.

> History is never composed of so-called bare facts. As human history, events are always intertwined with understanding, in hope and remembrance, and the transformations of understanding are themselves historical events. These elements are not to be separated from the happenings of history, as they originally occurred. Thus history is always "the history of the transmission of traditions"; and even the events of nature, which are included in the history of a people, have significance only with reference to their positive or negative relationship to the traditions and expectations in which those men live. The events of history speak their own language, the language of facts, but this language is hearable only in the context of the interpenetration of the traditions and expectations in which the occurrences actually happen.[71]

History, therefore, is essentially the interweaving of events and meanings within the history of traditions. The traditions provide the linguistic context—the concepts, the memories, and the expectations —wherein new events are meaningfully experienced and through which they are subsequently transmitted.

Pannenberg explicitly rejects the idea of splitting up the historical consciousness into the detection of facts and an evaluation of them, the dividing of history into history as known and history as experienced. Such a procedure is intolerable, he argues, because it is the reflection of an outmoded and inadequate historical method. Against the positivistic historiography espoused by neo-Kantian philosophy and assumed by dialectical theology, Pannenberg emphasizes the original unity of fact and meaning. "Every event, if not artificially taken out of context (out of its historical environment, stretching into the past and the future), brings its own meaning for each particular

---

[71] "Dogmatische Thesen," *OaG*, p. 112 [*RaH*, pp. 152–153].

inquirer, brings it with its context, which, of course, is always a context of tradition." [72]

Though every event does not have equal clarity, each event has its original meaning within the context of circumstances and tradition in which it took place and through which it is connected to the present for its historical interest. To be sure, the meaning of a past event can be determined only from the vantage point of the inquirer, for the historical continuum within which an event has meaning also includes the present, but that does not include the validity of attaching whatever meaning one will to a given event. On the contrary, the facticity of the event must remain the norm for measuring the multiplicity of its interpretations. Yet the content to be interpreted in its facticity always contains more than is immediately available in it. Hence, Pannenberg reasons, the content implies "an anticipation of meaning . . . and does so in such a way that this anticipation of meaning cannot be expressed exhaustively and definitively within any limited horizon of meaning or in any particular interpretation." [73] Thus the criteria that govern interpretations are also subject to reformulation in the transmission of the interpretations. Yet the meaning of an event in the realm of history has its criterion in the facticity to which it adheres, though the meaning as such may transcend the fact. Speaking theologically, Pannenberg pointedly concludes: "All interpretations of the historical Jesus—past as well as present—must allow themselves to be tested with regard to whether or not they explicate the meaning warranted by this history itself." [74]

Pannenberg's understanding of history as the transmission of traditions denotes "a hermeneutical process involving the ceaseless revision of the transmitted tradition in the light of new experiences and new expectations of the future." [75] Tradition initially provides the context in which and through which the meaning of new events comes to expression. The resurrection of Jesus constitutes the classic example of this hermeneutical function of tradition: Though Jesus' resurrection breaks apocalyptic expectation, it is only within apocalyptic tradition that resurrection itself can be understood. In addition, traditions themselves are reinterpreted in the light of the ongoing process of history, not arbitrarily, but precisely for the purpose of explicating

[72] "The Revelation of God in Jesus," *TaH*, p. 127.
[73] "On Historical and Theological Hermeneutic," *BQiT* I, p. 140.
[74] *Ibid.*, p. 150.
[75] "Foreword," *BQiT* I, p. xviii.

the meaning of a past event in a new historical context. Thus the reformulation of the Jesus tradition in the Fourth Gospel represents a conscious effort to present the significance of Jesus of Nazareth to the Hellenistic world. As a hermeneutical process, therefore, the history of traditions provides the context for understanding new events, and it is itself continually reinterpreted in the changing course of history.

The reports and interpretations of events transmitted in tradition are supposedly of some general import, of some relevance for others. Since the recipients of the ongoing tradition experience life differently in the light of new events, however, the tradition itself is continually modified. Pannenberg observes:

> It is a consequence of the language-character of historical experience that human history always accomplishes itself as history of the transmission of traditions, in dialogue with the heritage of a past which is either adopted as one's own or else rejected, and in anticipation of a future which is more than the future of the particular individual concerned.[76]

The history of traditions cannot be equated with "traditionalism," as though what has been transmitted were inalterably valid. The history of the transmission of traditions includes the *transformations* in tradition, "not only with the process of their formation, but also with the processes of their criticism, modification, and dissolution." [77] Hence, the "history" of the transmission of traditions, as a material process and as a theme of historical reconstruction, accomplishes the critique of traditional self-understanding by bringing to consciousness the transformation of the transmitted tradition. Only in the process of transformation is historical continuity actually to be found.

Pannenberg acknowledges that the concept of the history of traditions which he utilizes represents a revision of the concept as it is usually understood in exegetical and form-critical research. While the form critics define "the history of the transmission of traditions" essentially as a technical methodological concept for tracing the history of literary and oral materials, Pannenberg construes the history of traditions as a systematic concept through its extension by and reference to the philosophy of history. Over against the methodological conception,

[76] "Response to the Discussion," *TaH*, p. 256.
[77] *Ibid.*, p. 258.

the systematic concept does not begin with the final stage of
a text in order to inquire about the derivation of the material that has been fashioned into it. Rather it begins at
the points of origin reached through such historical research
and inquires into an *open future* of transformations, mixtures,
or ramifications of traditions, and what is more, it inquires
in such a way that the "materials" cannot be separated from
the concrete behavior of the individuals.[78]

Hence, beyond the technical analysis of the history of the transmission
of traditions (literary and oral), the systematic concept accentuates
the investigation of the behavior of the bearers of tradition as well
as the realities that shaped their behavior. Thus the history of traditions, systematically conceived, enables the historian to ask what stands
behind the phenomena that are being studied.

Though the history of traditions is neither conceptually nor materially identical with universal history, there is a viable impulse
toward universal history in the history of the transmission of traditions. First, as a conception of history anchored in the Biblical experience of history, the history of traditions is characterized by an
eschatological orientation. Indeed, the predictive word of the prophet
did not always precede the events revealing Yahweh's deity, but the
prophetic word of promise is an essential and vital part of Israel's
traditions. The promise becomes an event in history which points
history forward; subsequently, the promise itself is modified through
its historical transmission; and, finally, it is transformed in its fulfillment—a fulfillment that retroactively redefines the promise. The
thrust toward the future accomplished by new prophetic words (and
apocalyptic visions) as well as the occurrence of surprising events pointing beyond the present continually turned Israel's eye to the horizon
of the "not yet." Moreover, while the proleptic revelation of God in
the "past" of Jesus now qualifies and defines the eschatological hope
of the church, expectation for the future remains, because only the
End itself can clarify what the prolepsis of the End in the Christ event
ultimately means. Hence, the history of the transmission of traditions,
derived from the Biblical experience of history, reflects an eschatological impetus toward the horizon of universal history.

Second, the idea that God is present in an event which will be

[78] *Ibid.*, p. 257, n. 63.

overtaken by other events and revised by them with regard to its initial content points beyond the specific event (transmitted in the history of traditions) to a universal-historical horizon. When historical event participates in language, Pannenberg observes, it has already transcended the particular occasion with which it began.

> The word, which reaches beyond the particular event in selection and in anticipation, also says that—and how— God, the power over all things, is present in the individual event. The word can be corrected by further events, which in a similar way give occasion for experiences that reach beyond themselves, precisely because in this way the word comprehends the "general" in the individual.[79]

The participation of events in language ultimately suggests a conception of universal history, for only the End defines how God is present in the individual events of history. Therefore, the word giving expression to the significance of an event in the history of traditions, while transcending the moment of its occurrence, strains toward the horizon of universal history wherein the significance of the event is finally realized.[80]

[79] *Ibid.*, p. 256. While the whole of reality is not yet complete, which denotes the proleptic structure of all cognition and meaning, Pannenberg contends: "Nevertheless words ascribe to events, things, and even persons whom we encounter their essence, their meaning. . . . That implies an *anticipation* of the whole of reality. Though it is a question whether the attributed meaning proves correct—which is often debatable and always a question which remains open—all occurrence has to be understood, right into its ontological structure, as anticipation of future finality (both for the good and for the evil), insofar as the event already has any such meaning attributed to it by the word. The word brings to expression this essence, which is not immediately to be found in the event. The category of anticipation or prolepsis, which was originally introduced to describe the distinctive structure of the history of Jesus, especially of his resurrection, thus shows itself to be a fundamental structural element both of cognition and of language, and of the being of beings in their temporality. Thus the task is also posed of distinguishing the prolepsis of eschatological future in the ministry of Jesus and above all in his resurrection, in its distinctiveness over against other sorts of ontic and noetic anticipation of eschatological fulfillment." *Ibid.*, pp. 260–262.

[80] Since history continues after the prolepsis of God's revelation in Jesus of Nazareth, other historical events supersede the Christ event, *but only temporally.* No event will *surpass* the revelatory significance of the history and destiny of Jesus. While the content of the Christ event will not be fundamentally "revised" by new events in history, the depth of its content must be continually reformulated. Cf. "On Historical and Theological Hermeneutic," *BQiT* I, pp. 157–158.

IV

REVELATION, HISTORY, AND FAITH

A CONTEMPORARY SOLUTION to the problem of faith—of faith and doubt, of Easter faith and history—underlies the entirety of the program of *revelation as history*. Pannenberg insists that knowledge and faith are inseparable, observing: "Only unconditional trust in Jesus and in the God whom he reveals can truly be called faith. But such trust involves believing certain things to be true; from that it cannot be separated and without that it cannot exist."[1] Indeed, Pannenberg acknowledges that one encounters God in the personal experience of life, but he doubts whether personal experience in and of itself can substantiate the identification of "the power over everything" with the Biblical God, the Creator of heaven and earth whom Jesus called "Father." On the contrary, Pannenberg argues:

> If we take our bearings solely from the experiences of our personal life, the decision to believe or not to believe always retains an ultimately arbitrary, emotional element. It is the breadth of total experience of every and all reality which provides the field where we have to enquire whether the divine nature of the God of the Bible can stand up to verification; it is not the narrow bounds of an entirely personal experience of life, taken in isolation.[2]

The justification for talking about the all-powerful God engages one's understanding of the whole of reality beyond special individual

[1] *AC*, p. 6.
[2] *Ibid.*, p. 35.

experiences. Hence, Pannenberg says: "Immediate religious experience cannot *by itself alone* establish the certainty of the truth of its content." [3] *The truth of personal religious experience has its criterion and point of reference in the historical actuality of God's self-disclosure as "the power over everything"—not, conversely, in the subjectivity of an immediate experience of God.* Whether one has really experienced God, or whether "God" might be a convenient designation from one's culture or imaginative experience for something quite different from the Biblical God, requires critical reflection which relates one's experience of God to the whole of reality. Only thereby are personal religious experiences actually confirmed as genuine experiences of God. Therefore, Pannenberg's conception of *revelation as history*—which refers revelation to history's End and defines history as the interweaving of events with meaning on the horizon of universal history—has implications of profound consequence for the perception and appropriation of God's revelation in Jesus Christ.

THE ACCESSIBILITY OF REVELATION TO HISTORICAL RESEARCH

Though revelatory history is usually distinguished from critical history because the former supposedly lies beyond the grasp of the historical-critical method, Pannenberg considers such a distinction contrived. If a more satisfactory path to knowledge of past events really exists, he reasons, it should be declared the right historical method; moreover, if God has actually revealed himself in (or through) history, the truth of that revelation must be subjected to historical inquiry.[4]

The Connotations of Historical Revelation

Many, indeed most, men do not recognize God's revelation in the Christ event, but that is no reason in and of itself to dispute revelation's historicity; correspondingly, simply to assert the claim of God's revelation in the history of Jesus does not establish its veracity. Christian faith, which issues from and depends upon an actual past event, cannot remain untouched by the results of historical-critical research; the question of the facticity of revelatory events cannot be avoided. So Pannenberg says:

[3] "Response to the Discussion," *TaH*, p. 239.
[4] "Redemptive Event and History," *BQiT* I, pp. 38–39.

> The reference of the Christian faith to history unavoidably carries with it the demand that the believer must not try to save himself from historical-critical questions by means of some "invulnerable area"—otherwise it will lose its historical basis.[5]

With these words Pannenberg distinguishes himself from Herrmann and Kähler, who attempted to establish the basis of faith independent of the shifting currents of historical research and thereby fell victim to the fatal consequence of actually building faith upon faith itself. Moreover, he differs from Künneth and Althaus, who consider the historical as the *conditio sine qua non* of faith but not the authentic foundation of faith. If history is essential to revelation but not the basis of faith, if the revelatory significance of historically ascertainable events is visible only to the eyes of faith, Pannenberg reasons, "then it is impossible to see how the historicity of the pure facts should be able to protect faith against the reproach that it rests upon illusion and caprice." [6] Only when revelatory significance is inherent in and derived from the history of Jesus itself can one actually speak of incarnation, of the entrance of God into the mode of human existence. "But then," Pannenberg argues, "it will be impossible *in principle* to reject out of hand the idea that historical investigation of this event, even in its particularity, could and must discover its revelatory character." [7] Whether historical research can *in fact* apprehend the destiny of Jesus of Nazareth as the revelation of God is an entirely different question. Indeed, Pannenberg acknowledges, the category "revelation of God" poses a most difficult problem, because it seems to lack a proper place in the realm of historical interpretation.[8] However, when the concept of God is correlated with the whole of reality (though the whole of reality remains incomplete and unfinished), when reality is conceived as a process of history moving toward a still open future (which defines the all-determining reality, if personal, as the God of history), Pannenberg argues that it is possible within the framework of universal history to recognize the eschatological history of Jesus as the anticipatory revelation of God.[9]

[5] *Ibid.*, p. 56.
[6] *Ibid.*, p. 60.
[7] *Ibid.*, p. 61.
[8] "On Historical and Theological Hermeneutic," *BQiT* I, p. 156.
[9] *Ibid.*, p. 159. Cf. "Kerygma and History," *BQiT* I, p. 94, n. 20.

The Components of the Historical Method

While an anthropocentric element is inherent in the structure of the historical method, Pannenberg contends that the principles of historical research do not have to be essentially and unavoidably imprisoned within an anthropocentric world view (which would preclude any transcendent reference). To justify such a conclusion, he analyzes the basic components of the historical method, namely, the presupposition of universal correlation and the application of analogy.[10]

The principle of the universal correlation of all historical phenomena affirms that every historical occurrence is reciprocally connected with the circumstances in its environment and cannot be segregated from the other events related to its happening. Thus, the events that the Bible describes as God's relevatory deeds cannot be isolated from the rest of history; instead, the historical documents recording the faith of Israel and the church must be interpreted against their respective backgrounds, for they are inseparably bound to them. God's redemptive history did not happen outside the universal interrelatedness of history; consequently, revelatory history cannot be differentiated from ordinary history, as though it occurred in a different realm, but must be understood in reciprocity with its historical environment. Hence, Pannenberg contends:

> The conception of a redemptive history severed from ordinary history, as in Hofmann's view or in the sense of Barth's "primal history," is hardly acceptable on theological grounds, and is judged not to be so in the first instance because of historical presuppositions. It belongs to the full meaning of the Incarnation that God's redemptive deed took place within the universal correlative connections of human history and not in a ghetto of redemptive history, or in a primal history belonging to a dimension which is "oblique" to ordinary history . . . if, indeed, it has not remained in an archetypal realm above the plane of history.[11]

Though universal correlation includes the acceptance of causal re-

<hr/>

[10] "Redemptive Event and History," *BQiT* I, pp. 45–50. Pannenberg accepts Troeltsch's identification of the components of the historical method but criticizes the latter's definition (and application) of both principles.
[11] *Ibid.*, pp. 41–42.

lations between historical phenomena, the contingency of historical events (and the openness of history to the future) qualify the causal principle, invalidating all attempts to understand history essentially as evolution. Therefore, only a misuse of the causal principle, not universal correlation itself, could pose a fundamental conflict between the historical method and a theological conception of history.

The decisive problem for the relation of historical method to theology lies with the principle of analogy, or, more precisely, with the application of analogy by modern historiography. As a principle of historical research, analogy means that phenomena difficult to understand, comparatively opaque, should be conceived and evaluated in terms of the investigator's experience and observation. Proceeding from the known to the unknown is fundamental to analogy as a way of knowing, for analogy demonstrates its power of disclosure through the illumination of "what is obscure" by referring it to "what is plain." An obvious anthropocentric structure inheres in the use of analogy, Pannenberg concedes, but that poses no fundamental problem to a theology of history, for an anthropocentric methodological structure does not constitute an anthropocentric world view. An unnecessary constriction of historical inquiry through anthropocentrism does occur, however, when, instead of specifying concrete analogies from case to case, the historian—appealing to the "omnipotence of analogy"—postulates the fundamental homogeneity of all reality, which makes man's usual experience the norm for understanding history.[12] Since historical events are contingent and more or less unique, Pannenberg argues, the attempt to comprehend all historical dissimilarity within a universal homogeneity illegitimately restricts the historical question and effectively distorts the openness of the historical method.

The cognitive power of analogy depends upon its ability to teach one to see beyond the similar to the dissimilar, thereby illuminating but accentuating the distinction between the phenomena compared. Focusing upon the individuality and contingency of an event, the historian recognizes that he is dealing with the dissimilar, which can be illuminated by *but not restricted to* known analogies. Yet to concentrate upon the uniquenes of phenomena, first obtruded by analogy, does not dispute the cognitive power of analogy; instead, the more sharply the limitations of a particular analogy are recognized, the greater is its power of disclosure. Actually the historical method has

[12] *Ibid.*, pp. 45–46. Cf. "Response to the Discussion," *TaH*, pp. 264–265.

experienced its greatest triumphs where it could exhibit concrete mutuality between items, but never where it extrapolated analogies rather absolutely. With profound insight Pannenberg observes:

> The most fruitful possibility opened up by the discovery of historical analogies consists in the fact that it allows more precise comprehension of the ever-present concrete limitation of what is held in common, the particularity that is present in every case in the phenomena being compared. A genuine extension of knowledge takes place in this way. The fundamental anthropological disposition of being able to transcend any given content, the power of concrete negation, is expressed in ability to evaluate discovered analogies right up to their limits.[13]

Pannenberg reasons further:

> If the analogies discovered are employed in full knowledge of the limits of their validity, then they can hardly serve as criteria for the reality of an event affirmed in the tradition . . . [even when] a reported event bursts analogies with otherwise usual or repeatedly attested events.[14]

Thus a negative judgment about an alleged occurrence will not issue from the unusualness of the event reported but because of a positive analogy to some form of consciousness that does not have an objective referent.

The methodological significance of Pannenberg's analysis of the basic principles of historical research is noteworthy. The validity of the principle of universal correlation excludes a supernatural conception of salvation history, which would disengage revelatory history from the reciprocity of historical events by means of transcendent intervention. Furthermore, when the cognitive power of analogy is defined specifically with reference to its ability to illuminate the uniqueness of historical phenomena (thus liberating the principle of analogy from the doctrinaire tutelage of a radical anthropocentrism), the application of analogy can point history beyond itself to the possibility of a transcendent reference.

[13] "Redemptive Event and History," *BQiT* I, p. 47.
[14] *Ibid.*, pp. 48 f.

The Conception of Historical Knowledge

Historical research does not begin with a detached gathering of facts; rather, an assumption about the historical course of events guides the historian's interest from the outset. Following Collingwood, Pannenberg emphasizes that the spontaneity of historical imagination in the formation of a sketch of history constitutes the actual starting point for historical research. Subsequently, the specific evidence accessible to the researcher through historical documents counts for or against the historian's spontaneously projected theory of the model of the course of events. Pannenberg observes:

> All reported details, which are always to be understood as expressions of the view of the reporter, obtain historical significance only through relationship with the conception of the course of history which the historian brings with him. Depending on the findings concerning the particulars, this conception will be confirmed, modified, or else abandoned as inadequate in order to make room for a new one.[15]

An imaginatively projected theory of the whole of history and concrete historical investigation in terms of the theory—these two steps constitute Pannenberg's theory of historical knowledge. Recognizing the priority of historical imagination, the historian eschews historical positivism; referring the projected theory of the whole to verification by historical research, the theologian avoids any dualism between revelatory history and critical history.[16]

Though a subjective element is involved in the projection of a sketch of the course of events, Pannenberg insists upon the cognitive value of the imaginatively conceived theory of the history involved.

> To the extent that the projection of a historical course of events is verifiable by its agreement with the available findings on the particulars, it is obviously no mere individually conditioned perspective in the consciousness of the historian but rather a recounting of the event itself in its own context.[17]

---

[15] *Ibid.*, p. 70.

[16] Pannenberg acknowledges the similarity between an imaginative conception of the whole of history and historical intuition (*ibid.*, p. 70, n. 138); however, he rejects historical intuition as an independent avenue to knowledge of the past alongside historical investigation, for "intuition always needs confirmation by detailed historical observation" (*ibid.*, pp. 50 f., n. 91 [cf. *JGaM*, p. 99]).

[17] "Redemptive Event and History," *BQiT* I, p. 71.

Indeed, the historian must be aware of the "subjective conditioning" of his own historical viewpoint; nevertheless, he cannot arbitrarily change his picture of the course of events without waiving the cognitive value of his historical sketch. If the historian is to remember his own involvement in the event that he describes and if he is not to abandon the cognitive claim of his historical sketch, he can only interpret his sketch as the spontaneous reproduction of a previously given unity of history, which, to be sure, becomes conscious of itself only in this reproducing act. Therefore, the historian must maintain the cognitive value of his sketch of history until the evidence requires its modification or elimination. While the theory of knowledge that Pannenberg describes offers no absolute certainty—indeed, it is characterized by provisionality—it is the only option available for historical knowledge of the past. Theology is in no position to say what actually happened in the past when such knowledge remains inaccessible to the historian.

THE APPREHENSION OF REVELATION IN UNDERSTANDING

Since history is composed of events and meanings interwoven in the history of traditions, historical research impinges upon the hermeneutical quest for understanding.[18] Though the historical problem (the difference between the Biblical text and the event to which it refers) and the hermeneutical problem (the distance between the thought world of primitive Christianity and that of the interpreter) imply distinctive approaches to a transmitted text, they actually constitute two aspects of a single problem, namely, the significance of the traditions of the past for the understanding of the interpreter in the present.

The Delimitation of History and Hermeneutic

Since the text to be interpreted refers to an event that is distinct from the text itself, the hermeneutical endeavor must eventually inquire behind the text to the essential content it expresses—an inquiry wherein hermeneutic encounters historical investigation. Similarly, historiography is constantly guided by an interest of the present, a hermeneutical concern: Historical study entails more than simply a reconstruction of the past event to which the text refers, for the historian comprehends the past in the context of meaning wherein

[18] Pannenberg, "Hermeneutic and Universal History," *BQiT* I, p. 96.

the event occurred, a context that ultimately embraces the present age of the historian. Such convergence between historical investigation behind the text and hermeneutical bridges from the text suggests an orientation of historical study and hermeneutical theory to the horizon of universal history.

Recent hermeneutical theory—from Schleiermacher to Bultmann—reflects an attempt to bridge the historical distance between the text and the interpreter by reference to some nonhistorical, pre-given structure of human existence.[19] When the hermeneutical question is so formulated, however, hermeneutic conceals and/or depreciates the radical historical distance between the past of the text and the present of the interpreter. Indeed, hermeneutic avoids the problem of universal history when the historical distance of the text is so obscured, but the hermeneutical endeavor itself is subsequently damaged, for the rich diversity of the "claim" of history is circumscribed through reference to some formal structure of human existence. Therefore, if historical study entails more than a detached reconstruction of the past to which the text refers, and, correspondingly, if the hermeneutical bridge must span the historical distance between the text and the interpreter through the continuum of history, Pannenberg hypothesizes, the historical and the hermeneutical problems require the single horizon of universal history for solution.

The Dynamic of Merging Horizons

To resolve the problematic relationship of historical research and hermeneutical inquiry, Pannenberg seizes upon Hans-Georg Gadamer's concept of understanding as a "fusion of horizons." [20] Gadamer

---

[19] Ibid., pp. 100–115. Against Bultmann's existentialist interpretation, Pannenberg argues: "Such a hermeneutical obscuring of the intentio recta [direct intention] of the statements about God, the world, and history in favor of the meaning of the text as an expression of an understanding of human existence evidences an anthropological constriction in the formulation of the question, in the pre-understanding" (ibid., p. 110). Furthermore, Bultmann also fails to maintain the profound historical distance between the interpreter and the ancient text by reference to an existential type of questioning. Pannenberg constructively argues: "What happened then [das Damalige] cannot be stripped of its 'then-ness' [Damaligkeit] and in such a way construed as a contemporary possibility; for in that case its 'then-ness' would be missing. On the contrary, it must be related to the present precisely in its character as having happened then" (ibid., pp. 111–112). With these words Pannenberg moves toward a hermeneutical conception of universal history.

[20] Ibid., p. 117. Cf. Hans-Georg Gadamer, Wahrheit und Methode: Grundzüge einer philosophischen Hermeneutik, 2d ed. (Tübingen: J. C. B. Mohr [Paul Siebeck], 1965).

incorporates historical thinking into the hermeneutical achievement, for he makes the historical distance between the past of the text and the present of the interpreter a constitutive element in the process of understanding. Relating the past to the present through the dynamic of merging horizons, Gadamer significantly advances hermeneutic beyond recent hermeneutical theory.[21] First, the radical difference between the horizon of the text and that of the interpreter is not obscured but deliberately developed and accentuated. Second, the interpreter projects a new historical horizon that is distinct from but comprehends the initially contrasting horizons of the text and the interpreter—an action that occurs only in the process of understanding itself. Third, as he projects a comprehensive horizon, *the interpreter's own horizon is set in motion,* enabling the interpreter to transcend the limits of his original preconception and formulation of the question.

When Gadamer's insights are applied to the New Testament texts, Pannenberg observes, everything hinges upon the capacity of the newly projected horizon to encompass all the rich complexity of the New Testament texts as well as the radical distance of the interpreter from the text. To enable one to test whether or not the comprehensive horizon is actually capable of including both the horizon of the text and that of the interpreter, the newly projected horizon requires explicit formulation. The attempt to formulate a comprehensive horizon compels the interpreter to project a conception of reality as a whole; moreover, the essential historical differentiation between the text and the interpreter requires the projection of a concept of reality as history, i.e., universal history. But Gadamer, eschewing the shadow of Hegel, refuses to follow the direction of his reasoning and turns instead to the linguisticality of the hermeneutical experience (which suggests "conversation" as the model for the hermeneutical process).[22]

The Demand for Declarative Language

While affirming Gadamer's characterization of the hermeneutical process as a linguistic process, Pannenberg considers the difference between textual interpretation and a conversation fatal for Gadamer's hermeneutic. The interpretation of a text is not a language event comparable to conversation: "The text does not 'speak,' but rather

---

[21] "Hermeneutic and Universal History," *BQiT* I, pp. 118–119.
[22] *Ibid.,* p. 122–123. Pannenberg considers Gadamer's entire discussion a debate with Hegel, an attempt to demonstrate that linguisticality instead of universal history provides the "mediation of past and present" (*ibid.,* p. 121, n. 55).

the interpreter finds a linguistic expression which combines the essential content of the text with his own contemporary horizon." [23] Hence, the fusing of horizons is not primarily an *accomplishment* of language, but the formation of a new manner of speaking is the *expression* of a fusion of horizons accomplished by understanding. Though the hermeneutical process is articulated in language, it has its roots in the creative formation of language in understanding, whereby the interpreter translates the essential content of the text into an assertion or statement.

Gadamer, however, attempts to separate the language event of understanding from the linguistic form of statement, to disengage the linguistic character of understanding from the declarative function of language. Predicative language, Gadamer argues, fails to maintain the unity of meaning between the "what is said" and the "what is unsaid" of the original utterance; the assertion allows the original (if unspoken) horizon of meaning and the situation of the author, who formulated the text, to disappear. Yet, Pannenberg argues, that does not justify the depreciation of assertion for a hermeneutical inquiry into the text. First, "the implicit unspoken horizon of meaning [accompanying the text] is accessible to the understanding only on the basis of the assertion and not without it," and second, "the interpreter can only become clearly conscious of the unity of that [unspoken] background of meaning made accessible by assertions [of the text], if this unity, for its part, also becomes the content of assertions." [24] Hence, the unspoken horizon of meaning that accompanies every text does not devaluate the significance of predicative language, for that horizon can be grasped only when *everything* from the initial formation of the text to the unanticipated dimensions of its horizon of meaning is objectified into statement. Since the transmitted statement of the text is not understood so long as its unspoken horizon of meaning is disregarded, Pannenberg reasons: "The *interpretation* of the assertion must take into account the situation in which it arose, and to that extent the interpretation goes *behind the assertion* to its original conditions in order to be able to understand the assertion." [25] The necessity of transposing the entirety of the content intended in

[23] *Ibid.*, pp. 123–124.
[24] *Ibid.*, p. 126. The debate over predicative language is crucial, because without it a theological conception of universal history becomes a dubious, even hopeless, undertaking.
[25] *Ibid.*, p. 128.

the text into statement(s), including the unspoken horizon of meaning that accompanies the text—the priority of "assertion" for hermeneutic —binds the interpretation of the texts transmitted through history to historical research.

The Drive Toward Universal History

Pannenberg's reasoning drives him to postulate a conception of universal history as the horizon wherein understanding occurs. The rationale of his projection of a universal-historical horizon includes the following elements: (1) The radical historical distance between the horizon of the text and that of the interpreter must be maintained when the hermeneutical bridge is built. (2) The interpreter must inquire behind the statement of the text to its unspoken horizon of meaning in order to find the linguistic expression commensurate with its actual content. (3) The past horizon of the text and the present horizon of the interpreter, which are differentiated historically, can be merged only through the continuum of history that binds them together. Assuming the accuracy of these propositions, Pannenberg concludes:

> Only a conception of the actual course of history linking the past with the present situation and its horizon of the future can form the comprehensive horizon within which the interpreter's limited horizon of the present and the historical horizon of the text fuse together. For only in that way are the past and the present preserved in their historical uniqueness and difference in contrast to one another within the comprehensive horizon. Nevertheless, they are preserved in such a way that they are as moments which enter into the unity of a comprehensive continuity of history that embraces them both.[26]

The conception of universal history that Pannenberg proposes issues from the horizon of the open future, a dynamic horizon which precludes any unchanging conception of reality. Indeed, Pannenberg declares: "The concept of truth itself is to be defined essentially as history." [27] While that does not signify the relativistic dissolution of truth, it does mean that the unity of truth can be conceived only as

[26] *Ibid.*, pp. 129–130.
[27] *Ibid.*, p. 131.

the whole of a historical process. Hence, an understanding of the essential content of a text requires a projection of the history of that content, for only within the horizon of such a projection can the historical perspective of the text on its content and the contemporary perspective of the interpreter on the same content be adequately related to one another. Furthermore, since the divergent contents transmitted in tradition are all interrelated, the hermeneutical task not only requires the projection of the history of a specific subject matter but also a projection of universal history which encompasses the changing relationships of all the various subject matters.

When the content of a text is referred to the horizon of the future in order to discover new possibilities for understanding it, the *concept* of the "claim" that a transmitted text makes upon the present becomes intelligible. To be sure, the claim of the text issues not only from the horizon of the future but also from the linguistic expression of the text itself. However, the words always transcend the original occasion wherein the claim emerged through the universality of the claim expressed therein. Such a claim must prove itself anew in every period by the power of the transmitted text to illuminate current problems,

> [but] the fact that such a power of disclosure can proceed from a transmitted text at all is linked to the fact that the current understanding of the matter in question is not yet absolute but is itself bound to a finite perspective and is thus submitted to questionableness. In its questionability, and in view of the openness of the future, the current understanding of a matter is referred to tradition. This means that the matter about which one is presently concerned cannot be understood without looking back to what was written and spoken about it in the past.[28]

When the application of what is transmitted moves beyond the historically ascertained self-understanding of the text to a consideration of its current possibilities, however, it flows into the problem of universal history. To be sure, the projection of a concept of universal history (because of its speculative claim) can obscure the possibilities for understanding and action contained in the transmitted text, but that simply demonstrates the finitude which qualifies all human

---

[28] "Hermeneutic and Universal History," *BQiT* I, p. 133.

thought, including projections of universal history; it does not mean that a conception of universal history is impossible, only that it is necessary to produce ever better projections of universal history.

Pannenberg insists that the theological conception of history dare not be sacrificed because of the failure of the Hegelian solution. Instead, it is essential to develop a conception of universal history which, in contrast to Hegel's, would preserve the finitude of human experience, the openness of the future, and the intrinsic validity of the particular. Pannenberg poses a conception of universal history wherein the end of history, which gathers history into a whole, is only known provisionally: The eschatological activity and destiny of Jesus of Nazareth constitutes the prolepsis of the *eschaton* wherein the meaning of the entirety of history is anticipated. Accentuating the eschatological horizon of Jesus' history, Pannenberg contends:

> It is just this, at first sight so seemingly alien, basically apocalyptic characteristic of the ministry and destiny of Jesus that, by means of its anticipatory structure, can become the key to solving a fundamental question facing philosophical reflection in the problematic post-Hegelian situation in which we still seem to be involved. It is possible to find in the history of Jesus an answer to the question of how "the whole" of reality and its meaning can be conceived without compromising the provisionality and historical relativity of all thought, as well as openness to the future on the part of the thinker who knows himself to be only on the way and not yet at the goal.[29]

THE APPROPRIATION OF REVELATION THROUGH FAITH

When historical research and the hermeneutical quest converge upon the horizon of universal history, a theological conception of history emerges in which it is possible to recognize Jesus of Nazareth as the final revelation of God. Hence, Pannenberg says that "historical revelation is open to anyone who has eyes to see, it has universal character." [30] Avoiding the supernaturalism of salvation history and its concomitant of a *supplementary* illumination of the Holy Spirit, Pannenberg conceives a vital interpretation of the work of the Spirit

[29] "On Historical and Theological Hermeneutic," *BQiT* I, p. 181.
[30] "Dogmatische Thesen," *OaG*, p. 98 [*RaH*, p. 135].

in the appropriation of revelation without disparaging the universality of God's revelation on the one side or the responsibility of the man confronted thereby on the other.

The Mediation of Knowledge for Faith

The knowledge of the revelation of God in the Christ event is not apprehended apart from but through natural knowledge. Pannenberg says:

> Nothing must mute the fact that the truth lies before everyone's eyes, that its perception is a natural consequence which emerges solely from the facts. [The perception of God's revelation in Christ] does not require an additional perfection of man, as though he could not focus upon such a "super-natural" truth with his normal cognitive facilities.[31]

Thus Pannenberg's conception of the appropriation of revelation is specifically directed against the necessity of any supplementary condition for the recognition of God's revelation in the history of Jesus.

First, Pannenberg argues, the kerygma does not represent a supplementary revelatory word which interprets an otherwise ambiguous revelatory event. Neither as an inspired interpretation nor as the vehicle of encounter does the kerygma qualify as revelatory speech. Instead, Pannenberg contends:

> The kerygma is to be understood exclusively from its content, from the event which it reports and explicates. The kerygma does not actually add something to the event. The events wherein God has demonstrated his deity, *when perceived inside their historical context*, are self-evident. An inspired interpretation—supplementary to the event—is not first required to make the event recognizable as revelation.[32]

---

[31] *Ibid.*, p. 99 [*RaH*, p. 136].

[32] *Ibid.*, pp. 113–114 [*RaH*, p. 155]. Italics added. Yet Pannenberg's reference to God's revelation as "self-evident" in its original context refers primarily to the meaning inherent in the revelatory event and not directly to the event's historicity. Pannenberg clarifies the issue, observing: "Naturally the historicity of an event belongs to the self-evidence of the divine revelation which demonstrates itself therein. However, the historicity is the *condition* of the significance which proves itself therein; the historicity of the events cannot, conversely, be deduced from an experience of such significance" (Wolfhart Pannenberg, April 6, 1971: personal communication).

Pannenberg understands the kerygma positively as the "report" of the self-demonstration of God in the activity and destiny of Jesus—not simply a detached chronological description of the Christ event but the articulation of the meaning inherent in that event. Since the revelation of the universality of Israel's God cannot be conceived apart from the universal proclamation of that revelation, the promulgation of the kerygma is itself a moment in the fulfillment of the revelatory event. The kerygma, therefore, is the means whereby men hear the announcement of the revelation of God in the Christ event, but it is not revelatory in and of itself. Yet Pannenberg does not minimize the importance of proclamation, for preaching is the report of the revelatory history and a linguistic explication which the facts of this history communicate. As a reporting of the Christ event, therefore, the sermon enters into every situation as appeal and exhortation.

Second, Pannenberg argues, one may not appeal glibly to the Holy Spirit to justify the *truth* of the message of God's revelation in the history of Jesus. Since the revelation of God in Christ took place within the sphere of human history, the Holy Spirit is not a *supplementary condition* or *additional factor* that the Christ event requires in order to be known as "revelation." The message of Christ, if unconvincing in itself, cannot attain convincing power through an appeal to the Holy Spirit. Pannenberg declares: "The fact that the one who is convinced by the message confesses that this apprehension was affected in him by the Holy Spirit must not be misunderstood as if the Spirit were taken to be the criterion of the truth of the message." [33] When the content of the message itself lacks convincing power, it accomplishes nothing to appeal to the Holy Spirit.

Pannenberg explicitly rejects any appeal to the Spirit for the legitimation of the truth of the kerygma, but he does not mean that the Spirit has nothing to do with the origin of faith. In order to clarify the issue, he says: "The Spirit does not join itself to the gospel as something additional. It is rather the case that the proclaimed eschatological event and, proceeding from it, even the process of proclaiming the gospel is itself Spirit-filled." [34] Since the Spirit inheres in the content of the gospel, the Spirit himself is mediated through the reporting of the Christ event; consequently, the Spirit is essential to the perception of revelation, but he is not a separate court of appeal along-

---

[33] "Insight and Faith," *BQiT* II, pp. 34–35.
[34] *Ibid.*, p. 34, n. 11.

side the message of Christ. The Spirit is not a "haven of ignorance" for pious experience, exempting one from all accountability for its contents. The Spirit's presence, like the truth of the kerygma itself, is referred to and depends upon the historicality of God's revelation in Jesus Christ.

The Movement from Knowledge to Faith

When the historicality of God's revelation in Jesus Christ is perceived apart from a revelatory "word" or a supplementary work of the Holy Spirit, does that not make faith superfluous? On the contrary, Pannenberg argues, it makes faith possible: "Faith does not take the place of knowledge," but "it has its basis in an event which is a matter for knowing and which becomes known to us only by more or less adequate information." [35] Yet a man does not come to God by his own reason and strength, for faith is the response of man to God's revelation: "The events which reveal God and the message which reports these events bring man to a knowledge which he does not have in himself." [36] Though one cannot always comprehend the truth of the Christian message, one must be able to presuppose that the message about Jesus Christ is true. So Pannenberg reasons:

> In the sense of a logical presupposition (though not always a psychological antecedent), the knowledge of Jesus' history, including his resurrection from the dead, is the basis of faith. Furthermore, this knowledge has the peculiarity that it leads on to faith. Knowledge is not a stage beyond faith but leads into faith—and the more exact it is, the more certainly it does so.[37]

The individual moments of the act of faith may be distinguished but not isolated from one another, because every act of trust reaches backward and/or forward for a foundation of trustworthiness. If one returns to the concept of faith in classical Protestantism, knowledge of the content of faith (*notitia* with *assensus*) remains the logical presupposition for trust (*fiducia*). Hence, Pannenberg concludes:

> Whether one follows the Reformation's linguistic usage and concentrates the concept of faith upon the element of trust, or

[35] "The Revelation of God in Jesus," *TaH*, p. 128.
[36] "Dogmatische Thesen," *OaG*, p. 100 [*RaH*, p. 137].
[37] "The Revelation of God in Jesus," *TaH*, p. 129.

whether one takes it in such a broad sense that it includes the knowledge connected with the act of trust: in either case, one has to speak of a grounding of *fiducia* by means of *notitia* and *assensus*. If one takes faith and *fiducia* as synonymous, one will have to speak of a grounding of faith by a presupposed knowledge, as I have done. If one takes faith in a broader sense, it becomes a matter of speaking of a relationship of grounding between the individual elements, i.e., of a grounding of *fiducia* by *assensus* and *notitia*.[38]

Through the knowledge of Jesus' history as the prolepsis of the End of history (which is more than a preliminary knowledge of Jesus of Nazareth), men are led to faith: "He who understands [the promissory] meaning inherent in the history of Jesus is drawn, by knowing Jesus as the prolepsis of the coming general salvation, into the movement which is faith." [39] Hence, faith is finally directed toward the future, which justifies or disappoints it. "Nevertheless," Pannenberg argues, "one does not trust blindly but on the basis of an event which can be appropriated as one considered reliable." [40] Forsaking himself to the future of God, the Christian risks his trust and life and future on the presupposition that God has actually revealed himself in Jesus. Thus the act of faith presupposes the trustworthiness of the knowledge of God's revelation in the Christ event; otherwise, Pannenberg contends, "faith would be blind gullibility, credulity, or even superstition." [41]

Pannenberg rejects the equating of faith with a subjective conviction that would supposedly compensate for the uncertainty of the believer's historical knowledge of Jesus the Christ. Faith is not "subjectivity's fortress" into which the Christian can retreat when threatened by scientific knowledge: "Faith can breathe freely only when it can be certain, even in the field of scientific research, that its foundation is true." [42] To be sure, reason cannot absolutely and finally com-

---

[38] "Insight and Faith," *BQiT* II, pp. 30–31.

[39] "The Revelation of God in Jesus," *TaH*, p. 130. Yet Pannenberg reminds the reader: "One can understand the history of Jesus only if one understands the future salvation of mankind as having already appeared in and with him and as having been made accessible through him"; through knowledge of Jesus' history, including his resurrection from the dead, one is "led to faith, to trust in God's future" (*ibid.*).

[40] "Dogmatische Thesen," *OaG*, p. 101 [*RaH*, p. 138].

[41] "The Revelation of God in Jesus," *TaH*, pp. 130 f.

[42] *Ibid.*, p. 131.

prehend the truth of God's revelation, because the history wherein he
has revealed himself retains an open future. However, if the decision
of faith must finally guarantee the historical truth of God's revelation
in Jesus Christ, or if faith is rendered independent of the historical
facts that constitute its foundation, faith ultimately depends upon the
believer and the decision to believe, reducing faith to a work of self-
redemption. Thus, when the decision of faith becomes crucial for
the truth of faith, the believer falls victim to the pious self-deception
of salvation by works.[43] Ultimately, therefore, the knowledge of God's
revelation in the history demonstrating his deity (the history of Jesus
of Nazareth) constitutes the foundation of and presupposition for faith.

Furthermore, Pannenberg's treatment of the certainty of faith
helps to clarify the structural relationship of knowledge (faith's presupposition) to trust (faith's essence). Since Lessing and Kierkegaard,
it has become almost axiomatic that the certainty of faith cannot be
derived from the provisionality of historical knowledge. Addressing
himself to the issue, Pannenberg distinguishes between the certainty of
faith and historical certainty, for these two lie on different levels. Thus
the unconditional revelatory summons to faith is not compromised
by the provisionality that characterizes the knowledge of historical
revelation; consequently, he argues, there is no essential contradiction in basing trust on an event that can be known historically only
with probability. Though historical research into the history of Jesus
can never achieve definitive certainty but only greater or lesser probability, the certainty of faith consists in the completeness of trust,
which in turn is grounded in the distinctive eschatological significance
of the Christ event. So Pannenberg reasons:

> This special eschatological character of the history of Jesus
> demands and undergirds unrestricted trust: because *in Jesus
> it is a question of the whole,* here total trust is required de-
> spite the relative uncertainty of our historical knowledge of
> Jesus.[44]

Although the faith-establishing knowledge of God's revelation in
the history of Jesus varies with the shifting currents of historical research, faith itself is not shaken, "so long as the current image of the
facts of history permits faith to recognize anew and to appropriate

[43] *AC*, pp. 9–10.
[44] "Response to the Discussion," *TaH*, p. 273. Italics added.

again the event which establishes faith itself." [45] Transcending the specific historical picture which constitutes its foundation, faith achieves a certain independence from the historical knowledge of the event out of which it emerged; while rooted in the event revealing God's deity, faith itself relies upon *the God* who has revealed himself therein. Yet the independence of faith from knowledge is never absolute but always relative. Pannenberg insists: "Faith does not cling to its own form of knowledge, but abandons itself to the event from which it lives, though always by means of the knowledge through which it holds fast to this event." [46]

The critical knowledge of the history of Jesus which supports faith determines whether faith has a basis in fact; however, only unconditional trust beyond knowledge, wherein faith abandons itself, secures participation in the salvation of God. Pannenberg says:

> No mere knowledge of the object of faith is capable of granting a part in the saving event; that belongs to faith alone. For only in the act of faith do I forsake myself in order to anchor myself in the reality in which I trust. In this act of trust, faith goes beyond its own criteria, abandoning not only [it]self but the particular form of knowledge of its object from which it started, and laying itself open to a new and better knowledge of the truth on which it relies.[47]

The knowledge upon which faith is grounded is always provisional; consequently, faith cannot stop the constant probing and examination of its foundation. Since doubt questions the knowledge that establishes faith, ultimately tempting faith itself, the historical foundation of faith requires continuous but honest certification. Trenchantly Pannenberg observes: "Hence the process of knowing in which faith makes sure of its foundation is usually directed and held in progress by faith —by a trust which to some extent anticipates the results of the cognitive process." [48] Such anticipation is not really unique to the inquiry of faith, because all "knowing" operates in the anticipation of its results. The anticipatory structure of the cognitive process, however, does not represent "a storm-free area of faith." The possibility cannot be excluded that someday the historical features establishing Jesus'

[45] "Dogmatische Thesen," *OaG*, p. 101 [*RaH*, p. 138].
[46] "What Is a Dogmatic Statement?" *BQiT* I, p. 209.
[47] *AC*, p. 12.
[48] "Dogmatische Thesen," *OaG*, p. 102, n. 15 [*RaH*, p. 157, n. 15].

eschatological significance might become more or less *improbable*, that a conception of the historical Jesus might arise which would convincingly deny the faith of the early church its basis in the history of Jesus. If such a position of historical research should emerge, the foundation for the certainty of faith, trust in the eschatological power and significance of Jesus' history, would be removed. Though the possibility would remain that one could in the future build a "better" knowledge of Jesus, the certainty of faith (even as anticipation) would be rendered most tenuous and faith's proclamation at best precarious. The certainty of faith, therefore, while achieving relative independence from historical research, is not finally independent of but contingent upon the shape of historical knowledge. Hence, Pannenberg candidly says:

> [The] results [of historical research] can bring faith into dispute, and threaten it with the loss of its foundation; and where the conflict with knowledge is unequivocal and complete, hardly anyone could base faith on a future better knowledge without the loss of his intellectual and personal integrity.[49]

Without minimizing the crucial results of historical investigation into the foundation of faith, Pannenberg constantly refers the truth of God's revelatory disclosure in the history of Jesus to the understanding of the whole of reality. The fundamental criterion of the veracity of God's revelation in Jesus of Nazareth remains whether or not the whole of reality continually unfolds itself more deeply through the Christ event than without it. Therefore, Pannenberg concludes:

> As long as the whole of reality can be understood more deeply and more convincingly through Jesus than without him, it proves true in our everyday experience and personal knowledge that in Jesus the creative origin of all reality stands revealed.[50]

---

[49] "Response to the Discussion," *TaH*, p. 274. While such a possibility cannot be excluded, Pannenberg sees "no occasion for apprehension that such a position should emerge in the foreseeable future" (p. 272).
[50] "The Revelation of God in Jesus," *TaH*, p. 133.

V

CHRISTOLOGY "FROM BELOW"—
THE ESCHATOLOGICAL
HISTORY OF JESUS

THE CENTRAL AFFIRMATION of the Christian church is "that in dealing with Jesus we are dealing with God himself." [1] Though a provisional knowledge of God exists apart from Jesus, Christians confess Jesus Christ to be the final revelation of God. Indeed, the message of Christ presupposes a preliminary knowledge of God, but the revelation of God in Jesus of Nazareth suspends its own presupposition, insofar as speaking of God *himself* ultimately means talking about Jesus. The goal of Christology is to develop the interrelatedness of the doctrine of God and the doctrine of Jesus the Christ, but it is a task burdened by many historical and theological difficulties.

Pannenberg affirms as his starting point: *"Christology deals with Jesus as the basis of the confession that he is the Christ of God."* [2] Yet the "Jesus" of which Christology speaks is not immediately identifiable, for "Jesus" may refer to the historical Jesus of the past or the Jesus of contemporary proclamation. Asking methodologically whether Christology should begin with Jesus himself or with the kerygma of the church, Pannenberg contends that the diversity of the New Testament witnesses to Jesus precludes equating the apostles' witness to Jesus with Jesus himself, as Kähler suggested in the formula "the whole Biblical Christ." Instead, Pannenberg argues:

> One can and must get back to Jesus himself from the witness of the apostles by trying to recognize, and thus making

[1] Pannenberg, "The Revelation of God in Jesus," *TaH*, p. 101.
[2] *JGaM*, p. 21.

129

allowance for, the relation of New Testament texts to their respective situations. It is quite possible to distinguish the figure of Jesus himself, as well as the outlines of his message, from the particular perspective in which it is transmitted through this or that New Testament witness.[3]

While a biography of Jesus is not possible, the quest for the historical Jesus is both feasible and mandatory. First, the quest for the historical Jesus is necessary in order to anchor the basis of faith. Concurring with Ebeling against Bultmann, Pannenberg contends that the kerygma threatens to appear as the product of faith unless it is established in the historical Jesus himself (though the question of "how" Jesus of Nazareth is the basis of the kerygma and faith remains open). Second, Pannenberg moves behind the kerygma to Jesus himself in order to establish the unity that binds the New Testament witnesses together: "The unity of Scripture will not be grasped in a comparison of the statements of the New Testament witnesses; it consists only in the one Jesus to whom they all refer, and will be recognizable, therefore, only when one has penetrated behind the kerygma of the apostles." [4] Third, Pannenberg necessarily turns to the history of Jesus in order to identify contemporary Christian experience as association with the risen Christ, for knowledge that Jesus lives as the exalted Lord presupposes the identity of the risen Christ with the earthly Jesus. Pannenberg insists:

> No one now has an experience of [Jesus] as risen and exalted, at least not an experience that could be distinguished with certainty from illusion. . . . The *experience* of the presence of Christ is promised only for the end of time. Therefore, also, whatever concerns the certainty of the present life of the exalted Lord is based entirely on what happened in the past.[5]

Against Althaus, who maintains that faith primarily involves what Jesus *is* as he encounters one in proclamation, Pannenberg argues that faith pertains basically to what Jesus *was* (which defines what he is for the believer today).

The thrust of Pannenberg's arguments denotes that Christology must

[3] *Ibid.,* p. 23.
[4] *Ibid.,* pp. 24–25.
[5] *Ibid.,* p. 28.

substantiate the church's historic confession of faith in Jesus Christ: "Christology is concerned, therefore, not only with *unfolding* the Christian community's confession of Christ, but above all with *grounding* it in the activity and fate of Jesus in the past." [6] Such an attempt to establish the true understanding of Jesus' significance from his history involves the reconstruction of the particularity of Jesus' history on the one side and the evaluation of the Christological tradition by the critical norm of Jesus' history on the other. The church's historic Christological confessions remain instructive for the contemporary theological task, but the Biblically derived norm of Jesus' history remains decisive for an evaluation of all historical and current Christological statements: "All dogmatic statements about [Jesus'] universal meaning constantly require grounding in and confirmation by the historical particularity of the message, way, and figure of Jesus." [7]

Insisting upon Jesus' history as the point of departure for Christology, Pannenberg posits a distinction between a Christology "from above" and a Christology "from below." When Christology begins "from above," with the divinity of Jesus, the concept of incarnation is central; conversely, when Christology originates "from below," moving from the historical Jesus to the *recognition* of his divinity, the ministry and destiny of Jesus take precedence, while the incarnation emerges as a conclusion. An incarnational Christology "from above" presupposes the doctrine of the Trinity, asking how the eternal Son (the Logos) has assumed a human nature. Pannenberg rejects this methodology for three formidable reasons.[8] (1) Arbitrarily presupposing the divinity of Jesus, a Christology "from above" ignores *the most important task* of Christology, which is to present the reasons for the confession of the divinity of Jesus. (2) Taking the divinity of the Logos as its point of departure—which locates the essential problem of Christology in the *union* of "God" and "man" in Jesus—a Christology "from above" devaluates the constitutive significance of the real historical man, Jesus of Nazareth, especially his relationship to Palestinian Judaism and the Old Testament so fundamental to an understanding of his life and message. (3) Finally, Pannenberg rejects a Christology "from above" because the believer always must think in the context of a historically determined situation: He can neither stand in the position

---

[6] *Ibid.*
[7] "What Is a Dogmatic Statement?" *BQiT* I, p. 199.
[8] *JGaM*, pp. 34–35.

of God and follow the path of God's Son into the world nor comprehend the incarnation apart from the historical reality of Jesus. Though the incarnational Christology which has dominated the historical development of Christological doctrine was not simply a mistake, the divinity of Jesus may not be presupposed, for it is neither self-evident nor self-explanatory to modern man; consequently, a Christology "from below" is required to substantiate the church's confession of the incarnation of God in Jesus Christ.

The method "from below" impinges upon another dimension of Christology, namely, the relation between Christology and soteriology. Although soteriology (Jesus' saving significance) and Christology (the divinity of Jesus) are intertwined, the relatedness of these concepts must obscure neither their distinctiveness nor the logic of their conceptualization. Hence, Pannenberg thematically declares: *"The confession of faith in Jesus is not to be separated from Jesus' saving significance for us. The soteriological interest cannot, however, be the principle of Christological doctrine."* [9] Underscoring the logical primacy of Christology, he continues: "The divinity of Jesus remains the *presupposition* for his saving significance for us and, conversely, the saving significance of his divinity is the reason why we take *interest* in the question of his divinity." [10] The soteriological concern that inheres in almost every Christological formulation accurately reflects the interpenetration of Christology and soteriology. The danger is, however, that Christology will be constructed out of the soteriological interest of the theologian instead of the history of Jesus. Against the recurring tendency to project contemporary soteriological concerns upon the historical Jesus, Pannenberg argues: "Jesus possesses significance 'for us' only to the extent that this significance is inherent in himself, in his history, and in his person constituted by this history." [11] Hence, the question about the history of Jesus himself remains prior to all questions about his saving significance. The soteriological concern is not eliminated, however, for the meaning inherent in Jesus' history is itself soteriological. When Christology and soteriology are oriented methodologically to the history of Jesus, Pannenberg observes: "Christological research finds in the reality of Jesus the criterion for the critical examination of the Christological tradition and also

[9] *Ibid.*, p. 38.
[10] *Ibid.*
[11] *Ibid.*, p. 48.

the various soteriological concerns that have determined Christological presentations." [12]

THE ACTIVITY OF JESUS OF NAZARETH

Examining the exegetical foundation that has been used to comprehend Christology under the offices of prophet, priest, and king, Pannenberg considers only one of the three, namely, the "prophetic office," to characterize (to some extent) the earthly work of Jesus. Nevertheless, unlike Ritschl, Pannenberg prefers the concept of office to that of vocation to describe Jesus' actively pursued ministry, because it contains the aspect of commissioning. Since the idea of the "free choice" is usually connected with vocation, Pannenberg thinks "the concept of office is more appropriate for expressing the fact that Jesus understood himself entirely from God." [13] Jesus' dedication to his office, it must be emphasized, was not passive but active. Hence, the office of Jesus represents his actively pursued mission in dedication to God (in contrast to the crucifixion and resurrection, which "happened" to him).

Pannenberg defines Jesus' unique office plainly: "*The office of Jesus was to call men into the Kingdom of God, which had appeared with him.*" [14] Through calling men into the Kingdom of God, Jesus stood with his people in the history of the God of Israel. "Jesus' activity is understandable only from this history," Pannenberg argues, "for Jesus called Israel back into the nearness of the God who was Israel's God from Egypt on and for whose coming the pious Jew prayed daily." [15] Hence, the presupposition for Jesus' work was the election of Israel by God and the expectation of the future revelation of God's glory. An understanding of Jesus' proclamation of the Kingdom of God, therefore, requires an investigation into the Jewish traditions that comprised the context of Jesus' ministry, namely, the horizon of Jewish apocalypticism.

Jesus' Apocalyptic Orientation

Though Jesus was neither a prophet nor an apocalyptist, Pannenberg contends that "the views of the apocalyptic traditions are every-

[12] *Ibid.*, p. 49.
[13] *Ibid.*, p. 194, but cf. pp. 212–225, esp. pp. 215–217.
[14] *Ibid.*, p. 212.
[15] *Ibid.*, p. 193.

where the presupposition of what he said and did." [16] Jesus wrote no apocalypse, but he certainly thought in apocalyptic categories. So Pannenberg refers positively but carefully to the apocalyptic horizon of Jesus' ministry, observing:

> Only to the extent that the situation in the Jewish history of traditions out of which Jesus emerged with his message must be seen as determined by Jewish apocalyptic does it become necessary to describe the significance of the activity and destiny of Jesus in relation to the background of apocalyptic theology. *This does not mean that the figure of Jesus melts into this background. Rather, it means primarily that his uniqueness is set off from this background. But constant reference to it is necessary precisely for the sake of making this uniqueness stand out.*[17]

While affirming Jesus' relation to the horizon of apocalyptic, Pannenberg considers Jesus' activity to be profoundly different from that of apocalyptic visionaries.[18] (1) Unlike the apocalyptists, Jesus did not hide his person under a pseudonym, but was conscious of bringing something *new*. (2) Similarly, Jesus (like John the Baptist) probably expected the End to be so imminent that he did not describe the path to it but only issued a call to repentance. (3) While judgment was dominant in the Baptist's apocalyptic call to repentance, eschatological salvation actually appeared in Jesus' activity and future participation in salvation was promised through him; in distinction from the Baptist, therefore, Jesus' own person stands in the center. (4) Though the apocalyptists announced a visionary *pre-cognition* of the End, Jesus' activity and destiny represent the *pre-happening* of the End. These observations suggest profound differences between Jesus and the apocalyptic prophet, differences which suggest why the apocalyptic pictures of the End are lacking in Jesus' proclamation. Yet apocalypticism remains the intellectual context of the Baptist's preaching of repentance and of the proleptic appearance of God's rule through Jesus.

Proclaiming the immediate nearness of what the apocalyptists described as the End of history, Jesus called the people to repentance

---

[16] *Ibid.*, p. 217.
[17] *Ibid.*, p. 13. Italics added.
[18] *Ibid.*, p. 61.

in view of the imminence of the End. Pannenberg insists: "John the Baptist had already done this, and both materially and temporally Jesus stands closer to John's work than to that of anyone else." [19] As preachers of repentance, the Baptist and Jesus exhibit elements of an apocalyptically stamped prophecy wherein the call to repentance involves the content of the general apocalyptic-eschatological expectation. Yet Jesus' continuity with John the Baptist specifically and with the Old Testament prophets generally must not obscure Jesus' uniqueness. Describing that distinctiveness, Pannenberg observes: *"[Jesus] was certain that in his activity the future salvation of God's Kingdom had broken into the present time.* This distinguishes Jesus basically from the Baptist as well as from all the prophets." [20] Hence, while Jesus lived and thought in close relation to the apocalyptically influenced prophetic tradition (through which he was related to John the Baptist and also to the Old Testament prophets), he significantly qualified and substantially modified apocalyptic theology by granting eschatological salvation in the present.

Jesus' Proclamation of the Kingdom of God

The central feature of Jesus' proclamation and activity was the emphasis upon and concern for the nearness of God's Kingdom. Pannenberg says: "The coming Kingdom of God—this was the single, pulsating reality of Jesus' existence." [21] Pannenberg's conception of Jesus' understanding of the Kingdom includes several interrelated, but distinctive elements. First, Jesus' concept of the Kingdom of God was stamped by apocalyptic expectations: The coming of the Kingdom meant not only the termination of history (the *End*) but also the transformation of the entire cosmos (the *eschaton*). Though Jesus did

[19] *Ibid.*, p. 217. Ernst Käsemann, "The Beginnings of Christian Theology," in *Apocalypticism*, Vol. VI of Journal for Theology and the Church, ed. by Robert W. Funk (Herder and Herder, 1969), pp. 17–46, acknowledges that Jesus did take his start from the apocalyptically determined message of the Baptist but denies that Jesus' preaching was constitutively stamped by apocalyptic (pp. 39–40). Conversely, Pannenberg argues: "It should be said, against Käsemann's detachment of Jesus from the apocalyptic atmosphere that preceded and followed him, that such a postulate is historically not very probable. It must be considered more probable that in his own thought Jesus also had been connected with the apocalyptically determined message of the Baptist" (*JGaM*, p. 62).

[20] *JGaM*, p. 217. Italics added. Pannenberg considers the apocalyptic tradition wherein Jesus and the Baptist stood to have been a development of the prophetic movement (cf. "The Revelation of God in Jesus," *TaH*, p. 122).

[21] "The Kingdom of God and the Foundation of Ethics," *TaKoG*, p. 102.

not engage in eschatological speculation, he probably associated the arrival of God's Kingdom with the coming of the Son of Man, the Last Judgment, and the resurrection of the dead. The Kingdom of God, therefore, is not restricted to an internalized "reign of God" but embraces the whole of reality.[22] Second, Jesus recognized that the Kingdom of God could not be established by men but by God alone, an imminent cosmic revolution surpassing anything conceivable as man's accomplishment. Exposing every present condition to the light of God's inbreaking future, Jesus expected that this future would come "in a marvelous way from God himself," and that it would not be "simply the development of human history or the achievement of God-fearing men." [23] Third, Jesus considered the Kingdom of God to be temporally imminent, so imminent that it was already dawning in and through his eschatological message. Referring to Johannes Weiss and Albert Schweitzer, Pannenberg contends: "It is scarcely possible to ignore the fact that the imminence of God's reign, even in the sense of temporal nearness, was constitutive for Jesus' expectation and for his ministry as a whole." [24] While many of his Jewish contemporaries believed that God's Kingdom lay in the distant future, Jesus was convinced of the imminence of God's universal Lordship. Thus the sharp apocalyptic distinction between the modes of time nearly disappears in Jesus' proclamation, which enabled him to transcend the scope of possibilities in apocalyptic theology.[25] Fourth, in Jesus' proclamation of the coming Kingdom, God's rule is not "simply" future, but the future and the present are inextricably interwoven. Over against the typical affirmation of Jewish eschatological hope, Pannenberg emphasizes: "Jesus underscored the *present impact* of the imminent future." [26] Thus Jesus conceived the inbreak of God's Kingdom as the presence of the *coming* Kingdom. *Futurity is fundamental,* for only within the horizon of the expectation of the future coming of God's

---

[22] Cf. *JGaM*, pp. 365–378, esp. p. 368. Pannenberg does not sharply distinguish between the form of God's Kingdom (realm) and its substance (kingly rule); instead, the Kingdom itself means the open reference of all power and control to God.

[23] "Theology and the Kingdom of God," *TaKoG*, p. 52.

[24] "The Revelation of God in Jesus," *TaH*, p. 113. However, while emphasizing Jesus' imminent expectation, Pannenberg candidly acknowledges that "Jesus erred when he announced that God's Lordship would begin in his own generation" (*JGaM*, p. 226).

[25] "Dogmatische Thesen," *OaG*, p. 92 [*RaH*, p. 127].

[26] "Theology and the Kingdom of God," *TaKoG*, p. 53.

Kingdom could it be recognized that the Kingdom was already dawning in Jesus' ministry. Hence, while recognizing the intertwining of the futurity and the presence of God's reign in the ministry of Jesus, Pannenberg insists:

> But the future remains future. There is no "realized eschatology," as if the future had faded out. The presence of God's reign in Jesus was founded . . . only in the exclusiveness in Jesus' pointing to the *future* of God. . . . The present reality of the reign of God, thus mediated by the exclusiveness of Jesus' message, is to be considered a proleptic reality. Nevertheless, even as anticipation the ministry of Jesus referred in its very essence to the complete coming of the reign of God— the fulfillment of his expectation of the near End.[27]

Therefore, Pannenberg does not understand Jesus' activity as *establishing* the Kingdom of God but as calling men into the anticipatory *dawning* of God's future Lordship.

Unlike the Baptist, Jesus not only called men to repentance in the face of impending judgment but also directly granted eschatological salvation: *"The nearness of the Kingdom of God that he proclaimed is itself salvation for those who take notice of it."*[28] While the nearness of God's Kingdom signified a threat of judgment for those who closed themselves to it, salvation became a present reality for those yearning for the nearness of God proclaimed by Jesus, for those hearing and accepting Jesus' message of God's imminent Kingdom.

Jesus' Relativization of the Law

Pannenberg argues that Jesus' message did not offer anything completely new, for its roots were entirely in Israel's tradition; however, Jesus' message was new insofar as it radically stressed the central content of that tradition, namely, "the pre-eminence of the Israelite God over all powers and interests and . . . the hope for the future realization of God's will on earth."[29] With Jesus the coming of the reign of God, so imminent, became ultimate. Compared to the imminent coming of the God of eschatological hope, Jesus considered the detailed regulations of the law and the cultic traditions of Israel of

[27] "The Revelation of God in Jesus," *TaH*, p. 113.
[28] *JGaM*, p. 227. Cf. *ibid.*, pp. 227 ff., esp. Pannenberg's discussion of the power of love, pp. 233–234.
[29] "The Revelation of God in Jesus," *TaH*, p. 111.

little consequence. Suddenly Jesus' hearers had to choose between God and the law, the urgent message of God's coming Kingdom and the law given Israel by God. So the message of Jesus forced Jewish tradition into a conflict with itself, effecting an ambiguity which could only be resolved by an act of God that would vindicate or invalidate Jesus' claim. Therefore, the whole of Jesus' activity required divine confirmation and only by anticipating it could his disciples trust in him.

Jesus' opposition to the absolutizing of the traditional law was made possible through the vitality of the apocalyptic tradition. Pannenberg refers to Ulrich Wilckens, who says: "Only where interest in God is not directed toward the Torah but rather to history and its End, can polemics arise against the rabbinical understanding of law, as happened in Jesus' case." [30] The prophetic-apocalyptic circles were already accustomed to claiming God's own authority for a visionary announcement of God's future; consequently, the apocalyptic tradition of proleptic revelation provided the precedent for Jesus' claim to authority over the traditional norm of the law.

Since he gave himself completely to his message, Jesus' person and message ultimately became one. Rejection of Jesus, who lived only to announce the nearness of God's reign, necessarily meant the rejection of God's nearness itself; conversely, where Jesus was accepted, the message of the Kingdom was received. "Therefore," Pannenberg concludes, "without any further conditions, Jesus could pronounce forgiveness of sins upon those who opened themselves to his message of the nearness of God or even upon those who only trusted in him personally." [31]

Jesus' Expectation of God's Vindication

Proclaiming the nearness of the Kingdom of God and granting eschatological salvation, Jesus asserted a claim to authority that implied an unusual consciousness of personal unity with God. Following Käsemann's analysis of the antitheses of the Sermon on the Mount, Pannenberg notes that Jesus set himself above the authority of Moses and essentially claimed the unconditional authority of God. The "amen" with which Jesus introduced his sayings emphasizes his own sense of God-given certainty. Furthermore, as Ernst Fuchs has shown,

[30] Ulrich Wilckens, "Das Offenbarungsverständnis in der Geschichte des Urchristentums," in *OaG*, pp. 53 f. Cited in Pannenberg, "The Revelation of God in Jesus," *TaH*, pp. 111–112.
[31] "The Revelation of God in Jesus," *TaH*, p. 103.

Jesus' celebration of the eschatological meal with publicans and sinners—which Jewish tradition reserved for the future and only for the righteous—demonstrated Jesus' distinctive understanding of God as merciful and gracious toward any repentant sinner. Indeed, forgiving the sins of those who accepted his message of the imminent Kingdom of God and offering eschatological salvation to them, Jesus asserted the astounding claim that the mercy of God is extended through his person.[32] Therefore, exercising the office of calling men into the Kingdom of God, Jesus claimed authority belonging only to God himself— the assertion of a claim of divine authority that was either blasphemous or the indication of the promissory grace of God.

Yet Jesus' claim of divine authority does not presuppose that he understood himself as Messiah, Servant of God, Son of God, Son of Man, or the eschatological prophet. Pannenberg concurs with Hans Conzelmann that Jesus' consciousness of a unique unity with God did not express itself directly in the Christological titles but only indirectly in Jesus' activity.[33] Since Jesus did claim to speak and to act on God's own authority, the pre-Easter Jesus knew himself functionally to be one with God's will in pre-actualizing the future reality of the Kingdom. The disavowal of Jesus' self-identification with the traditional Christological titles, therefore, does not mean that he stumbled around Palestine not knowing who he was or what he should do. Devoting himself entirely to God and the office given him by God, Jesus apparently had no identity crisis that required the defining of his self-understanding through direct appropriation of the titular images provided in Israel's tradition.

While Jesus did indeed assume the authority of God in his proclamation and work, Pannenberg argues that Jesus' claim to divine authority was not self-authenticating but ultimately required God's vindication. Conversely, other theologians who construct a Christology "from below" usually do so on the basis of the *absoluteness* of Jesus' pre-Easter claim to authority—a claim they perceive either directly in Jesus' self-identification with the Christological titles or indirectly in Jesus' proclamation and activity in the name of God's Kingdom. Pannenberg, however, refers Jesus' pre-Easter claim to the horizon of the future. Though Jesus' claim emerged through the exercise of his office of calling men into the Kingdom of God, the claim itself could

---

[32] *JGaM*, pp. 56–58.
[33] *Ibid.*, pp. 327–328.

be confirmed only at the End when the Kingdom of God finally arrived. Hence, Pannenberg contends: *"Jesus' unity with God was not yet established by the claim implied in his pre-Easter appearance but only by his resurrection from the dead."* [34]

Against Conzelmann, Pannenberg argues that the temporal dialectic between the future expectation and the presence of salvation in Jesus' ministry cannot be eliminated. Rather, "the tension between present and future in Jesus' proclamation makes the proleptic character of Jesus' claim apparent; that is, Jesus' claim means an anticipation of a confirmation that is to be expected only from the future." [35] *This proleptic structure of Jesus' claim to divine authority* is reflected in Jesus' interpretation of the future judgment of the Son of Man: Jesus asserted that survival or destruction in the coming judgment of the Son of Man would be decided on the basis of a person's present attitude toward him (Luke 12:8). Though Jesus did not think of himself as the Son of Man, he did anticipate a correspondence between the attitude of men toward what he claimed and the future verdict of the Son of Man.[36] Therefore, just as prophetic words and apocalyptic visions required confirmation by their future fulfillment, Jesus expected his claim to be confirmed in the future when the resurrection of the dead occurred and the judgment of the Son of Man actually took place. The proleptic character of Jesus' claim expressed in the future Son of Man sayings converges with the background of Jewish apocalyptic in Jesus' preaching of the Kingdom of God and coheres with Old Testament prophetic inspiration in requiring future confirmation.[37]

Indeed, Jesus was probably asked to present a confirmation of his claim to authority (as reflected in the episode transmitted as the Pharisees' demand for a sign "from heaven"). Though Jesus rejected

[34] *Ibid.*, p. 53.

[35] *Ibid.*, p. 58. Cf. Hans Conzelmann, "Present and Future in the Synoptic Tradition," in *God and Christ*, Vol. V of Journal for Theology and the Church, ed. by Robert W. Funk (Harper & Row, Publishers, Inc., 1968), pp. 26–44.

[36] *JGaM*, pp. 58–63. The authenticity of the third-person Son of Man sayings is an important aspect of Pannenberg's understanding of the proleptic structure of Jesus' claim and receives strong support from H. E. Tödt, *The Son of Man in the Synoptic Tradition* (The Westminster Press, 1965). However, cf. "A Theological Conversation with Wolfhart Pannenberg," *Dialog*, Vol. XI (1972), pp. 291, 292–293.

[37] *JGaM*, p. 63. Cf. Pannenberg, "The Revelation of God in Jesus," *TaH*, p. 120, where he says of prophetic announcements: "Those words about the future are finally proven to be Yahweh's words only by their coming to pass (I Kings 22:28; Deut. 18:9–22; Jer. 28:6–9)."

the demand for "a sign from heaven," that does not mean he rejected every request for legitimation. In response to the Baptist's inquiry, Jesus pointed to the saving deeds of the End time that were already happening in his ministry as the verification and confirmation of his claim to authority. Hence, Jesus' refusal to produce a "sign from heaven" does not mean that he rejected all legitimation for accepting his message; however, it does mean that his earthly deeds could authenticate his claims *partially but not completely*. Only the coming of the Son of Man at the End could demonstrate conclusively whether Jesus was the one in whom salvation or judgment is ultimately decided. Unable to give a "sign from heaven" on his own initiative, therefore, Jesus rejected any inquiry about it. Since the whole of Jesus' activity aimed at the future verification of his claim to authority, which was bound to the arrival of the End, Pannenberg observes:

> The question about such a future confirmation of Jesus' claim by God himself is held open by the temporal distance between the beginning of God's rule, which was already present in Jesus' activity, and its future fulfillment with the coming of the Son of Man on the clouds of heaven.[38]

Precisely the question of Jesus' claim to authority explains Jesus' journey to Jerusalem, apparently to force a decision for or against his message. While not in the sense of the passion predictions, it would be very peculiar if Jesus had not already reckoned with the possibility of his death in Jerusalem. The journey was not one of despair, however, for Jesus expected God to justify him even in the case of his own failure. Since Jesus anticipated the immediate arrival of God's Kingdom, which included the resurrection of the dead and the judgment of the Son of Man, Pannenberg argues: "Measured by the imminent nearness of these events of the end, it must have been of secondary significance for Jesus whether he himself would have to endure death before the end came." [39] Though Jesus did not intend to die, death would not preclude the ultimate vindication of his message through the imminent fulfillment of all history at the appearance of the Son of Man. Therefore, the claim to authority of the pre-Easter Jesus was characterized by a proleptic structure wherein

---

[38] *JGaM*, p. 65.
[39] *Ibid.*, p. 66.

everything hinged upon God's ultimate confirmation of his proclamation and activity.

THE DISASTER OF JESUS' EXECUTION

Pannenberg employs the concept of destiny to refer to Jesus' crucifixion and resurrection, for both were "sent" to him. While the destiny of Jesus culminates in the resurrection, it includes the tragedy of the cross as something that "happened" to him. To be sure, Jesus' path of suffering included his acceptance of it, but the passion of Christ must be distinguished from his office of calling men into the inbreaking Kingdom of God. Jesus was not the acting agent in his death; consequently, his death should not be understood "as his own action in the same sense as his activity with its message of the nearness of the Kingdom of God." [40] Though the character of Jesus' passion as something that befell him is relegated to the background by means of the Gospel passion predictions, Pannenberg judges these predictions to be *vaticinia ex eventu.* Jesus' death was the *consequence* of the exercise of his office, but it was not *constitutive* for it. Therefore, the office of Jesus refers to the mission that he actively pursued, and the destiny of Jesus refers to the crucifixion and resurrection as events that "happened" to him.

The motivation behind the governmental decision to crucify Jesus is the basic historical question that guides Pannenberg's reconstruction of Jesus' execution. He rejects the historicity of the stylized Gospel portrayal of Jesus "embracing" death as the product of Easter reflection. For him the portrait of Jesus as the acting agent in his death represents the early church's transfer of the Messianic vocation of the exalted Lord back into the path of the pre-Easter Jesus. The passion theology of the early church must not obscure the character of these events as genuine, unforeseeable experiences. To be sure, there are indications that Jesus on his own initiative provoked the outbreak of the latent conflict that resulted in his death. Yet Jesus' fatal trip to Jerusalem was not to offer himself deliberately as a sacrifice but evidently to bring about a decision regarding his claim concerning the nearness of God's Kingdom and the centrality of his person in the anticipation of it. That Jesus virtually forced a decision regarding his claim to authority is reflected in the narrative of the cleansing of

---

[40] *Ibid.,* p. 245.

the Temple, "at least the kernel of which may be historical." [41] Thus Jesus most likely reckoned with the possibility of his death in Jerusalem (like the prophets and John the Baptist before him). Regardless of what happened in Jerusalem, however, Jesus expected God to verify his claim to authority. When it became obvious that death was his likely fate, perhaps Jesus even considered it to be of an expiatory nature, but he did not approach the cross as the supreme moment of fulfillment of his God-given vocation. Instead, Pannenberg insists: "The idea that the death of Jesus was an expiation of the sins of the world must be seen as a retrospective interpretation of the event, rather than an effect deliberately brought about by Jesus." [42]

Though Jesus was crucified as a rebel, as a Messianic pretender, Pannenberg regards the charge of sedition against him as slanderous. The Jewish authorities arrested, cross-examined, and condemned Jesus prior to delivering him to Pilate on the false charge of rebellion. Pannenberg has consistently interpreted the action of the Jewish leaders in the following way:

> Perhaps the Jewish leaders were afraid that the stir which Jesus had made among the people might, if they did not intervene, bring them under suspicion of a seditious attitude themselves. But in addition a conflict already existed in any case between Jesus and the custodians of the Jewish tradition, for other reasons: the claim to authority which was expressed in Jesus' whole demeanour, the claim with which Jesus set himself above the authority of the Law, was bound to appear as positive blasphemy to those Jews who only judged his behaviour from the outside and who did not permit themselves to be captured by the passion of his message about the kingdom of God.[43]

Since Jesus' activity really lacked any politically revolutionary accent, the accusation of rebellion against Jesus by the Jewish authorities would not be understandable unless he had earlier come into conflict with them. Hence, Pannenberg emphasizes: "Only this conflict, the character of which is understandable from the nature of Jesus' activity and teaching, provides the motive that permitted Jesus'

[41] *Ibid.*, p. 65.
[42] *AC*, p. 80.
[43] *Ibid.*

popularity among the people to serve as a welcome excuse for accusation before Pilate." [44] That the Jewish authorities did not execute Jesus for blasphemy by stoning but delivered him to the Romans to be condemned under a fraudulent accusation probably does not indicate the Sanhedrin's inability to implement the death sentence but the desire of the Jewish authorities "to avoid the indignation of Jesus' supporters." [45] Yet the indictment brought against Jesus probably involved some concrete incident, a saying against the Temple or his willful activity in the Temple. Though the details of the indictment cannot be definitely established, Pannenberg concludes:

> The reproach of blasphemy (Mark 14:64) through the claim of an authority properly belonging only to God was probably the real reason why the Jewish authorities took action against Jesus, *regardless of what the pretexts may have been in detail in the indictment itself.*[46]

While Jesus' offense against the law had not been envisioned by the law itself, the charge of blasphemy against him was not simply malevolent slander. Jesus could actually appear to be a blasphemer to the tradition-minded Jew who considered the law the ultimate criterion of salvation. To question the authority of the law, as Jesus did, *apparently* meant to those who absolutized the law nothing other than to question God himself as the One who had revealed his will in the law. Although Jesus' interpretation of the law from the central perspective of love suggests a certain continuity between his message and the traditional law, Jesus' conflict was with the law itself, at least "with the positive legal tradition which had become *calcified as 'the law' after the exile.*" [47] Hence, the rejection of Jesus was practically unavoidable for the Jew who was unprepared to distinguish between the authority of the law and the authority of God, but the disciples of Jesus demonstrate that the repudiation of Jesus was not an inevitable consequence of Jewish tradition.

In his *Jesus—God and Man* (first German ed., 1964) Pannenberg tended to present the rejection of Jesus because of his conflict with "the law" as practically inevitable, and he unfortunately concluded

---

[44] *JGaM*, p. 252, n. 21.
[45] *AC*, p. 81.
[46] *JGaM*, p. 252. Italics added.
[47] *Ibid.*, p. 258. Italics added.

that the resurrection of the Crucified who had been denounced as a blasphemer meant that the foundations of the Jewish religion collapsed.[48] Pannenberg has subsequently modified this conclusion considerably. He now holds that, instead of the destruction of the Jewish religion, the resurrection of the crucified Jesus reveals the inauthenticity of certain forms of Jewish piety, namely, the absolutizing of the law as the criterion of salvation. Pannenberg records his fundamental change of mind in *The Apostles' Creed* (1972):

> [Earlier] I represented the rejection of Jesus by the Jewish leaders of his day as being the result of his criticism of the Law; and I went on to remark that the raising of Jesus, therefore, conversely put the Law in the wrong and to that extent meant (in principle) the end of the Jewish religion. Today I regret this conclusion, which seemed to me inescapable at the time. It involved the presupposition of a view widespread in German Protestantism, that the religion of the Law and the Jewish religion are identical. I have meanwhile learnt to distinguish between the two. I think that I can see how for the Jewish faith, too, the God of Jewish history can stand above the Law. For it is only in this way that the earthly activity of Jesus can be also understood as a Jewish phenomenon.[49]

Pannenberg maintains nonetheless that Jesus' conflict with the Jewish authorities who had absolutized the law constitutes the deeper reason for Jesus' condemnation as a blasphemer by the Sanhedrin and crucifixion by the Romans on the slanderous charge of sedition.

Although Jesus knew that his death would not affect the final vindication of his claim at the coming of the Son of Man, the condemnation of Jesus as a blasphemer and his subsequent execution as a rebel constituted nothing less than a catastrophe for him personally and for his disciples vocationally. Pannenberg vividly portrays Jesus' tragic experience of the crucifixion in the imagery of hell's torment:

> To be excluded from God's nearness in spite of clear consciousness of it would be hell. This element agrees remarkably with the situation of Jesus' death: as the one who proclaimed

---

[48] *Ibid.*, p. 255. Cf. Neuhaus, "Profile of a Theologian," *TaKoG*, pp. 33–38.
[49] *AC*, p. viii. Cf. "A Theological Conversation with Wolfhart Pannenberg," pp. 291–292.

and lived the eschatological nearness of God, Jesus died the death of one rejected.[50]

The catastrophe that befell Jesus also enveloped the disciples, for they traumatically lost the assurance of Jesus' presence that God would actualize what he had preached. Jesus' condemnation and execution radically called into question the truth of his proclamation and the legitimacy of discipleship. Since Jesus had been rejected in the name of Israel's God, only the Judge of the last days could now say whether he had been right in spite of the disaster of the cross, only a confirmatory act of God could justify Jesus' activity and legitimate discipleship. The return of the disciples to Galilee, Pannenberg observes, is an eloquent expression of the disaster that Jesus' death signified for their continued discipleship: "After the crucifixion of Jesus the question of the legitimacy of his mission was no longer open; on the contrary, until something else happened, it was negatively decided." [51]

THE RESURRECTION OF JESUS THE CHRIST

Whereas Jesus had proclaimed the nearness of the End, it did not come—at least not in the way Jesus and his contemporaries had expected it. Instead of the general resurrection of the dead, the appearance of the heavenly Son of Man, and the commencement of the Last Judgment, there was "only" the pre-actualization of the End in Jesus' singular resurrection. Hence, Jesus' proclamation of the imminent coming of the Kingdom of God did not really fail but was confirmed in his own person. Pannenberg concedes that some difficulty inheres in this explanation. Yet the fulfillment of prophetic expectation seldom corresponds exactly to the announcement preceding it; furthermore, the unfamiliarity of the resurrection of a single man within apocalyptic theology suggests a special event undergirding the apostolic Easter message, an event which produced a decisive change in the traditional apocalyptic expectation of the End. Pannenberg reasons: "Evidently something had happened to the witnesses of the appearances of the Risen One for which their language had no other

[50] *JGaM*, p. 271. Cf. *AC*, pp. 90–92.
[51] Wolfhart Pannenberg, June 23, 1971: personal communication.

word than that used to characterize the eschatological expectation,
i.e., resurrection from the dead." [52]

The Significance of Jesus' Resurrection

Though contemporary theology does not usually locate the foundations of Christology in Jesus' resurrection, Pannenberg interprets New Testament research to say: "For primitive Christianity the resurrection of Jesus was the foundation of salvation and with great probability the starting point of all Christological confessions." [53] Hence, Pannenberg urges a thorough rethinking of the fundamental significance of the resurrection of Jesus for contemporary Christological statements. Only when the significance of Jesus' resurrection for the confession of the incarnation is recognized, he reasons, does the historical problem of the resurrection become decisive.[54] If the historicity of the resurrection of Jesus is momentarily assumed, the significance inherent in it emerges generally through the apocalyptic horizon that Jesus shared with his contemporaries and specifically through the shape of Jesus' pre-Easter activity. Pannenberg summarizes the immediate significance inherent in Jesus' resurrection with six concrete theses.

1. If Jesus has been raised, then the end of the world has begun.[55]

2. If Jesus has been raised, this for a Jew can only mean that God himself has confirmed the pre-Easter activity of Jesus.[56]

3. Through his resurrection from the dead, Jesus moved so close to the Son of Man that the insight became obvious: the Son of Man is none other than the man Jesus who will come again.[57]

4. If Jesus, having been raised from the dead, is ascended to God and if thereby the end of the world has begun, then God is ultimately revealed in Jesus.[58]

[52] "The Revelation of God in Jesus," *TaH*, p. 115.
[53] "Dogmatische Erwägungen zur Auferstehung Jesu," *Kerygma und Dogma*, Vol. XIV (1968), p. 105.
[54] *Ibid.*, pp. 105–108. Cf. *JGaM*, pp. 66–106, where treatment of the significance of Jesus' resurrection precedes an investigation of its historicity.
[55] *JGaM*, p. 67.
[56] *Ibid.* Cf. *ibid.*, pp. 106–108, where Pannenberg relates the resurrection to the delay of the parousia.
[57] *Ibid.*, p. 68.
[58] *Ibid.*, p. 69. Pannenberg affirms: "The translation of the apocalyptic understanding of Jesus as the one in whom the glory of God is ultimately revealed, because in him the end event has occurred in advance, into the Hellenistic concept

5. The transition to the Gentile mission is motivated by the eschatological resurrection of Jesus as resurrection of the crucified One.[59]

6. What the early Christian tradition transmitted as the words of the risen Jesus is to be understood in terms of its content as the explication of the significance inherent in the resurrection itself.[60]

The Metaphor of "Resurrection from the Dead"

Before grappling directly with the historical problem of Jesus' resurrection, Pannenberg emphasizes the importance of understanding the expression "resurrection of the dead." The early Christian designation of Jesus' destiny as "resurrection" did not refer to a random miracle but to a very specific reality expected by postexilic Judaism in conjunction with the end of the world. Though it may be compared to awakening from sleep, resurrection itself eludes ordinary experience. Rising from sleep is a metaphor or parable for the completely unknown destiny expected for the dead. Pannenberg considers the metaphorical structure of the language of resurrection to be of profound consequence, because "the intended reality and the mode in which it is expressed in language are essentially different." [61] Unlike empirical knowledge, therefore, "resurrection" lies beyond the experience of the man "on this side of death" and refers metaphorically to an event whose essence remains hidden.[62]

The metaphorical structure of the language of resurrection requires a sharp distinction between resuscitation and resurrection: While the former refers to the *temporary* return of a dead person to this life, the latter involves an imperishable life no longer limited by death, the transformation of the physical body into a spiritual body. Paul told the Corinthian Christians that the transformation of resurrection occurs to the present mortal body, but the transformation itself is so radical that there is no substantial or structural continuity from the

---

of revelation as epiphany may also have been the path that led to the thesis of the true divinity of Jesus."

[59] *Ibid.*, p. 71. Continuity between Jesus and Paul is partially established through Jesus' claim of authority above the law in offering eschatological salvation and Paul's proclamation of freedom from the law in access to salvation.

[60] *Ibid.*, p. 72.

[61] *Ibid.*, p. 75.

[62] Cf. *WIM*, p. 53, where Pannenberg says: "Jesus' new reality, which appeared to the disciples at Easter, remains incomprehensible for us, as it was for them. We also are able to describe it only by the metaphor with which Jesus' disciples spoke about it."

old to the new existence. Though Paul does suggest historical continuity in "the resurrection of the body," such continuity refers only to "that connection between the beginning and the end point which resides in the process of transformation itself, regardless of how radically this process may be conceived." [63] Pannenberg applies Paul's "description" of the future resurrection of the dead to Jesus' past resurrection—an application justified by Paul's understanding of Jesus' resurrection and that of Christians as being in essential parallel.

Only the apocalyptic expectation of the End of history enabled Paul and the other apostles to designate the encountered reality of the living Jesus as "the resurrected One," which could not be confused with a revivified corpse. Paul called the expectation of the resurrection of the dead the presupposition for the recognition of Jesus' resurrection (I Cor. 15:16). The validity of Paul's evaluation of the primacy of the apocalyptic hope of resurrection is reflected in the primitive Christian missionary kerygma, which brought the Jewish apocalyptic expectation into the new Gentile congregations. Therefore, the freedom of the Gentile Christians from the law did not indicate that all Jewish traditions had become meaningless, because the apocalyptic expectation of the resurrection of the dead remained valid in its essential structure even for the Gentile churches.

The question remains, however, whether or not apocalyptic concepts can be binding in the modern world. Although the apocalyptic concept of the end of the world may be untenable in many details, Pannenberg considers its fundamental elements—the expectation of the End, the resurrection of the dead, and the Last Judgment—to be comprehensible to modern man. Emphasizing the importance of the apocalyptic expectation generally and resurrection particularly for the integrity of Christian faith, he contends:

> The primitive Christian motivation for faith in Jesus as the Christ of God, in his exaltation, in his identification with the Son of Man, is essentially bound to the apocalyptic expectation for the end of history *to such an extent* that one must say that *if the apocalyptic expectation should be totally excluded from the realm of possibility for us,* then the early Christian faith in Christ is also excluded; then, however, the continuity would be broken between that which might still

[6] *JGaM,* p. 76.

remain as Christianity after such a reduction and Jesus himself.[64]

If the original apocalyptic horizon of Jesus' history were eliminated, the foundation of Christian faith would be shattered; consequently, Pannenberg disavows any attempt to reduce the fundamental content of "resurrection" into myth. Instead, he values the concept of resurrection as an "absolute metaphor," which is neither interchangeable with other images nor reducible to a rational kernel but is the only appropriate expression for the issue in question, namely, Jesus' eschatological destiny.[65] Therefore, openness to the possibility of a future resurrection and to an understanding of reality that does not exclude such an event is essential to the credibility of the message of Jesus' resurrection. Pannenberg maintains:

> If one assumes that the dead cannot rise, that an event of this type can never happen, the result will be such a strong prejudice against the truth of the early Christian message of Jesus' resurrection, that the more precise quality of the particular testimonies will not be taken into consideration in forming a general judgment. Only if the expectation of the future general resurrection of all men from death, whether for life or for judgment, makes sense in itself, only if it also expresses the truth for us, will it then be meaningful to put the question of Jesus' resurrection as a question of historical importance.[66]

Hence, any discussion of the veracity of apocalyptic hopes impinges directly upon the basis of Christian faith, for it profoundly influences one's estimate of the eschatological destiny of Jesus. In order to establish (at least tentatively) the legitimacy of Jewish apocalyptic expectation, Pannenberg examines the foundations of the contemporary phenomenology of hope and concludes that the expectation of a resurrection from the dead does not appear meaningless from the presuppositions of modern thought, but that a continuity of current thought with the apocalyptic hope of resurrection destiny remains a viable option.[67]

---

[64] *Ibid.*, p. 82. Italics added.
[65] *Ibid.*, p. 187.
[66] "Did Jesus Really Rise from the Dead?" *Dialog*, Vol. IV (1965), p. 131.
[67] Cf. *JGaM*, pp. 83–88; *WIM*, esp. pp. 41–53.

The Problem of the Historicity of Jesus' Resurrection

Though the centrality of Jesus' resurrection for primitive Christianity is often recognized in New Testament research, it seldom penetrates the foundations of contemporary Christological formulations because of the problem of the historicity of the resurrection.[68] While this problem confronts any attempt to reestablish Christology upon the resurrection, Pannenberg considers the historicality of Jesus' resurrection to be the only adequate foundation for contemporary Christological statements. Furthermore, he reasons:

> As long as historiography does not begin dogmatically with a narrow concept of reality according to which "dead men do not rise," it is not clear why historiography should not in principle be able to speak about Jesus' resurrection as the explanation that is best established of such events as the disciples' experiences of the appearances and the discovery of the empty tomb.[69]

Since critically certain knowledge of past events is achieved only through the fires of historical criticism, Pannenberg exposes the inadequacy of those prejudgments which would exclude in principle an open historical investigation of the reports of Jesus' resurrection. (1) Hume's *a priori* assertion—that the resurrection of someone from the dead is simply unbelievable because it contradicts all analogies of human experience—is untenable, for every historical event is more or less unique and resists absolute comprehension through known analogies. (2) The negative evaluation of resurrection as an impossible violation of "natural law" is also illegitimate. Natural laws represent abstract models employed to describe the usual course of events, but they may not be absolutized in the consideration of the possibility or impossibility of a specific historical occurrence. (3) Finally, Pannenberg rejects the theological presupposition that places the inbreak of the new aeon in Jesus' resurrection completely beyond the vision of the old aeon as a subtle *denial* of the incarnation: "The Incarnation of God affirms that the life of the new creation has begun within the scope of the old world and is also perceived with the eyes of the old man, so indeed, that those eyes are renewed precisely through [the

---

[68] "Dogmatische Erwägungen zur Auferstehung Jesu," p. 108.
[69] *JGaM*, p. 109.

act of] perception." [70] Yet the disavowal of these prejudgments which exclude a consideration of the historicity of the resurrection does not guarantee a positive conclusion from the historical investigation into Jesus' resurrection; on the contrary, a negative judgment might ensue. Regardless of the results, however, the assertion that Jesus of Nazareth has been raised from the dead implies a historical claim about a past event and thereby lays itself open to historical inquiry and examination. Pannenberg insists that a historical-critical investigation of the reports of Jesus' resurrection is finally inescapable—for the historian who wants to understand the history of Christian origins and for contemporary Christians, who are denied appearances of the risen Christ but remain utterly dependent upon the credibility of the witness of the primitive church.[71] Addressing himself to the complex historical problem of Jesus' resurrection, Pannenberg says:

> Recently it has been correctly emphasized that discourse about the *resurrection* of Jesus in primitive Christianity generally depended upon an *inference,* namely, upon the . . . deduction from the appearances of the living Lord that Jesus was indeed buried but did not remain dead—a conclusion which combined with the tradition of the discovery of the empty tomb of Jesus to [substantiate] the affirmation, Jesus is raised from the dead. The conclusion issues from the *appearances* of the living Lord. . . . But the conclusion [itself] has an inner necessity: If Jesus (after he was dead) now lives, then he was—before he was seen for the first time as the living One—either resuscitated or, conversely (when the manner of the contemporary life excludes resuscitation and his death was undoubtedly certain), he has been transformed to another "life." [72]

The difficulty of what "life" means in this context introduces the complexities of the historical problem of Jesus' resurrection. Since a

[70] "Dogmatische Erwägungen zur Auferstehung Jesu," p. 110.
[71] *AC,* pp. 107–114.
[72] "Dogmatische Erwägungen zur Auferstehung Jesu," p. 111. Hence, Pannenberg distinguishes between Jesus' resurrection itself and the appearances of the risen One, "because the event of the resurrection as such, insofar as we know, had no human witnesses, and the appearances of the resurrected One could be characterized as experiences of the risen One but not as the experience of the event of his resurrection. The event of the resurrection is rather an inference which was deduced from the appearances" (Wolfhart Pannenberg, June 23, 1971: personal communication).

historical event occurs in time and space, it must be affirmed or denied in reference to a *specific* time and a *specific* place. If the death of Jesus on the one side and the first appearances and the discovery of the empty tomb on the other are datable, the resurrection of Jesus qualifies as an event in time. However, the characterization of the resurrection as an event in space—that it is locatable—is more complex and difficult. That the resurrection must have happened in Palestine, certainly in Jerusalem, and (presupposing the historicity of the empty tomb) in and by the grave itself, does not entirely solve the problem. Other events that occur in space usually require a direct relationship to the sequence of events that follow. Conversely, Jesus' resurrection in reference to Jesus himself did not occur within a successive series of events in space or time. Since the appearances are not an *immediate* succession of events, their relationship to the specific *reality* of the resurrected Jesus is thoroughly problematic. To set the problem in perspective, Pannenberg reasons:

> That the Easter appearances were, as experiences, events in space and time need not include that the appearing *Reality* —presupposing it was not a question of mere hallucinations— on its side was in space and in time. Hence, the resurrection of Jesus as an event [itself] is fixable temporally and spatially— but the continuous sequential relationship in which events are usually arranged, temporally as well as spatially, at this point evades our view. Plainly said: The wider course of the event, insofar as it concerns Jesus himself, remains unknown. If Jesus did not remain dead, but is resurrected to a . . . new "life," then the statement can hardly be avoided that he has since then *disappeared* out of our world.[73]

Ultimately, therefore, the historian has at best a *vague* conception of what actually transpired in Jesus' resurrection. The "eventness" of the resurrection only permits one to say that "Jesus—who had died— 'lives,' without saying, however, what the word 'life' exactly means here, beyond the affirmation, that Jesus did not remain dead." [74] The event of Jesus' resurrection confronts the historian as opaque. But such a restricted affirmation does not denote a negative response to the question of Jesus' resurrection. To conclude that the historian has

[73] "Dogmatische Erwägungen zur Auferstehung Jesu," p. 112.
[74] *Ibid.*

nothing to say to this question or that the historian *a priori* must deny such an event would be unwarranted. Instead, Pannenberg argues, the historian has something quite positive and theologically significant to say:

> An event has happened, whose more detailed qualities evade his judgment . . . [but] it is an event which relates to Jesus, and indeed, the *dead* Jesus—an event which in any case means that Jesus thereafter was no longer dead. With so critically delimited a statement, which in spite of its negative form is *eminently positive* through the exactness of its negation, history guards the mystery of the resurrection.[75]

Every attempt to say *what* the event itself of Jesus' resurrection actually was exceeds what is historically examinable. Hence, the historian who attempts to name the event of the resurrection (which the reality itself requires him to do) can do so only in a language that changes its meaning through application to "what happened" to Jesus. Furthermore, the linguistic concepts which the event itself requires must postulate a life or existence on the other side of death. Those who experienced appearances of the resurrected One utilized such a language to designate the reality which encountered them, namely, the language of Jewish apocalyptic. However, since the assertion of the appearance of an imperishable life in Jesus' resurrection transcends the verifiable, only the future can finally reveal the truth of it. Correspondingly, while it is possible to translate the message of the resurrection of Jesus into another eschatological language, it must be an eschatological conceptual world which is related to the problem of life beyond death—the fact of which constitutes the basis of the Easter traditions.

An Evaluation of the Easter Traditions

The examination of the primitive Easter traditions constitutes the decisive moment in evaluating the historicity of Jesus' resurrection. Pannenberg recognizes that the Easter traditions of primitive Christianity fall into two different categories: the tradition of the appearances of the risen Lord and the tradition of the discovery of the empty tomb. While these distinctive traditions are increasingly drawn to-

[75] *Ibid.*, pp. 112–113. Italics added.

gether in the formulation of the Gospels, the oldest stratum of tradition keeps them separate, suggesting thereby the necessity to investigate these two traditions individually. Since the appearances reported in the Gospels have such strong legendary character (so that scarcely a historical kernel of their own can be found), Pannenberg focuses the historical question of the appearances of the resurrected One primarily upon the Pauline report in I Cor. 15:1–11. Enumerating the appearances of the resurrected Jesus—chronologically to Peter, to the Twelve, to the five hundred, to James, to all the apostles, and finally to Paul himself—Paul clearly intends to give proof for the facticity of the resurrection by means of witnesses who are subject to interrogation. Obviously Paul is not disinterested in the events he reports, but he means to offer convincing historical proof by the standards of his time.[76]

To evaluate properly Paul's report of the appearances, one must recognize the proximity of the report to the events reported. Though I Corinthians was not written until ca. A.D. 57, Paul speaks from an earlier personal knowledge, which probably refers to his visit to Jerusalem ca. A.D. 36, only six to eight years after the events. Furthermore, Paul appeals to a formulated tradition of the appearances, which most likely arose even prior to Paul's visit to Jerusalem. Pannenberg says of I Cor. 15:1–11:

> In view of the age of the formulated traditions used by Paul and the proximity of Paul to the events, the assumption that appearances of the resurrected Lord were really experienced by a number of members of the primitive Christian community and not perhaps freely invented in the course of later legendary development has good historical foundation.[77]

Consequently, Pannenberg reasons, it is an "idle venture" to explain the *emergence* of the primitive Christian message about Jesus' resurrection through appeals to parallels in the history of religions.

To conclude that the apostles actually experienced the appearances of the resurrected Jesus, however, does not explain what sort of experiences these were. Posing the question of the content of the appearances, Pannenberg turns again to Paul (for the Gospel reports, which emphasize the corporeality of Jesus' risen body, reflect a polemic

[76] *JGaM*, pp. 89–91.
[77] *Ibid.*, p. 91.

against an incipient docetism). Analyzing the Pauline materials (Gal. 1:12, 16 f.; I Cor., ch. 15) and relating them to the accounts in Acts, Pannenberg posits five elements relative to the content of the appearances:[78] (1) Paul has seen the Lord Jesus Christ, God's Son. (2) Paul saw a spiritual body, not a person with an earthly body. (3) The experience was not an earthly encounter but involved an appearance from heaven. (4) Assuming the unity of Jesus' resurrection and ascension, it is probable that the Damascus appearance could have happened as a light phenomenon. (5) Paul's Christophany was connected with an audition, but the verbal content did not exceed the meaning of the appearance itself. With the possible exception of the fourth, the light phenomenon, these same elements may also be presupposed for the other appearances of the resurrected Lord. Paul undoubtedly thought that "he had been granted an appearance of the same sort as the other apostles before him." [79]

Since the appearances were not visible to everyone, Pannenberg describes the mode of the Easter appearances as extraordinary objective visions. When the term "vision" is used to describe the Easter appearances, Pannenberg insists: "The term 'vision' can only express something about the subjective mode of experience, not something about the reality of an event experienced in this form." [80] Hence, Pannenberg vigorously rejects the "subjective vision hypothesis"—the purely psychological explanation of the Easter appearances as the imaginative projections of the disciples. First, positive points of contact for the application of the psychiatric concept of vision are lacking. Second, the historical problems, namely, the origin of the Easter message of an eschatological resurrection within history, the number of the appearances and their temporal distribution, cannot be explained by the enthusiastically excited imagination of the disciples.

Obligated to reconstruct the historical correlation of events that led to the emergence of the primitive Christian church, the historian—if he is open to the "element of truth" in the apocalyptic hope of resurrection—must honestly consider the reality of Jesus' resurrection

---

[78] Ibid., pp. 92–93. Cf. Pannenberg, "Did Jesus Really Rise from the Dead?" pp. 132–133.

[79] JGaM, p. 77.

[80] Ibid., p. 95. Pannenberg attributes the positive assessment of vision in his Christology to Ulrich Wilckens, who suggested in the discussions of "the working circle" that the Easter appearances were special "apocalyptic visions" (Wolfhart Pannenberg, June 23, 1971: personal communication).

as the best explanation for the events in question. As a historian, therefore, Pannenberg concludes:

> Thus the resurrection of Jesus would be designated as a historical event in this sense: If the emergence of primitive Christianity, which, apart from other traditions, is also traced back by Paul to appearances of the resurrected Jesus, can be understood *in spite of* all critical examination of the tradition *only if* one examines it in the light of the eschatological hope for a resurrection from the dead, then that which is so designated [i.e., Jesus' resurrection] is a historical event, *even if we do not know anything more particular about it.* Then an event that is expressible only in the language of the eschatological expectation is to be asserted as a historical occurrence.[81]

Though the results attained in the discussion of the appearances of the resurrected Jesus are valid independently of the judgment about the empty tomb, the decision about the historicity of the tradition of Jesus' empty tomb is significant for the final conclusion. The authenticity of the report is unaffected by the fact that Paul does not mention it. Paul's eschatological proclamation indicates an assumption of the emptiness of the tomb whether he knew the Jerusalem tradition or not. However, the Christian community in Jerusalem could hardly have proclaimed Jesus' resurrection without a reliable testimony for the empty tomb; otherwise, the proclamation of Jesus' resurrection could have been easily refuted merely by inspecting the place of burial.[82] Furthermore, the Jewish polemic against the primitive Christian community "shared the conviction with its Christian opponents that Jesus' grave was empty." [83] Finally, the likely discovery of the empty tomb after the disciples fled to Galilee, indicating that the tradition of the empty tomb emerged independently of the appearances of the risen Lord, further substantiates the historicity of Jesus' resurrection as the most plausible explanation for the proclamation

---

[81] *JGaM*, p. 98. Italics added.

[82] "Did Jesus Really Rise from the Dead?" p. 134. Since Jesus did not remain buried for many years and subsequently decay, Pannenberg concludes that the empty tomb belongs to the singularity of Jesus' transformation—a singularity unique to the shortness of time between his death and resurrection (*JGaM*, p. 100).

[83] *JGaM*, p. 101.

of the Jerusalem church and for the development of the tradition of Jesus' empty tomb.[84]

The Credibility of the Report of Jesus' Resurrection

Without really knowing what happened to Jesus or what kind of existence the risen One may have in relation to earthly life, Pannenberg necessarily describes the resurrection of Jesus in metaphorical language. Hence, he says: "The most we can really know is whether or not the Easter witnesses were confronted by a reality which we too can comprehend only in terms of the parabolic word of eschatological expectation: resurrection from the dead." [85] Though the language Pannenberg uses to describe the resurrection reflects caution and reserve, the statement itself—the historical claim of a cognitive knowledge of Jesus' resurrection on the basis of the Easter traditions—is not so hesitating or restrained. Pannenberg's confidence is even more apparent when he evaluates the significance of the divergent Easter traditions:

> If the appearance tradition and the grave tradition came into existence independently, then by their mutually complementing each other they let the assertion of the reality of Jesus' resurrection . . . appear as historically very probable, and that always means in historical inquiry that it is to be presupposed until contrary evidence appears.[86]

The historical probability of the resurrection corresponds to the concept of verification that Pannenberg employs. Unlike Ebeling, who constantly impugns all efforts toward establishing a "proof" for the

[84] *Ibid.*, pp. 101–106.
[85] "The Revelation of God in Jesus," *TaH*, p. 115.
[86] *JGaM*, p. 105. James M. Robinson, "Revelation as Word and History," *TaH*, pp. 32–34, reports on a public debate between Pannenberg and Herbert Braun on February 19, 1965, concerning the historicity of Jesus' resurrection—a debate in which Pannenberg challenged the *a priori* ideological rejection of the possibility of resurrection and places the burden of proof upon those who would deny its historicity. Thesis 9: "The traditions of Jesus' resurrection would be subject to evaluation as unhistorical if: (a) the Easter traditions were demonstrable as *literarily secondary constructions* in analogy to common comparative religious models not only in details, but also in kernel; (b) the *Easter appearances* were to correspond *completely* to the model of self-produced *hallucinations* (owing to organic peculiarities or medicines); (c) the tradition of the *empty tomb* of Jesus were to be evaluated as a *late* (Hellenistic) *legend*." (Punctuation adapted.) These hypotheses reflect the logical structure wherein specific historical evidence is evaluated and from which the provisional verification of resurrection emerges.

ground of faith, Pannenberg insists that the basis of faith in Jesus' resurrection must be as certain as possible (for the essence of faith is not risk but trust).[87] However, the historical verification of the basis of faith in God's revelation through Jesus' resurrection always remains open to the eschatological future, the essence of faith is always preserved by the eschatological tension of the "not yet" wherein the believer lives. Therefore, when the concept of verification is applied to the historical ground of faith, it only refers to a *provisional but reliable* knowledge which nonetheless remains open to the promise and threat of the future. Hence, Pannenberg candidly refers final substantiation of the truth of the resurrection beyond historical to eschatological verification.

The ultimate divine confirmation of Jesus will take place only in the occurrence of his return. Only then will the revelation of God in Jesus become manifest in its ultimate, irresistible glory. When we speak today of God's revelation in Jesus and of his exaltation accomplished in the resurrection from the dead, our statements always contains a proleptic element. The fulfillment, which had begun for the disciples, which was almost in their grasp, in the appearances of the resurrected Lord, has become promise once again for us.[88]

While the expectation of eschatological verification hinges upon the positive results of historical investigation, Pannenberg acknowledges that prior to the End of history the affirmation of Jesus' resurrection will remain permanently controversial. The fundamental question of Jesus' destiny is not finally decided or decidable historically (which would make all further discussion about it superfluous); nevertheless, the historical actuality of Jesus' resurrection is neither refuted nor without reliable evidence. Indeed, the issue is sharply disputed not only because it finally eludes the category of the historical but also because it cuts so deeply into questions about the nature of reality itself. Yet strong phenomenological and historical arguments

---

[87] *JGaM*, pp. 109–110. Although theology can never speak of verification in an exact, scientific sense, Pannenberg refers to the broader conception of proof as "that argument which appeals to a reasonable judgment and makes possible at least a provisional decision between contrasting assertions" (*ibid.*, p. 110, n. 117). Such provisional verification neither contradicts the essence of faith by comprehending its object nor replaces the mysterious depth of the content of faith.

[88] *Ibid.*, p. 108.

sustain the credibility of the message of the resurrection of Jesus. While the evidence is not incontrovertible, a critical investigation of the early Christian traditions of Jesus' resurrection justifies the affirmation of its historicity: "The historical claim, which is already contained in the assertion that Jesus is risen, is a tenable one on objective examination, even in the context of our present experience of reality." [89]

THE SIGNIFICANCE OF THE DEATH OF CHRIST

Although the resurrection of the Crucified was an event easily defined by the context of Israel's traditions and by the activity of the pre-Easter Jesus, the early church had serious difficulty in understanding the "necessity" of the death of Christ. Grappling with the divine "must" of Jesus' execution, the primitive Christian church concluded that Jesus' death on the cross had unusual, even universal significance as "a service to humanity." Jesus' death was interpreted variously as prophetic rejection, expiation for sin, an expiatory sacrifice, a covenant sacrifice, and "the end of the law" (Paul).[90] However, these different interpretations were based upon a common acceptance of the authority of the Old Testament Scriptures, a presupposition which can no longer be assumed. Thus Pannenberg seeks to establish the justification for assigning universal significance to Christ's death on other grounds, namely, in the course of Jesus' historical activity which led to the cross as well as in the validity of the category of "representation" or "substitution" (Stellvertretung)[91] as a universal aspect of human experience. First, Pannenberg interprets the significance of Jesus' death from the historical vantage point of Jesus' conflict with the law as the ultimate criterion of salvation, which converges with Paul's theological insight that Christ is the end of the law. Second, Pannenberg defines the "vicarious" character of Jesus' death as a "service" to

[89] AC, pp. 114–115.
[90] JGaM, pp. 246–251.
[91] Ibid., pp. 258–269. Wilkins and Priebe translate Stellvertretung as "substitution" (JGaM, p. 258); however, without excluding the concept of substitution entirely, I consider "representation" or "representative" to be the better terms to describe the conceptualization that Pannenberg defines. Contrary to "the substitutionary theory of the atonement," Pannenberg disavows the elements of (1) propitiation and (2) mutual reconciliation in the interpretation of Jesus' death. Yet the translation of Stellvertretung as "representation" must also be distinguished conceptually from the "representative sacrifice" of much Biblical theology, which, unlike Pannenberg, identifies the cross as corresponding to and the climax of Jesus' mission as the incarnate Son of God.

humanity—fulfilling a need for man, which, apart from Christ's service, each would have to fulfill for himself.

While the Jewish people as a whole and for all times cannot be condemned for the action of the Sanhedrin in the trial of Jesus, the question as to whether or not the Jewish authorities involved in Jesus' execution acted in behalf of the Jewish people (and ultimately mankind itself) is decisive for the representative significance of Jesus' death.[92] Since Jesus' resurrection revealed that he died as a righteous man, not as a blasphemer, those who rejected him as a blasphemer emerge as the real blasphemers. Thus, Pannenberg reasons, Jesus bore the damnation inherent in blasphemy which was rightly deserved by his judges:

> This Jesus has, in the strict sense, died in their stead—for the crime of blasphemy, which his judges have committed through their verdict. And through the very fact that these judges did not only act as isolated individuals but as the office-bearers of their people, the vicarious power of Jesus' death on the cross also extends beyond their sphere to the whole people, and indeed to the whole of mankind, since the Jewish nation, as God's chosen people, stands before God for the whole of mankind.[93]

The solidarity of non-Jewish peoples with the Jewish authorities in the condemnation of Jesus is implied in the involvement of Pilate as the representative of Rome and of state authority generally. Although the action of the Roman authorities was not motivated by the essence of Jesus' claim, his eschatological message removed the "glitter of ultimacy" from every political system. Jesus' proclamation of the ultimacy of the rule of God robs every political order of its absolute claim on its people. So Pannenberg concludes: "Thus the cross of Jesus demonstrates the tendency of political rule to violate the majesty of God, a tendency which operates everywhere where political rule usurps absolute binding force.[94]

Yet Jesus' death can have vicarious significance for all humanity only if all men are disclosed as blasphemers by Jesus' cross. Therefore, if Jesus in his death suffered the abandonment of God as the effect

[92] *AC*, p. 83.
[93] *Ibid.*, pp. 84–85.
[94] *Ibid.*, pp. 85–86.

of pride of equality with God (which separates man *universally* from God) and if he has taken such abandonment away once for all, one can legitimately find non-Jewish humanity represented by the activity of the Roman procurator in Jesus' condemnation. According to Pannenberg, the apostle Paul suggests the path to this general legitimation. (1) Negatively, the vindication of the One whom the law condemned abolishes the law as the criterion of salvation, making possible salvation through Jesus apart from the law. (2) Positively, the general anthropological relationship between sin and death—all men die as a result of their sin (Rom. 3:23)—enables one to interpret Jesus' innocent death as a vicarious service for blasphemous humanity.[95] The universal validity of the vicarious significance of Jesus' death ultimately presupposes that "all men participate in their lives in that opposition to God which is shown in Jesus' condemnation by his judges."[96] Hence, Pannenberg reasons, because all live in the blasphemous condition expressed in the rejection of Jesus as blasphemer by the leaders of God's chosen people, the Jewish leaders represented mankind itself in rejecting and crucifying Jesus; consequently, Christ bore the tragic consequences of death deserved by the blasphemous existence of humanity in general.

Are other men spared anything by Jesus' death? Since Jesus died the death of a blasphemer, which all men deserve, Pannenberg affirms that "in this sense" he died for the sins of all men. Although Jesus' death does not mean that the believer no longer must die, it does mean that no one else must die in the complete rejection in which Jesus died—expelled by the great tradition of the divine law, excluded from the nearness of God. No other person has to die this death of "eternal damnation"; rather, through community with Jesus the believer dies in the hope of the coming resurrection that has already appeared in Jesus. Pannenberg concludes:

> This communion between our human dying and the dying of Jesus is the essential substance of the representative significance of Jesus' death. Because Jesus gathers up our dying into his own, the character of our dying changes. In communion with Jesus it loses its hopelessness and has already been overcome through the life which has appeared in Jesus' resur-

[95] *JGaM*, pp. 260–263.
[96] *AC*, p. 88.

rection. The death of the blasphemer, the one who is shut out from all communion with God, has been taken away by Jesus once and for all.[97]

Since it is not universally agreed that vicarious representation can actually take place in the sphere of personal life, the concept of representation for interpreting Christ's death requires fundamental justification. Arguing that the people of Israel lived with a completely different *conceptual* world than that of post-Enlightenment western society, Pannenberg emphasizes that "vicarious representation" lay at the center of Israel's corporate reaction to the problem of "guilt and punishment." [98] (1) Israel understood misfortune as something already built into an evil deed, a kind of natural-law relation between a deed and its consequences; hence, Paul could think of death as the "wages" of sin: Death is *built into* the essence of sin as the most extreme consequence of sin's desire for separation from God. Thus, when Paul speaks of Christ's being made "sin" for the sake of man (II Cor. 5:21), he means that death, the fatal consequence inherent in man's sin, has fallen upon Jesus. (2) Furthermore, Israel's conception of the extensive independence of the evil deed from the individual doer contributed to the necessity of the concept of representation. Since the consequences of an individual's evil deed could bring misfortune upon the wider circles of corporate society, Israel developed the practice of directing the catastrophe inherent in evil deeds toward some other entity in order to annul its effect on the community (Deut. 21:1-9; Lev. 16:21 f.). Such a practice presupposed the legitimacy of transferring the guilt inherent in an offense onto an innocent victim, but God had given this authorization in the cultic system.

Relating Israel's conceptualization and practice to Christ's vicarious representation for humanity, Pannenberg affirms that God himself— to the extent that Christ's death was authorized by the law given by God—laid on Jesus the tragic misfortune inherent in blasphemy, which rightly belonged to the Jewish authorities in particular and to humanity in general. Although God legitimated Jesus by raising him from the dead, before he did so he let Jesus go to his death in the place of blasphemous humanity. Through Jesus' death, therefore, the

---

[97] *Ibid.*, p. 89. Cf. *JGaM*, pp. 263–264.
[98] *JGaM*, pp. 265–266. Since Pannenberg understands misfortune as inherent to an evil deed, the term "punishment" is not entirely appropriate, for it implies an arbitrary penalty *added* to an evil deed.

Godforsakenness of death is overcome.[99] Nevertheless, the legitimacy of speaking of representation today does not depend upon a "miraculously supernatural uniqueness of Jesus" but upon the corporate, social nature of human existence. Quite candidly, Pannenberg concludes:

> If [representation] is not a universal phenomenon in human social relationships, if the individualistic interpretation of responsibility and recompense need not be rejected as one-sided because it overlooks the social relationships of individual behavior, then it is not possible to speak meaningfully of a vicarious character of the fate of Jesus Christ.[100]

Precisely because he believes that representation is a universal phenomenon in contemporary corporate society, Pannenberg affirms the legitimacy of speaking of Christ's death as vicarious representation.

[99] Ibid., p. 269. Pannenberg suggests a similarity between his interpretation of Jesus' death as vicarious suffering and that of Luther and the later formulations of Karl Barth (ibid., pp. 278–280).

[100] Ibid., p. 268. Translation altered within brackets. See note 91 of this chapter.

VI

CHRISTOLOGY "FROM BEFORE"— THE INCARNATION OF THE *ESCHATON* IN JESUS

POSITING A CHRISTOLOGY "from below," Pannenberg poses the question of Christology in a striking affirmation of the absolute significance of Jesus of Nazareth for Christian faith:

> As *this* man, as man in this particular, unique situation, with this particular historical mission and this particular fate—as this man Jesus is not just man, but from the perspective of his resurrection from the dead . . . he is one with God and thus is himself God.[1]

Pannenberg is aware of the gravity of his affirmation. He affirms that an obscure contemporary of the emperors Augustus and Tiberius, one conditioned by his time and culture, a Palestinian Jew living prior to the catastrophic Jewish War of A.D. 70, an itinerant Galilean preacher sharing the apocalyptic hopes of his people—that *this Jesus* is the unique Son of God, the final criterion of faith in God. The unequivocal founding of Christian faith and hence of Christology upon this particular historical man makes Christianity extremely vulnerable. First, the vulnerability issues from the constant questioning of the reliability of the historical portrait of Jesus which sustains Christian faith. Second, it roots in the radical historical distance and attendant estrangement of Jesus from the contemporary world—while Jesus remains central to the Christian understanding of man and God. Although theology has often attempted to evade the historical

---

[1] *JGaM*, p. 323.

vulnerability of Christian faith, these efforts ultimately prove futile.[2]

A Christology "from below" obviously confronts one aspect of Christianity's vulnerability, namely, the problem of the historical Jesus; however, the category "from below" does not immediately provide a conceptual solution to the other dimension of vulnerability, namely, the problem of Jesus' divinity and universality. The conceptual clue is Pannenberg's insistence: "But in the destiny of Jesus the End of all history has happened in advance, as prolepsis." [3] Thus a Christology "from below," which understands the history of Jesus as the ground and criterion of Christology, finally assumes the shape of an eschatological Christology—a Christology "from before," which derives from the prolepsis of the End in Jesus' eschatological destiny.

While Christology "from below" roots in the history of Jesus, Christology "from before" issues from the eschatological shape of that history. Since the eschatological revelation of God as "the power over everything" has occurred proleptically in the history of Jesus, Christology "from below" necessarily precedes and undergirds Christology "from before"—the incarnation of the *eschaton* in Jesus. To be sure, Pannenberg himself does not employ the construct of Christology "from before," but such an eschatological Christology inheres in the fundamental significance of the frequently used concept of prolepsis, which occasions Pannenberg's statement: "The eschatological function of Jesus as the anticipation of God's future forms the key to the central theme of Incarnation." [4] Assuming the reliability of Pannenberg's historical portrayal of Jesus' life and destiny, a systematic analysis of the import of the prolepsis of the End in Jesus Christ will be developed in conjunction with the basic themes of Christology.

THE SHAPE OF JESUS' SONSHIP

As the consequence of the prolepsis of the End in the resurrection of Jesus, the event of the history and person of Jesus constitutes the final revelation of God. The revelatory character of the Christ event

---

[2] *AC*, pp. 45–47.

[3] "Dogmatische Thesen," *OaG*, p. 98 [*RaH*, p. 134].

[4] "Foreword," *BQiT* I, p. xvi. Unlike Moltmann's Christology "from ahead" or "from before" (*von vorn*), Pannenberg's eschatological Christology of prolepsis, which I call Christology "from before," presupposes and depends upon the historical foundation established in Christology "from below." Otherwise, it is reduced to a novel Christological concept.

is the key to the explanation of Jesus' unity with God. Hence, the eschatological event of revelation, the resurrection, is not only crucial for the perception of Jesus' divinity, but it is ontologically constitutive for the reality of his divinity. "Apart from the resurrection from the dead," Pannenberg contends, "Jesus would not be God, even though from the perspective of the resurrection, he is retrospectively one with God in his whole pre-Easter life." [5] In order to develop the conception of Jesus' divinity more precisely, Pannenberg surveys the Christological tradition of the church and evaluates its diverse forms from the vantage point of Jesus' history—the activity and the execution of Jesus, which converge into a unified complex of meaning through the Easter event.

Jesus' Revelatory Unity with God

Pannenberg distinguishes several different conceptions of the mode of God's presence in Jesus: the Spirit's presence in Jesus, God's substantial presence in Jesus, the mediator Christology, God's apparent presence in Jesus, and God's revelatory presence in Jesus. Pannenberg himself specifies the mode of God's presence in Jesus as revelational presence.[6] Unlike a mere appearance, which does not include an identity of essence, revelatory presence presupposes the fundamental unity of appearance and essence. The union of these two is expressed conceptually by the definition of "revelation" as self-revelation. However, Jesus' essential identity with God in the revelatory event must be understood (at least initially) from the perspective of the functional unity of Jesus with God, which was prominent in the transmission of the Christological titles in primitive Christianity.

Although the restriction of "revelation" to self-revelation is a modern development, the concept of the revelational presence of God in Jesus does not do violence to but concurs with the Biblical traditions, which speak of the self-disclosure of God in history.[7] Affirming the convergence of the Biblical and the contemporary understanding of

---

[5] *JGaM*, p. 224.

[6] *Ibid.*, pp. 116–133.

[7] *Ibid.*, pp. 127–129. Pannenberg, "The Revelation of God in Jesus," *TaH*, p. 124, concedes that the idea of God's self-revelation through history *rarely* occurs directly in the New Testament writings, but he argues: "That the idea of God's eschatological revelation in Jesus Christ does not stand explicitly at the center of early Christian tradition is probably connected with the fact that it developed mainly through the traditional Christological titles when they were transformed and applied to Jesus. But the most important of these titles . . . imply that the eschatological revelation of God is already anticipated in Jesus."

revelation, Pannenberg specifies three steps that lead materially from the concept of revelation to the knowledge of Jesus' divinity: (1) Self-revelation, which reveals the deity of Israel's God as "the power over everything," occurs as the prolepsis of the End in Jesus' resurrection, the actual event of revelation. (2) Self-revelation excludes the possibility of numerous revelations, for none could otherwise qualify as God's absolute self-disclosure. (3) Self-revelation requires the "revealer" and the "content of revelation" to be identical. To speak of God's revelation in the Christ event, therefore, means that Jesus is essential to the definition of God himself, that he belongs to God's divinity. Reminiscent of Barth, Pannenberg concludes: "The *essence* of God is not accessible at all without Jesus Christ." [8] Only through Jesus does one know that the ground of all reality is identical with the God of Israel. Since the End that stands before all things has already happened proleptically to Jesus, the *revelation* of God as the all-determining reality has been disclosed in him.

Indeed, the delimitation of revelation to self-revelation and the centrality of Jesus' revelatory unity with God are unique to the modern period, but the issue of revelation itself is not so uniquely modern. The early church also struggled with the problem of revelation, namely, the revelatory identity of Jesus of Nazareth with the God of Israel. As the development of the primitive Christian tradition demonstrates, the early Christians finally understood who God is from the perspective of Jesus' history in a new way and really for the first time. Consequently, Pannenberg observes,

> the Old Testament idea of God became something preliminary, not in the sense that something was added to it, nor in the sense that something completely different had taken its place, but in the sense that in view of Jesus everything previously thought about God appeared in a new light.[9]

Thus the concept of the revelatory presence of God in Jesus—a revelatory unity of Jesus with the Father that includes an identity of essence—is to Pannenberg the most appropriate way for understanding the mode of God's presence in Jesus. Though the revelatory unity of

---

[8] *JGaM*, p. 130. Italics added.

[9] *Ibid.*, p. 132. Cf. "The Revelation of God in Jesus," *TaH*, pp. 102–109, where Pannenberg notes: "The Jewish tradition [of God] had been transformed from within by the appearance of Jesus" (p. 108). Prior to the revelation of God in Jesus, "the Jews knew their God, and yet did not know him aright; otherwise they would not have rejected Jesus. Only through Jesus does it become clear what the God of Israel really is and means" (p. 104).

Jesus with the Father does not invalidate other conceptions of God's presence in Jesus, they cannot be considered as fundamental to, but only as aspects of, Jesus' revelatory unity with God.

Jesus' Essential Unity with God

Turning to the "scope" of God's presence in Jesus' life, Pannenberg relates the revelatory event of Jesus' resurrection to the whole of his existence. The revelatory identity of Jesus with the Father implies a unity of essence, but the character of that unity requires concrete explication in conjunction with the problems of adoption, the virgin birth, the incarnation, and the Trinity.

1. The prominent but divergent New Testament usage of the title Son of God to express Jesus' unity with God poses the perennial problem of adoption. Did Jesus become the Son of God at some point in his history, or conversely, was he the Son of God from the beginning? Pannenberg suggests a promising approach through which the different New Testament answers can be unified without exegetical violence, i.e., through the unity of the primitive Christian history of traditions wherein these Christological concepts developed.

Undoubtedly the oldest Christian community understood Jesus' resurrection as the decisive point in the history of his relation to God. Jesus' resurrection proved foundational for the designation of Jesus as the Son of Man, the eschatological Messiah, and the exalted Lord. The crucial significance of Jesus' resurrection for Christology is expressed rather pointedly in the "two-stage Christology" (Rom. 1:3 f.): The resurrected Jesus is designated Son of God, but the pre-Easter Jesus is designated Son of David. Though a continuity of the pre-Easter Jesus with the exalted Lord is perceived, the Davidic sonship is followed by installation as Son of God. However, the idea of adoption, that Jesus received divinity in the resurrection, is inappropriate, for it obscures the confirmatory character of the Easter event with the reference to Jesus' pre-Easter life. Affirming the retroactive power of eschatological resurrection for the essential identity of Jesus, Pannenberg declares: "He was not only unrecognizable before Easter, but he would not have been who he was without the Easter event." [10] However, Pannenberg continues:

[10] *JGaM*, p. 137. Cf. *ibid.*, p. 321, where Pannenberg says: "Apart from Jesus' resurrection, it would not be true that from the very beginning of his earthly way God was one with this man. This is true from all eternity *because* of Jesus' resurrection. Until his resurrection, Jesus' unity with God was hidden . . . because the ultimate decision about it had not been given."

Jesus' unity with God, established in the Easter event, does not begin only with this event—it comes into force retroactively from the perspective of this event for the claim to authority in the activity of the earthly Jesus. Conversely, the pre-Easter Jesus' claim to authority is to be understood as an anticipation of his unity with God that was shown by the Easter event.[11]

The retroactive significance of the resurrection for Jesus' pre-Easter claim clarifies the emergence of the tradition of Jesus' "adoption" as the Son of God through his baptism. Though the developed tradition reflects the post-resurrection tendency to establish continuity between Jesus' resurrection and his pre-Easter activity, the baptismal tradition itself probably did *not* originate from a projection back into Jesus' earthly life as a consequence of the Easter event. As the Marcan tradition suggests, the historical baptism of Jesus by John *might* really have been a special case analogous to a prophetic consecration (though this is unlikely). Yet if Jesus had experienced the endowment of the Spirit when baptized by John, it would not constitute "the moment of incarnation." While Jesus' claim to authority might have originated in his baptism by John, it cannot be understood as the origin of his unity with God but at most as its anticipatory unveiling for Jesus himself. Apart from the resurrection there is no event which could justify the assertion that God is revealed in Jesus. Therefore, the concept of adoption ultimately says too little: Jesus' resurrection establishes retroactively that Jesus' person is not to be separated from God in any way or at any time.[12]

2. Unlike the tradition of Jesus' baptism, the core of which is historical, the legend of the virgin birth originated only from the interest in the history of traditions to affirm that Jesus was the Son of God from the beginning. Aside from historical difficulties, theological problems compound a positive assessment of Jesus' virginal conception. Whereas Paul referred to Jesus' birth as an expression of his equality with other men, the concept of the virgin birth intends to locate Jesus' uniqueness precisely in the mode of his birth. In addition, the content of the story of the virgin birth—that Jesus *became* God's Son through Mary's conception—irreconcilably contradicts the Christology of the incarnation of the preexistent Son of God who only bound him-

[11] *Ibid.*, p. 137.
[12] *Ibid.*, pp. 141.

self to the man Jesus. Consequently, Pannenberg rejects Barth's conception of the unity between the "secret" of incarnation and the "sign" that points toward it. Pannenberg maintains that the virgin birth does not point to the incarnation but contradicts its conceptual structure. Christologically, the legend of the virgin birth is significant only as a preliminary expression of a basic, fundamental truth, namely, that Jesus was the Son of God from the very beginning.

Like Althaus, Pannenberg considers it especially important to avoid placing the virgin birth on the same level as Jesus' resurrection. First, the basis for the historical evaluation of these two "miracles" at the "entrance" and "exit" of Jesus' life (as Barth calls them) is entirely different. The former bears all the marks of a legend, while the latter is recognizably historical. Second, the significance of the virgin birth does not compare with that of Jesus' resurrection which, unlike the virgin birth, is essential to the Christian kerygma. Ultimately, Pannenberg suggests, the place of the virgin birth in the liturgical confession of the church is tolerable only because of the antiadoptionistic and antidocetic tendencies which the virgin birth has historically represented.[13]

3. The revelatory event of Jesus' resurrection establishes Jesus' unity with God as a unity of essence, which introduces the problem of incarnation and its concomitant of preexistence. Since Jesus' unity with God precedes the time of Jesus' earthly life, preexistence becomes a meaningful *expression* for Jesus' complete union with God. Pannenberg observes that "Jesus' revelational unity with the God who is from eternity to eternity forces us conceptually to the thought that Jesus as the 'Son of God' is preexistent" (even if the concept of preexistence in itself is mythical).[14] Yet the transformation of the eschatological history of Jesus of Nazareth into the message of a preexistent divine being descending from and ascending to heaven constitutes a major problem in the history of early Christian traditions.

Reflecting upon the history of the transmission of the Jesus tradition, which increasingly expanded the "scope" of Jesus' unity with God through the light of the resurrection, Pannenberg considers the "inner logic" of Jesus' oneness with the eternal God to mean that God was always one with Jesus, even prior to his earthly birth. The history of the transmission of the title "Son of God" in primitive

---

[13] *Ibid.*, pp. 141–150. Cf. *AC*, pp. 71–77.
[14] *JGaM*, pp. 150–151.

Christianity illuminates the derivation of preexistence from Jesus' resurrection and the understanding established thereby that he was the coming Messiah, the Son of God. The concept of the "sending" of the Son, which may have initially referred only to Jesus' commissioning from God, ultimately implied the idea of preexistence. Hence, the "descent" of the preexistent Son from heaven, which always stood in relation to the "ascent" in Jesus' resurrection and ascension, implies the structure of incarnation. Yet Pannenberg does not disavow the representation of the Christ event as descent and ascent, as incarnation; indeed, the essential unity of the risen Jesus with God leads to the concept of preexistence through its own inner logic. Jesus' revelatory identity with God establishes Jesus' identity as the Son within God's eternity. Analyzing rather precisely what preexistence and incarnation mean, Pannenberg affirms the indivisibility of Jesus and God but disavows the distinction between Jesus' eternal community with God and the temporality of Jesus' historical person:

> The concept of preexistence stands under the suspicion of conceptually separating Jesus' community with God as a special *being* (the preexistent Son of God) and his temporal appearance. The two distinct things are then reunited through the idea that the divine being has, in the incarnation, joined himself at a particular point in time with the earthly corporeality of the man Jesus. Thus the distinction between a preexistent divine being and the man Jesus or his earthly appearance conceptually divides precisely that which belongs together in Jesus' existence. This constitutes the mythical element of the incarnational Christology: it conceptually divides the eternal Son of God and the earthly, human appearance of Jesus, which together constitute the concrete existence of Jesus, into two separate beings. Therefore, what is thus divided must be subsequently brought together again. But the dramatic concept of the uniting of the eternal Son of God with the earthly, human appearance of Jesus also has a mythical character, insofar as it presupposes that conceptual division of the elements that belong together in Jesus' activity and fate, in order to link them together again in this concept.[15]

[15] *Ibid.*, p. 154.

The conceptual division of the elements of eternal Sonship and earthly human existence which belong together in the concrete figure of Jesus reflects the uniqueness of mythical thinking. Lest such thinking be judged negatively, Pannenberg himself acknowledges the necessity of distinguishing conceptually the *eternal Son* from the *man Jesus:* The eternal Son, from whom all things originate and to whom all things are directed, cannot be combined without difficulty with the individuality of Jesus of Nazareth, who lived at one time and in one place. Yet Christology, which involves precisely the conjunction of these two elements, must always recognize that the eternity of the Son and the earthly mode of Jesus' existence constitute differing aspects of a single, concrete life.

Furthermore, the movement from God to man expressed in the concept of incarnation affirms a truth that cannot be abandoned. Since God is revealed in Jesus, no other event or man is united with God's essence in the same way as the Christ event. The unity of the divine essence with the man Jesus (which is expressed in the concept of revelatory identity) did not exist prior to Jesus' appearance. Therefore, Pannenberg affirms the incarnation from the perspective of revelatory history: "In Jesus, God himself has come out of his otherness into our world, into human form, and in such a way that the Father-Son relation that—as we know in retrospect—always belonged to God's essence now acquired corporeal form." [16]

Finally, Pannenberg questions the relation of the incarnational Christology to the apocalyptically determined exaltation Christology of the earliest Christian community. Through the influence of Hellenistic conceptions the incarnational Christology tended to emancipate itself from the foundation of Old Testament apocalyptic expectations and its theology of history. When incarnation is cut loose from the Old Testament and Jewish apocalyptic theology, a gulf develops between the incarnational Christology and the historical Jesus, and Christology becomes mythology. Conversely, the Old Testament and apocalyptic understanding of history clarifies the confession of incarnation in primitive Christianity and validates the final affirmation of God becoming man in Jesus Christ. Hence, Pannenberg understands God's eschatological revelation in Jesus ultimately to mean "that in the eternal God himself a becoming takes place, a path to incarnation,"

---

[16] *Ibid.*, p. 156. Elsewhere, Pannenberg says: "Out of his eternity, God has through the resurrection of Jesus, which was always present to his eternity, entered into a unity with this one man which was at first hidden" (*ibid.*, p. 322).

and "that the unity with God which acquired form only in the concrete path of the man Jesus . . . nevertheless precedes the earthly beginning of Jesus' life as unity with the eternal God." [17] Obviously these "final" assertions partake of paradoxical formulation. Yet paradox is necessary to express the proleptic appearance of the *eschaton* in Jesus' history, for speaking of the end of everything as having already happened in Jesus exceeds the capacity of language. If the paradox of incarnation is not to evaporate into myth, however, it must be established from the Old Testament, from the apocalyptic expectations, and from the earthly path of Jesus.

4. Though Jesus' person cannot be separated from God's essence, Jesus understood himself to be disinguished from the God whom he called Father (which initiates the problem of the Trinity). Since Jesus' history and person now belong to God's essence, Pannenberg observes: *"The distinction that Jesus maintained between himself and the Father also belongs to the divinity of God."* [18] When we apply "Father" and "Son" strictly to the relation between God and Jesus, "Father" means the God of Jesus of Nazareth and "Son" designates Jesus in his relation to God, a relation of obedience, mission, and trust. Though Father-Son language is figurative, it is justified because Jesus' relation to the God of Israel as his "Father" belongs to the essence of God himself, just as does the person of Jesus of Nazareth. The revelation of God's essence in the Christ event contains within itself the twofoldness, the tension, the relation of Father and Son; consequently, the differentiation of Father and Son, which is characteristic of the relationship of the historical Jesus to God, is inherent in the revelation of God's essence and must be maintained. Hence, the revelatory unity of Jesus with God, which establishes the essential unity of the Son with the Father, constitutes the foundation of the doctrine of the Trinity. [19]

THE STRUCTURE OF JESUS' SONSHIP

The unity of God and man in Jesus Christ, which ultimately identifies him as the Son of God, constitutes the crowning theme of Christol-

[17] *Ibid.*, p. 157.
[18] *Ibid.*, p. 159.
[19] *Ibid.*, pp. 160–168. Since the essential but distinctive unity of the Son with the Father occurs in Jesus' revelatory unity with God, Pannenberg affirms the intention of the Logos Christology but rejects its problematic form.

ogy. Seeking to explicate the interrelationship of the divinity of Jesus with his authentic humanity, Pannenberg examines critically yet creatively the internal structure of Jesus' divine Sonship.

The Impasse of the Two-Nature Christology

The relation of the Son's eternal divinity to the particularity of Jesus' authentic humanity has been a perennial problem in Christology. From the beginning Christian theology declared that Jesus is truly God and truly man. Dissatisfied, however, the Council of Chalcedon added that Christ is "one and the same" in two natures, which are unmixed, unchanged, indivisible, inseparable in the one Christ. The subsequent impasse in the Christological tradition, Pannenberg reasons, stems from the disparity between these two affirmations:

> The formula of the true divinity and true humanity of Jesus begins with the fact that one describes one and the same person, the man Jesus of Nazareth, from different points of view. The unity of the concrete person Jesus of Nazareth is given, and both things are to be said about this one person: he is God and he is man. The formula of the two natures, on the contrary, does not take the concrete unity of the historical man Jesus as its given point of departure, but rather the difference between the divine and human, creaturely being in general. . . . The pattern of thought thus moves in the opposite direction from the formula *vere deus, vere homo*. Jesus now appears as a being bearing and uniting two opposed substances in himself. *From this conception all the insoluble problems of the doctrine of the two natures result.*[20]

Like Schleiermacher, Pannenberg insists that a single person cannot participate in two completely different natures, two independent beings cannot together form a single whole. However, the history of Christology reflects an attempt to maintain the traditional two-nature doctrine; consequently, Christology has always tottered between two false alternatives: It has either combined the two natures to form a third or, conversely, it has split the two natures and oriented the concrete figure of Jesus exclusively to one or the other. Hence, the attempt to conceive the unification of independent divine and human

[20] *Ibid.*, p. 284. Italics added.

natures into a single individual wherein both natures nonetheless remain distinct *"leads inevitably to an impasse from which there is no escape."* [21]

Pannenberg justifies this conclusion through a brilliant critique of three stages in the two-nature problem: the antithesis between the Nestorian and Monophysite conceptions of the incarnation, the problematic solution of the *communicatio idiomatum,* and the kenosis of the Logos in the incarnation.[22] Ultimately, he concludes, the essential problem of the two-nature doctrine is not "nature" but the "two" natures. This doctrine portrays the incarnation as the synthesis of the human and divine natures in "one" man. Therefore, while the incarnation remains an essential *expression* for the unity of God and the man Jesus, it is not itself an *explanation* of this unity. The incarnation constitutes a false point of departure, dooming every attempt to construct a Christology therefrom a failure. As an alternative to the two-nature Christology, which presupposes the incarnation as its point of departure, Pannenberg poses a conception of Jesus' personal unity with God: *"Only his personal community with the Father demonstrates that Jesus is the Son of God."* [23] Though the initiative in the event of incarnation originates from the side of God, the perception of Jesus' unity with God emerges only from the perspective of Jesus' resurrection destiny: *"Jesus' unity with God is not to be conceived as a unification of two substances, but as this man Jesus is God."* [24]

An Inquiry Into Jesus' Self-understanding

Though Jesus' essential unity with God was ultimately (but retroactively) established in the resurrection, if Jesus is one with God in his person and thus in the whole of his concrete life, such unity could not happen entirely outside Jesus' pre-Easter life and consciousness. While self-knowledge may occur somewhat obscurely and anticipate a more adequate mode of expression, a man's knowledge of himself is crucial for the unity of personality. The person who is not related or is scarcely related in his self-consciousness to the individual elements of his actual existence lives in self-contradiction, for it is constitutive for the self that it have consciousness of itself. If the self-

[21] *Ibid.,* p. 287. Italics added.
[22] *Ibid.,* pp. 287–322.
[23] *Ibid.,* p. 323.
[24] *Ibid.,* p. 283.

understanding of the pre-Easter Jesus were not at all related to his unity with God, "he would not be one with himself and *to that extent* not one with God." [25] Hence, Christology cannot avoid the thorny problem of Jesus' self-consciousness.

Since the titles attributed to Jesus' self-understanding must be considered the work of the post-Easter community, Pannenberg concludes that Jesus' consciousness of a unique unity with God is not directly accessible through the Christological titles. The question of the ontological structure of Jesus' divine-human consciousness must be referred to the implications of Jesus' activity and destiny. Pannenberg accepts Karl Rahner's convincing interpretation of Jesus' reflective coming to himself as a personal and intellectual history. However, unlike Rahner, Pannenberg considers the elements of the Jewish religious tradition crucial for the development of Jesus' self-understanding: "It is certain that Jesus' self-consciousness was decisively stamped by his message of the nearness of God and his Kingdom." [26] Such considerations shift the reference of Jesus' consciousness from the Logos to the One whom Jesus called Father.

In addition, the temporal element of Jesus' self-knowledge must not be overlooked. Jesus' nonobjective, fundamentally given immediacy to God as the presupposition for his activity was not only historically conditioned but directed toward an incomplete future. Jesus expected the future coming of God's Kingdom, which had already begun in his ministry, to determine the validity of his message; however, Jesus' expectation was fulfilled in a way he had not predicted; his person was retroactively defined in a way he had not envisioned. Hence, Jesus' lack of knowledge included his own person as well. Yet that does not represent an imperfection in Jesus; on the contrary, Jesus' lack of complete self-knowledge required absolute dedication to God's eschatological future, constituting thereby the condition for his personal unity with God. In spite of these qualifications, Pannenberg reasons:

> The assumption is close at hand that Jesus knew himself *functionally* to be one with God's will in preactualizing the future full reality of the Kingdom of God and thus to be one

[25] *Ibid.*, p. 326. Therefore, the issue of Jesus' self-understanding transcends the problem of Gospel exegesis and apprehends the crux of Christology itself, namely, the identity of Jesus. However, that the issue of Jesus' self-consciousness *apprehends* the fundamental Christological problem does not require that it *comprehend* it, as the theology of salvation history sometimes all too quickly assumes.

[26] *JGaM*, p. 332.

with God himself, namely, *in the function* of his message and his entire activity determined by his message, which made up his public existence.[27]

Jesus' Indirect Identity with the Son

Jesus' self-consciousness has shown him to be related to God the Father rather than to the Logos; moreover, Jesus' unity with God, as implied in his mission, included an infinite distinction between his own ego and that of the Father. Thus the proper point of departure for understanding Jesus' Sonship is his relation to God as his Father. The question of the unity of Jesus with the eternal Son of God cannot be put and answered directly but results only from the *detour* of Jesus' relation to the "Father." Only the personal community of Jesus with the Father identifies him as the Son of God. The resurrection confirms Jesus' whole activity as dedication to God and to the will of God to establish the Kingdom. Jesus' trust in God culminated in the darkness of the cross, for in the failure of his mission Jesus' dedication to God became self-sacrifice (Heb. 5:8). God raised Jesus, therefore, as the One uniquely dedicated to him, not simply in his mission but amid the apparent failure of his mission. As the one wholly dedicated to the Father, Jesus is the Revealer of God's divinity and belongs inseparably to God's essence. Thus the divinity of Jesus as Son is mediated through his dedication to the Father, and he is not a synthesis of divine and human substances. These two aspects of Jesus' existence are as different from one another as God and man are different. "Nevertheless," Pannenberg concludes, "with the special relation to the Father in the human historical aspect of his existence, his identity in the other aspect—that of the eternal Son of the eternal Father —is given." [28]

The unity of Jesus of Nazareth with the Son of God was expressed in post-Chalcedonian Christology with the formula of the enhypostasis of Jesus in the Logos. In the abstract sense, the man Jesus did not have the ground of his existence in himself as a man but "in" the Logos, hence, "en-hypostasis." Though such dogmatic abstraction is necessary,

---

[27] *Ibid.*, p. 334. Italics added. Hence, Jesus' self-understanding in terms of the near Kingdom of God refers his self-knowledge to his unity with God, without losing thereby the open reference to the future (which a titular conception of Jesus' self-understanding tends to do). Thus Pannenberg's solution to the problem not only coheres with critical life-of-Jesus research but also with the demands of "Christology" as such.

[28] *JGaM*, p. 337.

Pannenberg urges caution. Jesus' unity with God is mediated through his human dedication to the Father—especially in the consummation of his dedication as self-sacrifice at the cross—and must be distinguished from the ontological dependence of the whole of Jesus' existence upon the Logos. Only in and because of his dependence upon the Father is Jesus identical with the Son. To correct the Neo-Chalcedonian tendency to depreciate Jesus' concrete humanity and historical dependence upon the Father, Pannenberg contends:

> The execution of Jesus' dedication which (confirmed by his resurrection) mediates his unity with God and is related to the Father, is thus to be distinguished from the fact established therein that Jesus' human being has its existence (its subsistence) in the person of the Son, the Logos.[29]

Defining "person" as a relational concept, Pannenberg summarizes his argument for a relational Christology wherein Jesus' identity as the Son occurs dialectically through his dedication to the Father:

> In dedication to the Father, Jesus lives his personality as Son. If this statement is correct, Jesus' divinity is not a second "substance" in the man Jesus in addition to his humanity. Then precisely as this man, Jesus is the Son of God and thus himself God. Consequently, he is not to be thought of as a synthesis of the divine and the human. The unity of God and man in him is much more intensive than the concept of a synthesis can express. Nor does something new, a third thing, result from a mixture of the two. Nor is the humanity absorbed in divinity so that it disappears. Precisely *in* his particular humanity Jesus is the Son of God. Thereby not only his divine Sonship constitutes the particularity of this man, but above all the converse is true, that the uniqueness of Jesus' humanity in his path of dedication to the Father has established the confession of Jesus as the Son of God.[30]

THE SINGULARITY OF JESUS' SONSHIP

The absolute uniqueness of Jesus the Christ consists in his identity as the eternal Son of God, which eventuates from his revelatory unity

[29] *Ibid.*, p. 339.
[30] *Ibid.*, p. 342.

with the Father. Pannenberg explores the uniqueness of Jesus by examining the historical particularity and eschatological significance of Jesus' destiny to Sonship.

Jesus' Fulfillment of Human Destiny

As the revelation of God, Pannenberg declares, *"Jesus is at the same time the revelation of human nature, of human destiny."* [31] That Jesus the Son is "true man" is fundamental to Christology generally, but Pannenberg uniquely extends authentic human fulfillment to eschatological union with God: "In Jesus himself the ultimate destiny of man for God, man's destiny to be raised from the dead to a new life, has been fulfilled." [32] Hence, beyond the wholeness of life that Jesus demonstrated in his ministry, resurrection is the content of salvation, the ultimate wholeness of life that man anticipates but never achieves this side of death. Indeed, the openness to God which characterizes Jesus is not alien to the humanity of man as such. On the contrary, affirming the authenticity of Jesus' humanity, Christian theology has historically portrayed Jesus as man's representative before God in a variety of conceptual patterns. These images are not essentially projections of the changing ideals of man upon Jesus, but reflect the universal significance of Jesus' humanity as the fulfillment of man's hopes and longings. [33] As the actualization of Sonship, as the "God-man," Jesus is the true man. Since the openness of man to God is characteristic of human destiny, there is no deformation of Jesus' authentic humanity when Christian theology asserts that Jesus received his life-integrating personality from personal community with the Father. Rather, Pannenberg reasons:

> Through [the Christ] event it becomes apparent that all human existence is designed to be personalized by its dependence upon God, to be integrated into a person through its relation to God the Father in such a way that men are constituted as persons by the Fatherly God in confrontation with him. [34]

---

[31] *Ibid.*, p. 191. Translation altered. Cf. *Grundzüge der Christologie*, p. 195.
[32] *JGaM*, p. 192.
[33] Cf. *ibid.*, pp. 195–208.
[34] *Ibid.*, p. 345; cf. pp. 235–244. Pannenberg judges that the particularity of Jesus' imminent expectation and unique destiny confronts every man through the changes of history with the ultimate decision concerning the coming God: "This constitutes the universal validity of [Jesus'] activity" (*ibid.*, p. 244).

The authentic humanity of Jesus the Son reveals "sonship" as man's eternal destiny. Though sonship became a historical reality only in Jesus' eschatological history, others may share Jesus' divine personality as Son *through* him. Unlike Jesus, in whom the Son of God has become an individual man, Christians become sons only to the extent that they participate in Jesus' Sonship. Though Christians participate indirectly in God's essence through him, Jesus alone is identical with the eternal Son of God. Therefore, through Jesus and only through Jesus, God has taken corporate humanity into community with himself.

Jesus' Freedom and Sinlessness

In his complete dedication to the will of the Father—a dedication that corresponded to the unconditionality of his earthly mission and that assumed the form of self-sacrifice in the face of the apparent failure of his mission—Jesus is the Son of the eternal Father. Since the fundamental unity of Jesus' will with the Father's will is the medium of his essential unity with God, Pannenberg considers the possibility of Jesus' choosing in independence from or indifference to God an "empty abstraction." The totality of Jesus' dedication to the Father through his eschatological mission precludes freedom of choice against God. While "other possibilities" may appear actual to a distant observer of Jesus' situation, they were present for Jesus only as possibilities excluded from the beginning: "Jesus' freedom consisted in doing the will of the Father and pursuing his mission." [35] Precisely because Jesus' mission seized him so unconditionally, he reserved no inner independence for himself over against it. Such dedication to his mission, which establishes his oneness with the Father, constituted Jesus' freedom.

Pannenberg contends that the possibility of decision against God must be related to human sin and not to human creatureliness. To be sure, there is a kernel of truth in the indeterminist concept of freedom of choice, for a person must choose from a plurality of possibilities the one most appropriate to his destiny; however, this does not necessarily include decisional indifference to God. If God is the One in whom man's destiny is fulfilled, indifference to God is not essential to such openness. Therefore, the man who lives in openness to God and in resolute dedication to him does not make an arbitrary "free choice" but follows the call of his human destiny. The clarity of

[35] *Ibid.*, p. 349.

Jesus' mission in proclaiming the inbreaking Kingdom of God must have defined the content of his freedom to such an extent that other choices could not remain open for his freedom beside it. Yet Pannenberg's interpretation of Jesus' freedom does not preclude temptation and doubt. Jesus' temptations probably involved the adjustment of his message and perhaps the evasion of his mission because of the controversial claim for his own person implicit in it. Such temptations were powerless, however, so long as he was certain of his life-determining message of God's nearness. Similarly, attacks of doubt apparently threatened Jesus with despair concerning his mission. Yet he endured the doubt caused by the rejection of his people in the name of God because he expected the decision about his mission to come from God. Trusting his message of God's coming Kingdom, Jesus resisted the temptation to be untrue to his mission and sustained the doubt that threatened him with despair.

The affirmation of the sinlessness of Jesus is only the negative expression for the reality of his dedication to God, which defined the content of his freedom. Since sin is essentially life in contradiction to God, in the self-closing of the ego against God, then Jesus' unity with God denotes his separation from all sin. Yet the precise conceptualization of Jesus' sinlessness remains problematic. When Christology hinges upon the man Jesus of Nazareth, the problem of original sin raises the question of Jesus' sinlessness in a most radical way. Although sin does not characterize the essence of humanness, sinfulness refers beyond specific deeds to the fundamental existential condition of man in his egocentricity and his ego-obstructedness toward God. Unable to disassociate the structure of egocentricity from man's existential situation, Pannenberg cannot conceive of a "natural" sinlessness of Jesus as though he were not stamped by the universal structure of self-centeredness which becomes sin only in man. Beyond the anthropological radicality of sin, the testimony of the New Testament that the Son of God assumed sinful flesh and in sinful flesh itself overcame sin contradicts an incarnation into a purified humanity. That Jesus overcame sin under the condition of man's existence in bondage to sin, that precisely therein he lived in complete openness to God, that Jesus' pre-Easter claim to authority could express the Son's complete dedication to God—became visible and actual only in the resurrection. The resurrection reveals that Jesus overcame this egocentric structure of sin by the dedication that pulled him beyond his own givenness. Thus Jesus' sinlessness was not a natural incapacity for sin, rooted in a special humanity; on the contrary, as his eschatological resurrection was to prove, Jesus of Nazareth overcame sin in sinful flesh decisively at the cross.[36]

Jesus' Eschatological Lordship

The revelation of Jesus as the Son of God ultimately identifies him with the Lordship of God. Pannenberg thematically declares: *"Shown to be the Son of God by his dedication to the Father, Jesus is the eschatological ruler toward whom all things are, so that all things are also through him."* [37] The dimensions of the Lordship of Christ include his kingship, his summation of humanity, and his mediation of creation.

1. The crowning aspect of Jesus' unity with God is his exaltation to participation in God's rule over the whole of creation. The transition from Jesus' proclamation of the imminence of God's Kingdom to the church's confession of Jesus' own kingly rule was not arbitrary but issued from the realization that the future eschatological salvation had already appeared in the destiny of Jesus. Pannenberg affirms: "Through the resurrection, the revealer of God's eschatological will became the incarnation of the eschatological reality itself." [38] As the unsurpassable incarnation of the *eschaton,* Jesus exercises kingly rule now out of the power of God's eternity. Yet the Lordship of Jesus and the Lordship of the Father which he proclaimed are not competitive. The Son rules as the Son, which means he rules in dedication to the Father and his Lordship; correspondingly, the Father establishes his Kingdom through the Son, not apart from or beside or after the Son's Kingdom. Only in the sacrifice of himself in dedication to the will of the Father is Jesus the eschatological ruler. Pannenberg contends: "The expectation of the coming Kingdom of God, the Father in heaven, thus remains the horizon for understanding the Lordship of Jesus Christ himself." [39] The coming Lordship of Christ, which establishes God's Kingdom on earth, is presently hidden on earth, for the full reality of the Kingdom of Christ still belongs to the future. The recognition of the rule of Christ in the church does not permit the identification of the church with the Kingdom of Christ. The church only anticipates the coming reality of the Kingdom which will fulfill the corpo-

[36] *Ibid.,* pp. 354–364.
[37] *Ibid.,* p. 365.
[38] *Ibid.,* p. 367.
[39] *Ibid.,* p. 370.

rate destiny of man, the destiny of the individual to community. As it awaits the consummation of God's Kingdom, the church must always transcend the barriers of its earthly life through reform and constantly seek to actualize the fulfillment of humanity under the Lordship of God through the restructuring of social and political orders.[40]

2. Jesus' participation in the Lordship of God over the cosmos includes the unique position of Jesus in the history of humanity. Pannenberg interprets the New Testament conception of God's plan in history thusly: "Everything is predestined toward Jesus, and he is predestined to the summation of the whole." [41] Hence Jesus' destiny is to reconcile the universe into Sonship, which mainly involves the summation of humanity into wholeness. The fulfillment of human destiny through the new man Jesus Christ relates the divine plan for history to the predestination of Jesus Christ to be the head of humanity. Seeking to maintain the conceptual unity of divine history and the election of Jesus Christ, Pannenberg emphasizes: (a) God's eternal election is not decided in a hidden decree outside of history but within history through Jesus Christ; moreover, Jesus is God's elect only in his historical mission of service to humanity toward the coming Kingdom. (b) The predestination of Jesus forms the keystone in the divine plan for history and is thereby the expression of Jesus' Lordship as the head of all humanity. Therefore, as the prolepsis of the eschaton, Jesus Christ is the goal of history which gathers all history into a whole: "Only from the perspective of the Christ event as eschatological event is human history to be understood as a unity." [42]

3. The predestination of Jesus within the divine plan of history eventuates in the perception of the Lordship of Christ over the cosmos, which includes the creation of all things "through him." The mediation of creation "through" Jesus Christ presupposes the eschatologically oriented Israelite understanding of truth, i.e., the essence of a thing has not always existed but is decided only by what becomes of it. Thus the final definition of all things, the ultimate place of every-

---

[40] *Ibid.*, pp. 371–378. Hence, without denying the eschatological character of Christ's Kingdom, which constitutes the enduring mandate of Luther's conception of the two Kingdoms, Pannenberg affirms the political consequences of faith in Christ's Lordship. Cf. "Facts of History and Christian Ethics," *Dialog*, Vol. VIII (1969), pp. 287–296; "The Church and the Eschatological Kingdom," in Pannenberg *et al.*, *Spirit, Faith, and Church* (The Westminster Press, 1970), pp. 118–123 (note esp. p. 120).

[41] *JGaM*, p. 381.

[42] *Ibid.*, p. 388.

thing in the whole of creation, is decided through the prolepsis of the End of history in Jesus' eschatological destiny; consequently, the creation of all things is mediated "through" Jesus Christ. Since God's eternal act of creation will first be completely unfolded in the End, the temporal unfolding of the divine act of creation is not established from the perspective of the beginning of the world but from its eschatological fulfillment. If the End has already appeared proleptically in Jesus, he is the One from whom all things come and through whom all things receive their essential nature. Indeed, concomitant New Testament affirmations contain an unresolved tension between the eschatological turning point of the world accomplished in Jesus' exaltation on the one side and the cosmological conception of the origin and enduring order of the world on the other. However, when the reality of the world process is conceived as a unique and irreversible course of events, as a history where everything is in transition to something other than itself, this problematic tension between eschatological-soteriological and archetypal-cosmological elements in Jesus Christ's mediation of creation may be resolved. Pannenberg concludes:

> The incarnation of God in Jesus of Nazareth forms the point of reference in relation to which the world's course has its unity and on the basis of which every event and every figure in creation is what it is. . . . Jesus' resurrection from the dead and thus the incarnation of the Son of God in Jesus is that event in time through which the Son mediates the creation of the world and executes God's royal Lordship.[43]

[43] *Ibid.*, pp. 396–397.

VII

THE FUTURITY OF GOD

THE WORD "GOD"—if identified with the Biblical God as the all-determining reality—threatens to become an empty word. God seems unnecessary for, and perhaps an obstacle to, understanding the actualities of the contemporary world as shaped by science and technology. The very question of God as the ultimate ground of all being has become fundamentally problematic. So Pannenberg contends: "Secular atheism, that is, life and thought without God, is evidently the given premise on which even the question of God is being debated today." [1] Contemporary Christian theology, therefore, must justify the reason for its speaking of God as well as the ground for its specific statements about him. Unless theology defends its God-talk in confrontation with atheism, theology as the knowledge of God must surrender its validity. However, theology cannot be expected to prove the reality of God beyond all doubt. Such expectation neglects, even misunderstands, the identity of the God of *Christian theology*. Pannenberg comments: "If the reality of God were already definitively decided—though the world lies in wickedness and the suffering of man cries to heaven—he would very probably not be the solution to the dark mysteries of life." [2] So long as theology speaks of the God of love whom Jesus proclaimed and the Christian faith believes, the reality of God will remain debatable.

The inability of Christian theology to demonstrate conclusively the reality of God within the ambiguities of history coincides with the

---

[1] "The Question of God," *BQiT* II, p. 202.
[2] "Wie kann heute glaubwürdig von Gott geredet werden?" in *Gottesfrage heute*, ed. by Friedebert Lorenz (Stuttgart: Kreuz-Verlag, 1969), p. 52.

Biblical affirmation of the hiddenness of God. Pannenberg contends that "hiddenness" is fundamental to the living God, the all-determining reality: "For Israel's faith, God is essentially hidden. This is not because he stays away from men, so to speak. On the contrary, God is hidden precisely in his historical acts." [3] The hiddenness or holiness of God, which prohibits every attempt to comprehend him, is not eliminated through his self-demonstration in the history of Jesus; rather, the majesty and hiddenness of God attains its profoundest depth precisely through his revelation in the eschatological destiny of Jesus. Thus primitive Christianity did not mitigate the holy otherness and incomprehensibility of God-revealed-in-Christ, but the indiscernibleness of the essence of God to human comprehension undergirds the entirety of its proclamation. Therefore, while the God of Israel has revealed himself in Jesus Christ as the God of all men, he transcends the world of human conceptuality and remains hidden even in his revelatory disclosure.

The hiddenness of God, which coincides with the inability of Christian theology to prove the existence of God, coheres with the understanding of God implicit in Jesus' eschatological message. Jesus proclaimed the imminence of the Kingdom of God as a future reality that already impinges upon the present; correspondingly, he portrayed God as the God of the coming Kingdom. Futurity was fundamental not only for Jesus' message about the Kingdom but also for the understanding of God himself. If, as Pannenberg believes, Jesus' proclamation and destiny signify the ontological priority of the future—the eschatological structure of all reality—the Biblical affirmation of the hiddenness of God and the modern experience of the question of God must be oriented to and defined by the futurity of God. Thus an analysis of Pannenberg's unique eschatological conception of God will be developed from the interrelatedness of the philosophical quest for ultimate reality and the revelation of God in Jesus of Nazareth.

GOD—THE INESCAPABLE PROBLEM

Many, perhaps most, modern men consider the question of God already decided and permanently shelved as one of the great illusions of humanity. Since such atheistic doubt has penetrated deeply into

---

[3] "The Appropriation of the Philosophical Concept of God as a Dogmatic Problem of Early Christian Theology," *BQiT* II, p. 154.

the ranks of Christian theology itself, Pannenberg insists: "Christian speaking of God can have credibility today only to the extent that it engages the arguments of atheism and shows itself equal to them." [4]

A New Anthropological Starting Point

The most recent past epoch of Protestant theology did not debate atheism, because the atheistic critique of religions was deemed applicable only to man's talk of God outside the sphere of Christian proclamation and not to the speaking of God that derives from God's own self-disclosure. Barth's rejection of natural theology as the opposite of a theology oriented to the revelation in Christ climaxed a growing criticism of the philosophical conception of God and its use in Christian theology. From Schleiermacher to Barth the concept of "natural" theology was progressively expanded into a polemical counterconcept to Christian revelatory theology, an expansion that paralleled a progressive delimitation of the understanding of the Christian revelation. However, Barth's rejection of natural theology had a new, special function: "It became an instrument of theological apologetics against the atheist criticism of the metaphysical idea of God, and of that which religions teach." [5] Hence, Barth valued atheism as the confirmation of the exclusiveness of revelation, as the corroboration of its claim to present exclusively the true knowledge of God.

While Barth and his followers accepted theologically Feuerbach's critique of religion (which Feuerbach himself had initially applied to Christianity and the Christian concept of God), they restricted such criticism to non-Christian religions and philosophies, claiming an exception for the Christian faith. Yet Pannenberg contends: "This assertion appears today as a desperate evasion considering the abundance of analogies between Biblical and non-Biblical concepts of God and divine powers." [6] Indeed, appealing to the uniqueness of the revelation in Christ, theology has been able to defend itself against external attack. However, the situation has become critical within theology itself "through the recognition that the use of the idea of God can itself no longer be justified on the basis of an exclusive theology of revelation." [7] When theology disengages itself from all philosophical

---

[4] "Wie kann heute glaubwürdig von Gott geredet werden?" p. 51.
[5] "Speaking About God in the Face of Atheist Criticism," *IGaHF*, p. 100.
[6] "Wie kann heute glaubwürdig von Gott geredet werden?" p. 51.
[7] "Speaking About God," *IGaHF*, p. 101. However, Pannenberg does not neglect the insights in the modern rejection of natural theology: "Schleiermacher's realiza-

theology, it cannot justify maintaining Jesus' statements about God. Rather, Jesus' concept of God is essentially reduced to a presupposition of his historical environment. The universality of the humanity of Jesus—if that humanity remains true to the centrality of Jesus' message of God's coming Kingdom—finally hinges upon the definition of man through his community with God. Pannenberg contends:

> If we reject a relationship between man and a reality which transcends him and everything finite, which to this extent is mysterious, and which we call God, as irrelevant for the understanding of the being of man, then it is also impossible to attribute general validity to the humanity of Jesus.[8]

Since the question of God is intrinsic to the possible universality of Jesus' humanity, the claim of Jesus' ultimate significance can neither be detached from Jesus' proclamation of God nor become the solitary basis for Christian speech about God. The authority of the person of Jesus is established only through his message of God and of his coming Kingdom, *which presupposes a preliminary knowledge of God.* Thus the dissolution of the idea of God would not really ease but would intensely aggravate the apologetic task, and perhaps make it altogether hopeless. Hence, Pannenberg declares:

> Only if man, even outside the Christian message, is related in his being as man to the reality of God on which the message of Jesus is based can fellowship with Jesus mean salvation to him. But if, even outside the Christian message, man already has a relationship with the God whom the message of Jesus presupposes, then man must always have had, in some form, a consciousness of this relationship which constitutes his being as man.[9]

If, as Pannenberg argues, a relation to the reality called God is constitutive for man as such, the world of religions must become the

---

tion that all concrete religion is historical, and that philosophical or 'natural' theology is the result of a process of abstraction; Ritschl's understanding that the idea of God cannot be based solely upon the world which exists here and now, and with which our theoretical knowledge is concerned; and finally, Barth's argument that the concept of revelation is emptied of significance if it is possible to find elsewhere what can seriously be called definitive knowledge of the God to whose revelation the scriptures bear witness" (*ibid.,* pp. 101 f.).

[8] *Ibid.,* pp. 102 f. Cf. *AC,* pp. 15–17.

[9] "Speaking About God," *IGaHF,* p. 104.

area where Christian theology engages in debate with atheism. When the religious situation of man is considered decisive for the justification of language about God, the self-understanding of man must ultimately determine the validity or indefensibility of such speech. It is not accidental, therefore, that the proponents of modern atheism have concentrated upon anthropology. Since the methodological atheism of modern natural science shifts the burden of the question of God upon man, atheism has sought to reduce the concept of God to an illusionary projection of man and to disavow the reality of God as a hindrance to the freedom of man. Hence, the first and fundamental issue between theology and atheism rests essentially in the understanding of man, because all other arguments are anthropologically founded. So Pannenberg reasons:

> Thus it is clear that in the conflict between theology and atheism, the decision about whether any way can be found to the idea of God depends upon the understanding of man, upon anthropology. This is true, even though the final tenability of any idea of God which is put forward depends in addition upon the understanding of the world, that is, upon how far the God who is asserted is comprehensible as the reality which determines everything.[10]

A New Method of Correlation

If anthropology is the sphere wherein the question of God is debated, the understanding of man is constitutive for the truth claim of the Christian faith. Furthermore, if theology disavows a special status for its God-talk and acknowledges its relatedness to theism, the claim of Christian proclamation to derive from man's experience of the reality of God must be capable of verification or remain a mere naked assertion. Yet Pannenberg insists: "Christian speech about God can be verified only in such a way that it is the revelation of God itself which discloses that about man and his world in relation to which its truth is proved." [11] Analyzing the recent history of theology, Pannenberg perceives a significant attempt to establish the integrity of the truth claim of the Christian faith in the works of the young Karl Barth, Rudolf Bultmann, Paul Tillich, and, more recently, Gerhard Ebeling. How-

---

[10] *Ibid.*, p. 107.
[11] "The Question of God," *BQiT* II, p. 207.

ever, while these different theologians are more or less agreed that the questionableness of human existence and of all finite reality can really be understood only from the perspective of the divine answer, the actual relationship of this questionableness to the divine answer remains problematic. The correlation of question and answer does not specify how far "knowledge of the human question is in fact irreversibly dependent upon the divine answer" and fails to say "to what extent the questionableness of existence really has something to do with the God of whom the Christian proclamation speaks." [12]

Pannenberg considers the formula of the questionableness of existence to constitute a comprehensive expression for the contemporary understanding of man, corresponding to "openness to the world." Man's characteristic ability to transcend every situation is expressed in the process of inquiry that underlies every human projection. Thus, the designation of questionableness as a basic structure of human existence is more than a metaphor, for every projection is an anticipation of an answer to a question that underlies it. Pannenberg understands man's inquiring openness thusly: "In questioning the reality he encounters and going beyond its currently given aspects to its very essence through this inquiry, thus disclosing *its* questionableness, man is in the last analysis asking about himself, about his own destination." [13] Since the question that strains for an answer proves to be dependent upon the answer that is the object of inquiry, the phenomenon of inquiry exemplifies the structure of human existence, wherein man is creatively free to transcend the world but remains dependent upon a ground outside himself that supports him and the world. However, Pannenberg recognizes:

> Whether this characteristic openness of human behavior presupposes such a supporting ground, different from the entire realm of existing beings (that is to say, from the world) precisely because what is being inquired into is man's openness to inquire beyond everything in existence; or whether this openness is only an expression of the self-creative power of man as an "acting being," is probably the central problem inherent in the modern idea of man's "openness to the world" or self-transcendence. [14]

[12] *Ibid.*, p. 215.
[13] *Ibid.*, p. 217.
[14] *Ibid.*, p. 221.

Although the question of man's existence does not refer directly to
a person (or to God), it indicates man's dependence upon a ground
that encounters and supports both him and the world. If man is to
avoid delusion, only access to such a ground can provide a solid
foundation for his living. Pannenberg observes:

> Therefore, man inquires after a ground which can support
> himself and all reality, which as the power over all reality
> is also able to carry him beyond the limits of his own present
> existence, and which therefore supports him precisely in the
> openness of his freedom.[15]

While man's quest does not have direct reference to a personal God,
it does refer to something, for every question implies an outline of a
possible answer. Consequently, the attempt has often been made to
deduce the answer from the question of human existence or the questionableness of the world's finitude, e.g., the proofs for the existence
of God. Such expressions elaborate the question of finitude, which
drives man beyond himself toward infinite reality; however, they do
not, as is often mistakenly supposed, constitute its answer. The con-
fusion exists because an awareness of the answer is implicit in the
question.

Although the answers arising from the question are always projections of the one who asks the question, it would be an abstraction to
think that man asks a question prior to all contact with the reality
he seeks. The question is always formulated through involvement with
the reality in question, especially the question which man not only
asks but actually is. Pannenberg judges: "[Man] already stands in the
experience of the reality about which he is concerned in his question
—the experience of a non-objective depth of reality, which underlies
all extant objects and supports his own life." [16] The power beyond all
reality, which brings human existence to fulfillment, appears especially
in those experiences that illuminate reality as a whole. Though the
answer to the question arising through such experience corrects the
way the question was initially asked, the questionability of existence
is often set free only through such an experience, which projects a
new answer to the question contained therein. The projection of
possible answers is always mediated through an experience of the

---

[15] *Ibid.*, p. 223.
[16] *Ibid.*, p. 225.

reality sought in the question. Hence, a philosophical doctrine of God which *concludes from* the questionableness of human existence and finitude *to* an answer implied in it discovers *only* those answers that have emerged from historical experience of reality which concerns the question of human existence: "It discovers the religious answers which always precede philosophical reflection and which are the first to reveal to it a specifically new understanding of the question of existence." [17]

To be sure, the questionableness of human existence neither constitutes a theoretical proof for the existence of God nor signifies an anthropological religious *a priori*. The power that man presupposes beyond himself in his openness to the world, in his self-transcending dependence, remains unknown apart from the experience of this power as a concrete meeting. Through religious experience, Pannenberg notes, man has designated the object of his infinite striving as God. However, whether man has actually or appropriately experienced the power beyond all reality is another question entirely. The truth of religious experience, therefore, cannot be derived from man's structure as question, "but from his *being met by* the reality that is experienced as the answer to the open question of his existence, and thus claims his ultimate confidence as the ground of his existence." [18]

A New Response to Atheism

Although there is an atheism of shallow superficiality which considers itself an indisputable fact, there is a studied, reflective atheism which seriously threatens the feasibility of belief in God. Pannenberg analyzes these atheistic arguments not just to refute them but to appropriate their insights into the reformulation of the Christian conception of God. [19]

1. The moral argument against the existence of God, which has its classic formulation in Fyodor Dostoevsky and its contemporary representative in Albert Camus, considers the given world with the power of evil and the extremity of suffering to be irreconcilable with the affirmation of an all-powerful and loving God. The argument seems convincing, especially if one thinks of God as the creator of an originally perfect world subsequently demolished by evil. From this perspective

---

[17] *Ibid.*, p. 226.
[18] "Response to the Discussion," *TaH*, p. 225, n. 2.
[19] "Wie kann heute glaubwürdig von Gott geredet werden?" pp. 53–58.

the God of fatherly love whom Jesus proclaimed often appears as a God of terror, who unnecessarily sends suffering and despair upon a humanity he supposedly loves. Theologians are partially responsible for the effectiveness of this argument, Pannenberg reasons, because they have spoken of the omnipotence of God too abstractly, namely, apart from the struggle of history. The issue of God's omnipotence in the world ultimately hinges upon the point of departure—an experiential foundation which exists only in the struggle of history where the reality of God remains debatable and the Kingdom of God unrealized. Since God is the strongest power available to man in the historical struggle against evil and suffering, the reality of God is not actually refuted by negativity and meaninglessness. Rather, man experiences God as the power of hope, whereupon Pannenberg concludes:

> The acknowledgement of God's omnipotence, the confession of him as the Creator of all things, is not the simple affirmation of something which is presently indisputable, but the expression of hope and trust in the superiority of divine love beyond all tears and all the absurdity of this world, even beyond death.[20]

If theology maintains this point of departure for conceiving God as the power over everything, all ideas of a divine concession to evil in the world appear as supplementary reflections that cannot penetrate behind the covenant of man with God against the power of evil and death.

2. Feuerbach, Marx, Fichte, and Freud have explained the concept of God as the projection of the human spirit onto an illusory object of religious experience. So conceived, the content of religious experience consists of the transfer of human experiences upon the mysterious power that religious experience supposedly perceives; that is, the idea of a personal divine reality originates through man's detaching a side of himself from himself and projecting another being beside or beyond himself. Indeed, there are many illustrations of this anthropological transfer in religions; however, Pannenberg insists that the whole phenomenon of divine reality (as it has been experienced in the different religions) resists singular explanation through the transfer of extrareligious experiences or the projection of the human self-experience. First, that religious concepts represent man's projec-

[20] Ibid., p. 55.

tions and do not simply describe the reality which encounters man does not require an atheistic judgment. Many modern theories of perception have recognized that all human experience and thought take the form of creative sketches, of projection. So Pannenberg contends: "If a prejudgment were not associated with the concept of 'projection' against an actual, corresponding referent of religious experience, the characterization of speaking of God as projection would not need to be rejected in principle." [21] Though all human conceptions of God are products of human reflection, the category of projection itself does not validate atheism. Rather, Pannenberg judges: "But the decisive question is whether the development of an idea of God is of the essence of man's being, or whether it can be shown to be a misunderstanding of man on his own part, and consequently an error." [22] Second, the history of the self-understanding of man is actually a dimension of the religious history of mankind, because men of all cultures have progressively understood the world and themselves in the light of divine reality. The understanding of man as personal, which is *presupposed* in the concept of the projection of divine reality from human self-experience onto a heavenly screen, originated in religious experience. Thus every theory that attempts to explain man's religious traditions as an illusory reflection of man himself stumbles over the historical priority of religious experience to each conception of man's understanding of himself. Before man could project a conception of a personal God, he had to understand himself as person, but precisely man's understanding of himself as person occurred in a religiously determined experience of reality. Although these observations do not verify the truth of divine reality, they preclude the elimination of the God-hypothesis through the assertion that man has created God in his own image.

3. Arguing that God and human freedom are mutually exclusive, Nietzsche, Nicolai Hartmann, and Jean-Paul Sartre have rejected the concept of God for the sake of the freedom of man. Pannenberg considers the question of freedom *the* crucial question whereby modern atheism stands or falls:

> Does man, in the exercise of his existence, assume a reality beyond himself and everything finite, sustaining him in the very act of his freedom, and alone making him free, a reality

[21] *Ibid.*, p. 53.
[22] "Speaking About God," *IGaHF*, p. 106.

to which everything that is said about God refers? Or does the
freedom of man exclude the existence of God, so that with
Nietzsche, Nicolai Hartmann and Sartre we must postulate
the non-existence of God, not his existence, for the sake of
human freedom? [23]

The atheism of freedom interprets the concept of an eternal, omnipotent God to exclude the possibility of anything happening in the
world which had not been foreseen and predetermined from eternity
by God. In such a view the reality of God means the impossibility of
freedom, and conversely, the experience of freedom excludes the
existence of God. This dilemma is a consequence of the futile attempt
to unite (a) the conception of God in analogy to existing objects and
(b) the Biblical concept of the all-powerful God acting in history.
Pannenberg observes: "An almighty and omniscient being thought
of as existing at the beginning of all temporal processes excludes
freedom within the realm of his creation." [24] Furthermore, Pannenberg reasons:

> Neither the solution that God foresees free actions as such,
> nor the consideration that the eternity of God is simultaneous
> at any point in time and therefore does not predetermine
> temporal events, could be convincing as long as the being
> of God was thought of as already perfect and complete in
> itself at every point in past time and therefore at the begin-
> ning of all temporal processes.[25]

If all events are already determined within God's providence from
the beginning, historical contingency and human freedom are essentially disallowed. Only when the eternity of God is conditioned by
the course of history does it permit human freedom. However, if one
affirms such a historical perspective and concurrently views creation
primarily from the beginning, God's own essence appears incomplete
prior to the beginning of the world—an idea that seemingly compromises God's eternity and makes him dependent upon his creation.
Theology has repeatedly refused to take that step. Therefore, the
classical concept of God in Christian theism has increasingly appeared
as a deadly threat to human freedom.

[23] Ibid.
[24] Ibid., p. 108.
[25] Ibid.

Yet Pannenberg argues that the atheism of freedom does not really embrace the God of Christian faith: "This God is the origin of freedom, not its enemy." [26] Through his redemptive acts in history God has revealed himself as the power that liberates man from all bondage. Theology has always recognized God as the origin of freedom; nevertheless, its formulation of the concept of the eternity of God has obscured the liberating power of God. An eternal God, it seems, must be unchangeably the same from the beginning of creation to the end, guiding the course of all things omnipotently and omnisciently. Under these circumstances, Pannenberg reasons, God necessarily appears as the enemy of freedom.

> Conversely, if God had been conceived as the origin of human freedom, then he could not simultaneously have been conceived as a being existing like the things of the world. He would have to be conceived as *the future* of the good and of true happiness, whose fullness is yet unrealized in the world— a fullness which must often appear improbable and at most occur in intimations and parables. The longing of freedom is turned to this future, because [the future] alone can become the origin of freedom.[27]

Obviously the suggestion that God may be conceived as the origin of freedom instead of its antithesis does not demonstrate the reality of God; nevertheless, it indicates a need to reevaluate the crucial issues in the projection of a concept of God, namely, the conception of God as the personal origin of freedom, a projection which is oriented to the future.

GOD—THE POWER OF THE FUTURE

Is theism dead? While the devastating criticism of the traditional conception of God does imply the "death of God," the crisis of *theology* could motivate a new and more profound approach to the mystery referred to in the significant word "God." In Jesus' eschatological message everything, including the understanding of God, is affected by the centrality of the imminent Kingdom of God. Neither Jesus nor the early church developed the implications of his eschato-

---

[26] "Wie kann heute glaubwürdig von Gott geredet werden?" p. 56.
[27] *Ibid.*, p. 57. Italics added.

logical message for the idea of God; however, the contemporary crisis concerning God requires the church to rethink its conception of God. In this task the undeveloped resources of Jesus' message for the Christian doctrine of God must not be ignored.[28] Therefore, without disregarding the central theological affirmations in the Christian tradition, Pannenberg reformulates the distinctive Christian understanding of God eschatologically.

The Futurity of God

Although the futurity of God was hidden in the early religious contemplation of nature, it emerged through Israel's experience of God within the dynamics of history. In the origin and crises of its history Israel recognized the divine action of God, which continually directed its expectations and longings to the future. Hence Pannenberg judges: "The biblical writings are documents of this path that leads to knowledge of the God of Israel as the God of hope through the history of the promises which Israel received." [29] As a consequence of its historical experience of God, Israel perceived with increasing clarity the necessity to distinguish the reality of God from the existing world, not only from the powers of nature but also from its own institutions. Finally, Pannenberg observes: "Everything existing appeared as an anticipation which did not attain the purposeful projection of the divine will and therefore must be surpassed by God's historical activity." [30] Hence, the action of God in history—a promissory history which strained toward future fulfillment—proved fundamental to Israel's understanding of God. Subsequently, Jesus concentrated the entirety of Israel's hope upon God's eschatological activity, the future of his Kingdom: "In Jesus' message it is only *as future that God is present*." [31] Through the appearance of the eschatological glory in Jesus' resurrection. a new light which beamed from the eschatological future was cast upon Israel's understanding of God.

However, Pannenberg concedes: "The idea of the future as a mode of God's being is still undeveloped in theology despite the intimate connection between God and the coming reign of God in the eschatological message of Jesus." [32] As his dialogue with Ernst Bloch indi-

[28] "Theology and the Kingdom of God," *TaKoG*, p. 55.
[29] "The God of Hope," *BQiT* II, p. 246.
[30] "Wie kann heute glaubwürdig von Gott geredet werden?" p. 62.
[31] "Theology and the Kingdom of God," *TaKoG*, p. 68.
[32] "The God of Hope," *BQiT* II, p. 242.

cates, Pannenberg attempts to develop the concept of the futurity of God from Jesus' eschatological proclamation of God's coming Kingdom:

> When the coming kingdom is designated in biblical terms as the kingdom of God, that is out of concern for the ontological primacy of the future of the kingdom over all present realities, including, above all, psychological states. This means that from the biblical standpoint the being of God and that of the kingdom are identical, since the being of God is his lordship. He is God only in the execution of this lordship, and this full accomplishment of his lordship is determined as something future. To this extent, the God to whom the hope of the kingdom refers is characterized in a radical and exclusive sense by "futurity as a quality of being" [*Seinsbeschaffenheit*].[33]

Thus Pannenberg insists, "Lordship belongs to the deity of God." [34] Since God's being and existence cannot be conceived apart from his rule, Pannenberg declares:

> Only the god who proves himself master over all is true. This does not mean that God could not be God apart from the existence of finite beings, for God certainly can do without anyone or anything else. It does mean that, if there are finite beings, then to have power over them is intrinsic to God's nature. The deity of God is his rule.[35]

Hence, omnipotence is not incidental to, but constitutive for, the being of God himself. Jesus proclaimed the exclusive rule of God as a future reality. He announced that God's claim on the world is to be understood with reference to his coming rule; consequently, Pannenberg says: "The futurity of God's rule implies that in some sense the *existence* of God himself is yet future." [36] Thus, "in a restricted but important sense God does not yet exist. . . . God's being is still in the process of coming to be." [37] The absence of God is then the

[33] *Ibid.*, p. 240.
[34] "Dogmatische Erwägungen zur Auferstehung Jesu," *Kerygma und Dogma*, Vol. XIV (1968), p. 115.
[35] "Theology and the Kingdom of God," *TaKoG*, p. 55.
[36] "Dogmatische Erwägungen zur Auferstehung Jesu," p. 115.
[37] "Theology and the Kingdom of God," *TaKoG*, p. 56.

negative side of his futurity.[38] If the mode of God's being is inextricable from his coming rule, God should not be conceived as an objectified being already existing in his fullness. He is obviously not locatable "somewhere" in present reality, and present reality certainly does not reflect his omnipotent Lordship. Instead, Pannenberg reasons:

> The God of the Bible is God only in that he proves himself as God. He would not be the God of the world if he did not prove himself to be its Lord. But just this proof is still a matter of the future, according to the expectations of Israel and the New Testament. Does this not mean that God is not yet, but is yet to be? In any case, he exists only in the way in which the future is powerful over the present, because the future decides what will emerge out of what exists in the present. As the power of the future, God is no thing, no object presently at hand, which man could detach himself from and pass over. He appears neither as one being among others, nor as the quiescent background of all beings, the timeless being underlying all objects.[39]

Hence, Pannenberg considers the protest of the atheism of freedom against the traditional concept of God as an eternally existing essence eminently valid: "An *existent* being acting with omnipotence and omniscience would make freedom impossible." "But," he continues, "such a being would also not be God, because it could not be the reality which determines everything, for the reality of freedom, of human subjectivity, would remain outside its grasp." [40] The Biblical portrait of an all-powerful God—the God who is the origin of freedom, the reality who makes possible the subjectivity of man—is irreconcilable with the conception of God as an existing being. Pannenberg warns: "If Christian theology is nowadays to think of God as the origin of human freedom, then it can no longer think of him as an existent being." [41] However, if God is not conceived as an *existing* being, the *reality* of God must be understood eschatologically, because the future offers the basic alternative to an understanding of reality oriented *only* to existing things. Insofar as the future determines

---

[38] *Ibid.*, p. 58.
[39] "The God of Hope," *BQiT* II, p. 242.
[40] "Speaking About God," *IGaHF*, p. 109.
[41] *Ibid.*, p. 110.

the present, the future is real though it does not yet exist. Therefore, the conception of God as "the power of the future" not only issues from the revelation of God in Christ but also transcends the legitimate protest of the atheism of freedom.

Yet the idea of the futurity of God cannot be championed simply to avoid the critique of atheism, that is, the concept of God cannot be salvaged just by moving him to the future because of a lack of room in the present. A positive evaluation depends upon whether or not the extant world can be understood more adequately in terms of the power designated "God." When God is conceived as the power of the future, the word "God" acquires new concreteness, for the future is not an empty but a dynamic category. Though the future may be partially foreseen and planned, man is constantly confronted by the future as by a mysterious power threatening his life or promising its fulfillment. The experience of the ambiguity of the future does not issue from a lack of understanding of the past or present but indicates the essential indeterminateness or vagueness of events yet to occur, "the contingency of events according to which, in a particular instant, something is decided that was only a possibility before." [42] Hence, the future is not the prisoner of past and present, but occurs as unforeseen contingency.

The contingency of events is crucial for understanding the future as personal (and speaking of God involves speaking of a personal power). As noted earlier, Pannenberg considers man's projection of personality upon "God" to presuppose a more basic idea of personality rooted in man's encounter with divine reality: "The basic idea of divine personality seems to be related to man's experience of the contingency of events [for] . . . only contingent events can be perceived as personal acts." [43] However, contingency as such is inadequate to give events a personal quality. In addition, there must be an identity of power, a unity behind these contingent self-expressions. The unity acquires the identity of a personal power only through exhibiting some meaningful connection in the sequence of events, which would exclude a deterministic model of reality.

The power of the future, which constitutes the unity behind the events that spring from the future, appears to be greater than the sum of individual contingent events, for the future confronting man is

---

[42] "Theology and the Kingdom of God," *TaKoG*, p. 57.
[43] *Ibid.*, p. 58.

more than a number of finite events that are yet to happen. The future communicating its lively indefiniteness, its unpredictability, is experienced as *mystery* which provokes anxiety and hope for more exuberant human fulfillment. When events that are anticipated in anxiety or hope do occur, the ambiguity that transcends the anticipation of single events congeals into finite and definite fact. Pannenberg reasons:

> In every event the infinite future separates itself from the finite events which until then had been hidden in the future but are now released into existence. The future lets go of itself to bring into being [man's] present. And every new present is again confronted by a dark and mysterious future out of which certain relevant events will be released. Thus does the future determine the present. If we, in our anxiety and hope, contemplate this power of the future, we recognize both its breathtaking excitement and its invitation to trust. For those who accept the invitation, the world is widened with new possibilities for joy. In every present we confront the infinite future, and in welcoming the particular finite events which spring from that future, we anticipate the coming of God.[44]

Pannenberg's argument presupposes not only the concreteness of the power of the future but also a single future for all events—a definitive unity toward which all events are moving, a common future wherein all events will converge. Three ideas are essential: unity, sovereignty, and the future. Since sovereignty establishes unity, the future coming of God to sovereignty over the world will unify the contingencies of its history (which is God's gift to the world), for the coming of God establishes his ruling power over the future of everything. As Jesus' message of the coming Kingdom implied, this unity of the world is to be expected from the future; consequently, the unity of all things should finally be understood in terms of a process of reconciling previous schisms and contradictions (which means that reconciliation is a crucial aspect of creation). The philosophical quest for the ultimate unity that integrates and unifies all things is the question "reaching" for God; correspondingly, the adequacy of a particular concept of God hinges upon its ability to account for the unity of all reality, to comprehend conceptually the power dominat-

---

[44] *Ibid.*, p. 59.

ing everything. Since unity and power belong together, power ultimately requires a future, for only he who has a future is in possession of power. So Pannenberg reasons: "The notion of the Kingdom of God evokes a vision of the unity of each being and the unity of the world as flowing from the future." [45] Therefore, God, the all-determining reality, must be conceived as the power of the future.

The Eternity of God

If the ultimate future of all creatures is a universal one, if each instance of reality has the same future, the historical present has the same future as that which confronted every earlier present now past. Hence, the events of the past eventuated from the same future that confronts the present; moreover, the specific events of the past, *which emerged from the power of the future,* were the finite future of still earlier events. Thus the past events did not occur necessarily but contingently; correspondingly, the past can be understood as the creation of the coming God. If the power of the future could not reach back to the past, it would be a limited power, which means the Almighty God would not be identical with the power of the future as derived from Jesus' proclamation of God's imminent Kingdom. However, God has been the future of all past events, giving the past a preliminary share of a finite future and of a finite destiny but holding to himself the ultimate future and ultimate destiny of the events that comprise the past and present. Pannenberg contends:

> In this way, God, through the realization of the historical future at a given time, pushed this away from himself as power of the ultimate future and in this way mediated himself to it in his own eschatological futurity. If God is to be thought of in this way as the future of even the most distant past, then he existed before our present and before every present, although he will definitively demonstrate his deity only in the future of his kingdom. He existed as the future that has been powerful in every present. Thus, the futurity of God implies his eternity.[46]

Yet the futurity of God does not "remove" God to the future, as though he were only in the future but not in the past or the present.

[45] *Ibid.,* p. 60.
[46] "The God of Hope," *BQiT* II, p. 244.

"Quite to the contrary," Pannenberg argues, "as the power of the future he dominates the remotest past." [47] As the coming one, God determines the historical present as well as that present which is now historically past. Precisely the coming God is the contemporary to all time. Hence, Pannenberg understands the eternity of God from the perspective of his futurity:

> The God of the coming Kingdom must be called eternal because he is not only the future of our present but has been also the future of every past age. God assigned to each present its own historical future; this future in turn has become a past for us. Because he is the power of the ultimate future, God has released to each single event its actual historical future. In relation to past and present, *God is constantly bringing himself back into his own eschatological futurity.*[48]

The temporality of God's being precludes the Greek conception of eternity as an everlasting present without change, the conception of a timeless eternity. Instead, Pannenberg insists that "the eternity of the one God who acts in history . . . can be understood only as powerful simultaneity with every time." [49] God's eternity, therefore, is closely associated with his omnipresence.

Since the essence of God implies time, only the future arrival of his Kingdom will ultimately validate the statement "God exists," which, however, will retroactively always have been true. Precisely as the power of the future the coming God was already the future of the remotest past, including the "nothing" that preceded creation. While the process philosophy of Whitehead and Hartshorne effectively incorporated time into the idea of God, Pannenberg disavows their suggestion that the futurity of God's Kingdom implies a *development* in God, for the future is not yet decided but remains open: "Therefore, the movement of time contributes to deciding what the definite truth is going to be, also with regard to the essence of God." [50] Unlike Whitehead, however, Pannenberg affirms:

> What turns out to be true in the future will then be evident as having been true all along. This applies to God as well as

---

[47] "Theology and the Kingdom of God," *TaKoG*, p. 62.
[48] *Ibid*. Italics added.
[49] "The Philosophical Concept of God," *BQiT* II, p. 174.
[50] "Theology and the Kingdom of God," *TaKoG*, pp. 62–63.

to every finite reality. God was present in every past moment as the one who he is in his futurity. He was in the past the same one whom he will manifest himself to be in the future.[51]

The conception of the futurity of God does not endanger but actually preserves God's powerful eternity. Therefore, instead of the fundamental primacy of past and present, which defines God essentially as "the One becoming," Pannenberg opts for the ontological priority of the future, which envisions the eternal God as "the coming One."

Analyzing the human experience of space and time, Pannenberg poses a conceptual model of God's eternity that includes time. Just as there is not an absolute center in space but only relations between bodies, the delimitation of past, present, and future—the modes of time—is relative to the perspective of the observer. The historical present of a person is the center from which he determines what is past and what is future. Time is divided only through the series of entities and events that follow one another in the sequence of time. The division of time into past and future is a consequence of the *irreversible* character of the course of time, which apparently (but not essentially) flows in a fixed succession from earlier to later. From the perspective of the absolute future of God, Pannenberg suggests, the distinctions between past, present, and future would disappear: "Only the series of events would remain, but they would be seen together as in a single present." [52]

The understanding of "the present" is crucial. When the present is viewed superficially, it seems to be only a *point* at which the past and future are adjacent. Since events plunge ceaselessly *out of the future, through the present,* and *into the past* (wherein they become fixed), the present point seems always to move further down the time line in the direction of the future. However, the now itself remains through the flow of time. Though what happens "now" changes with each moment, the now itself persists in the change of its contents. So the present, Pannenberg argues, is not simply a point but a more or less extensive vicinity: "Everything over which we still exercise control and which we can still meet with decisions is counted as present." [53] Hence, the unchangeable, completed past on the one side and the unforeseeable, unpredictable future on the other constitute the boundaries of the

[51] *Ibid.,* p. 63.
[52] *WIM,* p. 71.
[53] *Ibid.,* p. 72.

present. Therefore, only the absolute future, *the all-inclusive source of time,* would permit a knowledge of and power over the whole of time, constituting thereby an "eternal present." Pannenberg cogently reasons:

> The truth of time is the concurrence of all events in an eternal present. Eternity, then, does not stand in contrast to time as something that is completely different. Eternity creates no other content than time. However, eternity is the truth of time, which remains hidden in the flux of time. Eternity is the unity of all time, but as such it simultaneously is something that exceeds [man's] experience of time.[54]

Since the perception of events in an eternal present is possible only from the absolute future, eternity is God's time, for, as the source of time, he cannot be confined to the flow of time. As the one present to every time, God's action and power extend to everything past and future as something present. Pannenberg posits, therefore, a close relationship between omnipresence and eternity (cf. Ps. 139).

Since the idea of the future is relative to present and past, it might be argued that God merely seems to be future to the finite, time-bound perspective of man. However, Pannenberg contends:

> God is in himself the power of the future. The reason for this is that the very idea of God demands that there be no future beyond himself. He is the ultimate future.[55]

Therefore, unlike the Greek understanding of eternity as that which always is, in the sense of an unchanging universal, Pannenberg's conception of eternity does not exclude temporal dynamics from its definition. The particular, the unique, and the accidental are included in God's eternity. Hence, the eternity of God converges with his futurity, from which time itself eventuates. Ultimately, the differences between past, present, and future are overcome in the *eschaton,* for "the power of the future" itself is unsurpassable by any other future. Therefore, Pannenberg concludes: "The *eschaton* is eternity in its fullest sense, and this is the mode of God's being in the coming of his Kingdom." [56]

---

[54] *Ibid.,* p. 74.
[55] "Theology and the Kingdom of God," *TaKoG,* p. 63.
[56] *Ibid.,* p. 64.

The Personality of God

The eschatological conception of God confronts a fundamental but difficult question: Is it legitimate to identify the power of the future as "personal," as "God"? Though the word "God" is occasionally used to refer to an impersonal world principle, it is indestructibly personal. Pannenberg argues: "One cannot say the word 'God' without speaking of God as person." [57] Most religions consider the power that sustains all reality and transcends its finitude, that provides the ground of human existence and provokes the quest of man, to be personal. The questionableness of human existence is characterized by the question of God; consequently, the designation of the power determining all reality as God presupposes its conception as personal. However, the word "person" provokes an image that seems incommensurate with the idea of the power determining all reality. So Pannenberg observes: "The crisis of the idea of God since the eighteenth century is connected chiefly with the problem of how the power that determines all reality can be thought of as a person." [58]

In order to avoid the critical dissolution of the personality of God and thereby of the concept of God itself, Pannenberg investigates the source and structure of the concept of "the personal." He perceives the origin and development of the idea of "person" in the phenomenology of religious experience: (1) The Old Testament expression of "the image of God" in man (which signified man's participation in the majesty of God) approximates the concept of personality; (2) the Greek conception of the person as a spiritual individual portrays the religious understanding of man as a spiritual being participating in the divine reason of the world; (3) the uniquely modern concept of person in terms of an "I-thou" relationship reflects the development of Christian theology, namely, the problems associated with Christology and the Trinity. Therefore, Pannenberg concludes: "Man first experienced God as personal reality before he could understand himself as person." [59]

These observations suggest that personality is a primal category of the phenomenology of religion. Personality characterizes the mystery, the nonmanipulatability of the power encountered as well as its ability to make a concrete demand upon man. The correlation of con-

---

[57] "Wie kann heute glaubwürdig von Gott geredet werden?" p. 58.
[58] "The Question of God," *BQiT* II, p. 227.
[59] "Wie kann heute glaubwürdig von Gott geredet werden?" p. 59.

crete demand and nonmanipulatableness defines the power encountered in religious experience as personal. Pannenberg reasons:

> If the concept of the personal is originally based on a religiously determined experience of reality, or of the powers governing it, then it is not inherently anthropomorphic to experience and describe a concrete occurrence of being laid claim to by a reality beyond our control in personal terms. . . . But, on the other hand, the possibility of anthropomorphic speaking about the reality constitutive of religious experience could be grounded in the fact that man participates in the personal character of the divine power or has received this already from his creation.[60]

A basic example of anthropomorphic projection that is associated with the personality of divine reality is the use of the name "Father" for God. Reflecting upon its origin within the patriarchical structure of antiquity, Pannenberg notes: "Indeed, the name of Father for the God of the Christian tradition is quite sacred—through its use in the mouth of Jesus; however, an element of time-conditionedness adheres to it, a reflection of a vanishing social-historical situation." [61] While the relationship of human and divine fatherhood is one of reciprocity, that does not alter the fact that it represents primarily a transfer of human characteristics upon the divine, which is quite different from the experience of divine personality as such. Though men of earlier times vividly portrayed God's personhood in the concept of Father, the disintegration of the patriarchal structures of society increasingly reduces its value. "But still," Pannenberg observes, "Father is not arbitrarily replaceable, for it identifies the personal God as the God of Jesus, as the God whom *Jesus* called Father." [62]

With the fading of the father image, however, the personal reality of God for modern man has become more mysterious. Such mystery occurs in personal encounter, through intimations that are only partially articulated; nevertheless, unlike human encounters, intimations that signify the mystery of the personal life of God for man are more opaque. Yet Pannenberg considers the vitality of the concept of the

[60] "The Question of God," *BQiT* II, pp. 230–231.
[61] "Wie kann heute glaubwürdig von Gott geredet werden?" p. 60.
[62] Pannenberg, "I Believe in God the Father Almighty," in *A New Look at the Apostles' Creed*, ed. by Gerhard Rein (Augsburg Publishing House, 1969), p. 18.

will of God a basic intimation of God's presence to man. The ethical ideals of Christianity—the love of one's neighbor and the value of each individual man—continue to be effective beyond all doubt and skepticism about God. The compelling power of the Christian concept of love, which is inextricable from the picture of Jesus, remains an experience of the divine will in spite of its apparent independence of any conception of God. So Pannenberg contends: "In the illuminating power of the Christian idea of love a transcendent claim . . . manifests itself to the conduct of men, namely, the will of God, who has revealed himself through Jesus as love." [63]

Since personality manifests itself in the will, the experience of a divine will has been closely related to the belief in the personal reality of God. Man experiences with varying degrees of clarity a liberating or perhaps destructive will grasping his life. Such experience constitutes the root of experiences of a personal deity; consequently, the concept of the will must be kept free of all anthropomorphic characteristics, especially the identification of divine will with an anthropomorphic conception of knowing and decision-making. The experience of transcendence which breaks in upon man and seizes him—the experience of a transcending will—is prior to any conception of the human will. Thus the concept of a divine will, like that of a personal deity, is not essentially anthropomorphic. However, while the "person" refers to the whole man, "will" designates descriptively only one aspect of human behavior. So Pannenberg concedes: "Only a deep penetration into the phenomenon of the will—especially into the questions of the freedom of the will and the representation of the person as a whole through his will—can verify that speaking of a divine will is not simply an anthropomorphic reflection and projection." [64]

Since "God" is indisputably personal, the question of a reality that is not an existent being but future is relevant to a consideration of the personality of God. Pannenberg argues: "A person is the opposite of an existent being. Human beings are persons by the very fact that they are not wholly and completely existent for us in their reality, but are characterized by freedom, and as a result remain concealed and beyond control in the totality of their existence." [65] A man who could be grasped totally and anticipated completely would cease to be a person; moreover, where a man is considered an already existent

[63] "Wie kann heute glaubwürdig von Gott geredet werden?" p. 61.
[64] *Ibid.*, p. 62.
[65] "Speaking About God," *IGaHF*, p. 112.

being and is treated as such, his freedom, and hence his personality, is disregarded. Indeed, man's personal existence attains form in his present, bodily reality, but it does not become entirely visible. However, unlike man, who exists in a bodily sense, God exists only in his works, in the demonstration of his power. Therefore, if God's freedom means the power to transcend and transform the present, futurity as the condition of freedom constitutes the core of the personal—the mystery and nonmanipulatableness of the personality of God.

The Freedom and Faithfulness of God

Two concomitant distinctives of the Biblical God are his freedom and his faithfulness, which together define the historical action of God in history.[66] Every historical event wherein the future becomes finitely present must be understood as a contingent act of God, who gives that finite reality being by distinguishing it from his own powerful future. Yet God does not simply release the finite from his own absolute future; he also preserves the bond between the finite and himself. Since God is the ultimate future, no future can surpass him. Consequently, Pannenberg suggests:

> God should be conceived as *pure freedom*. For what is freedom but to have future in oneself and out of oneself? In his freedom, God is present to himself and keeps present to himself everything that is past, of which he has been the future. . . . Because there is no future beyond God, his having been the future of his past creatures has not, for him, passed away. He remains the future of the whole of the past and keeps present to himself his having been the finite future of every finite present which has now become past. *Thus he keeps his past creatures in the present of his future.*[67]

These observations indicate the unity of God's eternity, but more so, they reflect the freedom of God in his divine activity on the one side and the faithfulness of God to his creation and works on the other.

Accentuating the freedom of God, Pannenberg says: "The eternal God of the Bible is a living, active God. . . . He possesses an infinite

---

[66] "The Question of God," *BQiT* II, p. 232.
[67] "Theology and the Kingdom of God," *TaKoG*, p. 63. Italics added.

richness of attributes. He can act in a particular way, and at another time he can always act in a different way without detracting from his eternity by doing that." [68] Pannenberg has developed the conception of the freedom of the God-who-acts largely in dialogue with the concept of God in Greek philosophy. The universality of Israel's God, which was definitively decided in Jesus' resurrection, occasioned the appropriation of the philosophical concept of God by the apologists of the patristic church in the formulation of a Christian understanding of God. However, the critical relation of the freedom of the God-who-acts to the philosophical concept of God illuminates the need to maintain an eschatological conception of God.

Whereas the Greek conception of unchangeable being can be known inferentially from the world of existing things, the Biblical God acting contingently in the world is known only through his own self-disclosure. This difference in the mode of man's knowledge of God reflects a more profound difference between the Greek and the Biblical concepts of God, namely, the essential freedom of the Biblical God over against the world of existing objects. God's freedom to perform new, unheard-of actions in the world transcends the conceptual possibilities of the philosophical understanding of the divine origin, for the latter could not be conceived as the ground of something totally unprecedented. To be sure, the God-who-acts is also the creator of the world, but he is not essentially defined by or confined to this function. Pannenberg emphasizes the Biblical God's freedom of activity, observing:

> God, as the origin, is never merely the invisible ground of present reality, but the free, creative source of the ever new and unforeseen. This essential characteristic of the creator and of his historical acts is unambiguously revealed for the first time by the resurrection. He is the God "who gives life to the dead and calls into existence the things that are not" (Rom. 4:17). For this reason, the only bond man has to this God is in faith that "in hope . . . believe(s) against hope" (Rom. 4:18).[69]

Hence, the theological appropriation of the elements of the philosophical concept of God requires their transformation: "They must be remolded in the light of the history-shaping freedom of the biblical

---

[68] *WIM*, pp. 75–76.
[69] "The Philosophical Concept of God," *BQiT* II, p. 138.

God." [70] Though the utilization of the philosophical concept of God in patristic Christianity may not be rejected as such, the elements used were often appropriated with less than thorough transformation, especially those elements which relate to the freedom of the God-who-acts-in-history.

Since the Biblical God acts contingently in freedom, the essence of God cannot be isolated from his acts in history. Theology cannot reason analogously from God's historical action to speculate on the divine essence *in abstraction from* his historical activity. To be sure, a divine action or work without attributes is inconceivable. Thus God's activity is characterized by definite, distinctive attributes. However, if a specific result is not inevitably established in the essence of the cause but ensues contingently, one cannot *directly* conclude from the effect to the essence of the cause. "Therefore," Pannenberg reasons, "the otherness of God in contrast to creatures is radically protected on the presupposition of the contingency of the divine operation." [71]

Of course, these observations do not imply that God's contingent activity is unrelated to his essence. However, Pannenberg contends, contingency is not the *expression* of the essence of an underlying cause but the freedom of the God-who-acts in *producing* properties for himself.

He chooses himself as the one who so acts in that he "decides" for such an effect rather than for another. Thus, the one who acts contingently, completely differently from a necessarily operative cause, is himself present in his effects. . . . The contingently operative biblical God is present in his effects not by means of the participation of these effects in their origin, but in a "personal mode," i.e., by the choice of his acts he decides about the properties to which he binds himself precisely by this choice. . . . The one who acts contingently, however, produces a property for himself in that he chooses "this" specific act in its particularity and makes it his own, so that now it really is a property of his eternal essence. It is *in that way* that the the contingently acting God of the Bible demonstrates his essence in his act, and for this reason

[70] *Ibid.,* p. 139.
[71] *Ibid.,* p. 171.

his essence is not to be sought behind his acts as a propertyless entity.[72]

If, as Pannenberg believes, the Biblical God is essentially characterized by freedom, if the divine essence cannot be isolated or abstracted from God's contingent historical action, then the historicity of the God who comes precludes the conceptualization of the idea of God as an already existing essence. Rather, the Biblical God chooses how he will be God in relation to man only in the sphere of history. Therefore, the essence of God as such cannot be conclusively defined in the past or in the present but must finally be referred to the future—ultimately, to the absolute future, the *eschaton*, already anticipated in the eschatological destiny of Jesus.

Pannenberg's understanding of the absolute future of God does not preclude the temporal dynamics of change. On the contrary, he says bluntly: "The very essence of God implies time." [73] "The essence of God, though the same from eternity, has a history in time." [74] "In the eternal God himself a becoming takes place, a path to incarnation." [75]

In contrast to traditional Christian theism, therefore, Pannenberg speaks of faithfulness instead of immutability (or unchangeableness) to describe God's relationship to the world. Though the predicate of immutability belongs to the Greek philosophical concept of God, it is irreconcilable with the living God of the Bible. Such statements as Rom. 11:29, I Sam. 15:29, and Heb. 6:17–18 refer to God's faithfulness and integrity, but they are quite different from the concept of an immovable divine being. To be sure, immutability rightly affirms that God is not a thing which originates and perishes, for the existence of all things is grounded in him. Nevertheless, Pannenberg argues:

> But immutability says too little, since God not only immovably establishes and maintains present reality in its lawful course, but has within himself an infinite plenitude of ever new possibilities in the realization of which he manifests the freedom of his invisible essence. For this reason, while he is unoriginate and indestructible, God is nevertheless not immobile, but rather, in this inner plenitude, the living God.[76]

[72] *Ibid.*, p. 172.
[73] "Theology and the Kingdom of God," *TaKoG*, p. 62.
[74] "Dogmatische Thesen," *OaG*, p. 97 [*RaH*, pp. 133–134].
[75] *JGaM*, p. 157.
[76] "The Philosophical Concept of God," *BQiT* II, p. 161.

So, in contrast to those Scriptures that accentuate God's faithfulness, others affirm that he changes his mind (Jer. 18:8–10; Gen. 6:6). Indeed, the stability of the world depends upon God's maintaining his creative decisions instead of dropping them or leaping from one possibility to another. Pannenberg continues:

> But the fact that God does not change in his acts is an expression not of an immobility constitutive of his essence but rather of his free, momentary, humanly unanticipatable decision, just as much as is his creative activity. It is identical with the faithfulness of God. In his faithfulness, God does not simply allow his previous deeds to fall to the ground for the sake of the new possibilities of his freedom, but instead includes the prior ones in the new. This is what first makes possible duration and continuity in created being.[77]

Since the God who acts freely, who is the future of everything which is past, may not be defined as unchangeable but as faithful, the fundamental problem emerges of history's relationship to the being of God himself. Pannenberg says plainly that the movement of history contributes to the definition of the essence of God, that a becoming occurs in the being of the eternal God himself. The crucial instance of the movement of history, of becoming, eventuating *in* the divine life is obviously the "incarnation," the unity of Jesus with God. Pannenberg sketches several conditions for the incarnation which intimate the relationship of history as such to the essence of God. First, "God in all his eternal identity is still to be understood as a God who is alive in himself, who can become something and precisely in so doing remain true to himself and the same." [78] However, when God's becoming and his sameness are considered in their relatedness, it is inadequate to speak of a becoming "in the other," as if the inner essence of God were distinguishable so as to remain untouched from such becoming. Hence, Pannenberg says candidly:

> The maker himself is changed by the production and shaping of another being. The change cannot be held remote from God's inner being. But this does not necessarily affect his identity [or "sameness"].[79]

[77] *Ibid.*, p. 162.
[78] *JGaM*, p. 320.
[79] *Ibid.*, p. 320 [cf. *Grundzüge der Christologie*, p. 331].

The unity of such sameness with a becoming in God can be conceived only if time and eternity are not mutually exclusive: "Then the presence of eternity is to be thought of as including in itself and uniting what is separated in the succession of temporal events." [80] When the presence of eternity is so conceived, a becoming in God, such as the new action of God in the incarnation, can be conceived without endangering the divine eternity. However, Pannenberg insists that "the incarnation does not involve a becoming in general, but God's becoming one with something different from himself." [81] Second, in order to understand history's relation to God generally and the incarnation specifically, Pannenberg presupposes the dialectic of divine self-differentiation, namely, "that God can be himself in creating what is differentiated from himself, in devoting himself and emptying himself to it." [82] That such self-differentiation is possible does not constitute God's unity with what is differentiated from himself, but it is the presupposition of that unity. The solution to the fundamental problem of reconciling "the other" to God once it emerges radically over against him in creation lies in the understanding of God as the power of the future—the future from which every past issues and toward which it moves. Third: "That an element of God's becoming and being in the other, in the reality differentiated from himself, is one with his eternity requires that what newly flashes into view from time to time in the divine life can be understood at the same time as having always been true in God's eternity." [83] The concept of intention expresses the eternality of the incarnation; however, the truth of any such conceptuality depends upon its temporal actuality. Finally, Pannenberg affirms: "What is true in God's eternity is decided with retroactive validity only from the perspective of what occurs temporally *with the import of the ultimate*." [84] Only the occurrence of the ultimate can qualify the whole of history and thereby accomplish its truth in union with God's eternity.

The Love of God

Jesus proclaimed that Israel's eschatological hopes were to be fulfilled immediately, that God's Kingdom was imminent. Hence, he

[80] *JGaM*, p. 320.
[81] *Ibid.*, p. 321.
[82] *Ibid.*
[83] *Ibid.*
[84] *Ibid.* Italics added.

made the eschatological hope the only source of knowledge and the only guide for living. Identifying the God of the coming Kingdom as the God of fatherly love, Jesus indicated that the creative power of the future is finally conceivable only in terms of love. God's love was revealed through the manifestations of the presence of the Kingdom prior to its arrival in power. As Pannenberg observes, Jesus recognized therein the disclosure of God's love: "The present announcement of the Kingdom of God offers man a chance to participate in God's future rather than being overwhelmed by its sudden arrival and being conquered as an adversary of that future." [85] The proleptic offer of salvation reveals God's loving concern for man. Furthermore, the acceptance of the message of the imminence of God's rule means that "God has already come into power and man now has communion with God." [86] Thus Jesus offered the forgiveness of sins without prior conditions. In addition, Pannenberg contends:

> In this unconditional forgiveness, the power of the coming Kingdom revealed itself as creative love. Creative love, through forgiveness, opens the way to new life. *The creativity of genuine love is the power of the future overcoming past and present.*[87]

Thus love produces reconciliation. Also, while the concept of power itself is ambiguous, making possible both destruction and life, creative love is unambiguous in liberating the present to life.

> Love is the only real answer we have to the startling question, Why should there be anything at all rather than nothing? *Love* grants existence and grants it contingently. This means that love grants *new* existence, in spite of the self-asserting arrogance of that which already is.[88]

Again, the coming God does not rob man of his freedom to go beyond anything that is present. Although a presently existing, omnipotent being would destroy human freedom through its unsurpassable power, Pannenberg insists: "But the power of the future is distinguished by

[85] "Theology and the Kingdom of God," *TaKoG*, pp. 64–65.
[86] *Ibid.*, p. 65.
[87] *Ibid.* Italics added.
[88] *Ibid.*

the fact that it frees man from his ties to what presently exists in order to liberate him for *his* future, to give him his freedom." [89] As the origin of freedom, God lifts man beyond the existing world and liberates him from bondage to it; moreover, he turns man creatively toward the existing world, even as he is turned to the world and is already present in it as the coming One. The reality of God, therefore, is the creative arrival of his powerful future in the event of love. Through his creative and redeeming disclosure in the Christ event, the God of the coming Kingdom demonstrates his power as the power of creative love —power that gives life and freedom to man. Finally, the actualized promise of God's love in the Christ event sustains man's hope for the eschatological fulfillment of his destiny—the perfect community of man within the life of God himself.

GOD—THE ESCHATOLOGICAL CREATOR

The Bible portrays the creation on the way to its destined reality, wherein the essence of things is finally decided in the *eschaton*. Hence, Pannenberg reasons: "The creation occurs from the side of the end." [90] Yet he asks: "How can the physical finite entities be understood as having been created by the God whose power is the eschatological future?" [91] The concept of the Creator-God as the power of the future requires an eschatological conception of creation, a "theology of nature" which embraces the structures of the universe in the light of God's futurity.

The Dialogue Between Science and Religion

Since the God of Christian faith is also the Lord of nature, a sharp distinction between creation and nature proves intolerable; consequently, the task of theology is aptly defined in a "theology of nature," wherein "creation" is a possible but not a necessary result of a theological interpretation of natural reality. However, Pannenberg argues, creation must not be primarily conceived as or restricted to the beginning of the world: "A theology of nature must relate nature in its wholeness and in its present existence, not just the history of its origin, to the reality which forms the actual theme of theology—to the reality

[89] "The God of Hope," *BQiT* II, p. 243.
[90] "Analogy and Doxology," *BQiT* I, p. 237.
[91] "Theology and the Kingdom of God," *TaKoG*, p. 64.

of God." [92] Yet Pannenberg warns against the God-of-the-gaps approach to science and faith, for the advance of the theory of evolution has increasingly closed the gaps. While contemporary theologians are usually quite careful to avoid conflict with natural science by developing a theology of creation upon a special theological plane inaccessible to and beyond scientific criticism, Pannenberg charges that such a procedure threatens the relevance of theology for modern man: "The confession of the God of the Christian message as the Creator of heaven and earth remains empty, remains mere lip-service, so long as it cannot be asserted with good reasons that the [same] nature which concerns the natural scientist has something to do with this God." [93] Although the validity of the God-hypothesis is oriented more to anthropology than to natural science, the concept of God depends upon the whole of man's experience of himself in the world, which finally embraces man's understanding of nature. Since religion involves the experience of power which determines the reality of existence in its entirety, the truth claim of religion is all-inclusive. So Pannenberg reasons:

> The assertion of divine reality is justified only under the condition that the alleged reality can be understood as the origin of all actualities, including nature and its possible perfection, and indeed nature as we must see it today, namely, as the field of modern science. A God who was not the origin and perfecter of this nature could not be the power determining all the reality of existence and thus not the true God.[94]

Aware of the essential problem of speaking of an all-determining power that evades the perception of technical methodology, Pannenberg indicates a mutual plane wherein constructive dialogue can occur between the natural sciences and Christian theology without compromising the distinctiveness of either discipline, namely, the relationship of contingency and natural law.

The Dilemma: Contingency or Natural Law?

Israel and the primitive Christian church understood reality primarily through the category of contingency, indeed, the contingency

---

[92] Pannenberg, "Kontingenz und Naturgesetz," *Erwägungen zu einer Theologie der Natur* (Gütersloh: Gütersloher Verlagshaus Gerd Mohn, 1970), p. 34.

[93] *Ibid.*, p. 35.

[94] *Ibid.*, p. 36.

of events. The work of the almighty God was experienced in the new and unprecedented; consequently, all events were considered mysterious which, in turn, made prayer an authentic possibility. An understanding of nature as marked by such contingency stands in fundamental contrast to the concept of an invisible "order" in the course of nature. Indeed, the Israelites spoke of enduring orders of nature as in the human community; but Pannenberg argues:

> These orders were not only conceived with regard to their origin but also with reference to their continuation as dependent upon the contingency of the divine will. They are more comparable to the positive [administration of] justice, whose laws permit fundamental exceptions and can be changed by the lawgiver, than to the idea of natural law, which does not allow exceptions and is unchangeable.[95]

Whereas the search for natural law in the period of classical physics assumed an eternal order of the world and judged contingency negatively, the belief in such a deterministic conception of all events of nature has been shaken today. A certain provisionality characterizes the formulation of natural laws which are interpreted as approximations of general regularities; furthermore, the possibility exists that the natural laws known to man today are limited spatially and temporally in the scope of their application, that they are not applicable to every earlier or future time and, when applicable, are not always applicable in the same way. If the world process has the character of a unique and irreversible course, a temporal delimitation in the application of the formulations of natural law becomes more than a simple conceptual possibility.

If one reflects upon the limitation of regularity through the contingency of natural events, it is not a question of discovering gaps in the natural law explanation of events (upon which a "God-of-the-gaps" would depend). Gaps are continually closed through scientific research, so that even the question of the emergence of life from inorganic processes must remain open. To the extent that a question can be posed in the context of the natural sciences, it can be answered within the framework of those sciences, which would ultimately preclude any possibility for a "God-hypothesis" anchored in the "gaps" of scientific knowledge. However, with each scientific advance new problems

[95] *Ibid.*, p. 38.

emerge, raising the question of the relation of contingency and regularity in a new form.

The possibility of uniting contingency and regularity within a single perspective constitutes the fundamental problem. Is it possible to comprehend the regularity of events, which are described in statements of natural law, within the framework of contingency? Pannenberg puts the question ontologically: "Can the contingent event in its specific event character . . . apprehend regularity as its own element so that the existence of regularity can be conceived together with the contingency of the event—not just understood by abstraction from the contingency of the event?" [96] The task of authenticating the Biblical concept of God as the all-determining reality may be formulated in reference to such an understanding of nature. Whether or not the existence of order, the foundation of natural law, can be understood from the contingency of events is the basic issue. Only the comprehension of order within the framework of the essential contingency of all reality can preserve the concept of creation. Pannenberg contends:

> Therein and only therein could the understanding of reality established from the Biblical concept of God show itself to be more comprehensive than the interpretations of the universe in the sense of a timeless order, which originated from the Greek view of the whole of reality as cosmos.[97]

To be sure, the vindication of the Biblical conception of God is unavailable in the field of scientific argumentation. Natural science interrogates nature only under the aspect of natural law. Conversely, the theological task requires the observation of the regularity of nature from an angle that is different from it, namely, from the perspective of its understandableness through the contingency of events, from *the* concept of God wherein the contingency of events has become significant for an understanding of reality as a whole. The validity of the concept of God cannot be established through physics but only in anthropology, ultimately, in the history of religions. Hence, Pannenberg reasons: "The relation of the concept of God to the knowledge of nature formulated in the natural sciences emerges only through the question of the confirmation of religious answers in the whole of the experience of reality." [98] Yet the question of that relationship cannot

[96] *Ibid.*, p. 40.
[97] *Ibid.*, p. 41.
[98] *Ibid.*, p. 42.

be avoided. The deity of an alleged God hinges upon its ability to embrace the whole of reality as a unity and to illuminate the depth of that unity more profoundly than any other, including the realm of nature.

The Description of Reality as History

The first task of a theology of nature is to determine whether or not the order of events described as regularity can be understood as a kind of contingency, as established through contingent event. Thus Pannenberg devotes special attention to the particular contingency of time, of history. He suggests that the understanding of the contingency of history as the activity of the Biblical God throws light on the conceivability of order and regularity within the horizon of the contingency of events, including the events of nature. The Biblical understanding of reality as history developed progressively in the tension between the giving of the promise and its subsequent transforming fulfillment. Pannenberg specifies three crucial features of Israel's understanding of reality that are relevant to a consideration of contingency and natural law.

First, Israel recognized the fundamental element of the contingency of events in all that had happened, the continual occurrence of the new which previously did not exist. Hence, history appeared to Israel as the continual succession of unprecedented events wherein, in spite of similarities, the creative power of God was recognized. As the contingent work of God, moreover, history was unrepeatable.

Second, Israel perceived the connections between events only with reference to the end of a specific process. Every event cast light back upon earlier occurrences, which then appeared in a new relationship to the sequence of events itself. Thus Israel's historical thinking implied an eschatological ontology, i.e., the true essence of a specific occurrence eventuates only in the end. Since Israel's logic implied a final future, creation itself must be understood from the End. The continuity of history, therefore, does not exist primarily as evolution but must be established retroactively. So the contingency of events which redefines the succession of events converges with a "retroactive continuity" (*Kontinuität nach rückwärts*).[99] Such contingent, retroactive integration of events does not presuppose the striving toward a goal within the whole process nor does it contradict the general constancy of pat-

[99] *Ibid.*, p. 44.

terns of regularity within the process (which are describable only through abstraction from the contingency of events).

Third, Israel's conception of the retroactive continuity of history raises a crucial question: Does retroactive continuity express only the human perspective of man experiencing history, or, beyond human experience, does it reflect the peculiarity of the reality disclosed therein? Obviously retroactive continuity is closely related to the concrete human experience of time. Man never lives only in the now; rather, he experiences his present as the heritage and transformation of the past; moreover, he anticipates the future, and its anticipatory light illuminates his present and the heritage of his past. Since a contingent occurrence always enters a context of experience, a definite correlation of tradition, Pannenberg argues: "As a contingency which befalls us from the (until then) unrealized future, it forms anew the connection with earlier events, for it changes the correlation of experience which was already established in our historical experience." [100] The question of the relationship of the human experience of time—wherein the interrelation of contingent events with earlier ones is continually reestablished—to the reality of history itself is deeply rooted in the problem of cognition. Pannenberg contends that man's experience does not first create the unity of the events he experiences but already presupposes it; that is, events have the power to refer the human consciousness to earlier events and to establish a new relationship of continuity retroactively. However, the integrative power of contingent events does not issue from the events themselves but occurs as the precursor of a future which decides the essence of the past, a future which breaks into the past and which man's consciousness anticipates in the act of perception. So Pannenberg concludes: "The future, which breaks into present occurrences, would thus be the source of the perspective wherein what has happened in the past is transposed through each new experience." [101] In Israel's understanding of history it was not finally human experience or activity that effected the connection between world events but "the unity of God in his activity," namely, in the history of his promises on their way to fulfillment. Through his faithfulness Yahweh continually reestablished the unity of events, for he related each new deed to earlier works.

[100] *Ibid.*, pp. 45–46.
[101] *Ibid.*, p. 46.

The Distinctives of Creation Faith

Theology cannot immediately appropriate the formula "history of nature" or a model derived therefrom as an interpretation of God's contingent activity in creation, Pannenberg contends, "for all [such] models treat the contingent succession of events in the history of the cosmos under the category of regularity, not under that of contingency." [102] Each scientific model examines contingency only as a marginal problem, which corresponds to the fundamental situation in physics wherein the reality of nature is interrogated under methodological delimitation to the configurations of regularity. Whether or not the contingency of events illuminates the regularity and the unity of nature is not actually considered as a scientific question, and rightly so. However, the question of the unity of regularity and contingency is relevant for a philosophical understanding of reality, a question that the scientist cannot ignore in his work. Attempting to legitimate the concept of the Creator-God as the power of the future, Pannenberg explores three distinctive aspects of a theology of nature which is oriented to the reality of nature as the object of scientific research, specifically: the relation of contingency to belief in creation, the relation of contingency and natural law, and the understanding of nature as history.

1. The Christian can discover the expression of the creative activity of God in the scientific encounter with contingency as it searches for regularity and inquires into the origin of the world. Both contingency and regularity can be understood as the activity of the Biblical God, for the existence of specific laws and a regular order are observable through contingency. Though contingency and creativity are not synonyms, contingency in the sense of the unanticipated or unprecedented is an essential moment of creative productivity; moreover, the *continuation* of such production is itself an expression of creativity. Hence, the concept of creativity includes the combination of contingency and regularity. The world, therefore, can be conceived as creation, as the event of the continuous creative activity of the Biblical God, without requiring the natural sciences simply to concentrate exclusively upon the contingent factor of the world process. Yet Pannenberg resolutely affirms: "The concept of creation presupposes that the world process in its entirety as in its details is defined by the contingency of what

[102] *Ibid.*, p. 56.

happens, wherein all regularity represents only partial aspects." [103] Therefore, the concept of a constant world order or a deistic model of creation contradicts creation faith.

The modern knowledge that time and matter belong together has helped to illuminate the problem of the relationship of the temporal beginning of the world to time itself. The concomitance of time and matter precludes the existence of time prior to that of the world; consequently, the act of creation should not be conceived as a temporal act. Hence, Pannenberg suggests a new theological formulation of the concept of creation: "The divine act of creation does not happen in time, but it embraces the entire world process as an eternal act which is contemporaneous to all time; however, this world process itself has a temporal beginning, because it develops in time." [104] The understanding of creation as an eternal act coheres with the conception of eternity as contemporaneous to all time but describable in statements of time.

It appears that human perception, especially that of the natural sciences, participates in the perspective of eternity, for it anticipates and grasps the temporal sequence of events. Such participation in eternity is manifested in the function of human perception to construct unitary wholes within the brokenness of time, ultimately, through the anticipation of the whole of the process itself which flows in time. Therefore, the question emerges of the relationship of the function of eternity, which embraces everything temporal, to the world process itself, which proceeds in time. Pannenberg reasons: "*Insofar as the world process is characterized by a progressive unification, eternity enters into time from the future.*" [105] Hence, the future instead of the past is the mode of time nearest to the eternal act of creation. The world is created from the future, including the periods of the world process that are already past. Therefore, the understanding of the world as creation not only excludes the concept of an eternal "order" of the world but also the conception of the world process strictly in terms of evolution, because an evolutionary or teleological explanation would exclude the possibility of genuine contingency within the process and thereby the significance of the Biblical God for the understanding of nature.

Though there are thoughtful scientific hypotheses which would exclude the concept of creation, the understanding of the world as God's

103 *Ibid.*, p. 59.
104 *Ibid.*, p. 60.
105 *Ibid.*, p. 62. Italics added.

creation is not restricted to any specific scientific model but is more or less compatible with several. Utilizing the cosmological models of C. F. von Weizsäcker, Hermann Bondi, and Pascual Jordan,[106] Pannenberg demonstrates that the theologian can speak meaningfully of a creation of the world by the living God of the Bible. Thus each model maintains the difference between God and the world, Creator and creation:

> God distinguishes the world from himself, for his activity is conditioned by nothing which takes precedence to it; hence, [God's action] is contingent, contingent also in the further progress of events in relationship to what already exists. The activity of God goes beyond that which exists at any moment, produces something different (but also finite) from it, and demonstrates therein the difference of God from the world which originates through his activity.[107]

Furthermore, these models permit the theologian to speak of a continuing creative activity of God in the events of the world. All consider the origin of forms to be statistically exceptional, that is, contingent, but posit regularity in the development of the process. Hence, Pannenberg reasons:

> God has limited himself in his contingent activity by definite laws, and he works in the framework related to them. He presupposes the material processes, which converge into regular patterns within the [world] process, as the material for his subsequent work whereby . . . new patterns originate within the process.[108]

Although each model has theological limitations, they do not pose insurmountable problems for an affirmation of the creation of the cosmos by the Biblical God. Only the dissolution of the concept of the irreversibility of the sequence of events would threaten the integrity of creation faith. Yet Pannenberg concludes: "The concept of a world without the irreversibility of the sequence of events can presently be judged as an empty conceptual experiment, because all given reference points generally suggest the irreversibility of the world proc-

[106] Cf. esp. *ibid.*, pp. 47–56.
[107] *Ibid.*, p. 63.
[108] *Ibid.*

ess." [109] (Note especially the second law of thermodynamics and the concept of an expanding universe indicated by the "red shift" in the spectrum.)

2. The concept of the irreversibility of the world process has profound implications for understanding natural law, for under such a presupposition scientific hypotheses cannot evade the question of the origin of regularity described by natural laws in conjunction with the origin and transformation of the world itself. Then, however, the posing of the question of natural laws would remove them from the sphere of timeless valuation and thrust them into the comprehensive horizon of an originating and changing world. Therein the conception of "continuity from the end" instead of "progressive evolution" may also be realized for the regularity in nature described by natural law. Scientific law indicates a constant relationship between conditions as formulated in the hypothesis "When A, then B." Though it remains open whether or not A is given, if A is, then B follows. In order to discover the connection between A and B, the observer must (at least in his imaignation) move from A to B, but the connection itself appears in the consciousness only after he has grasped B—therefore, retroactively. Such observation becomes a natural law only through experimentation or continued observation, for the repeatability of occurrences is the prerequisite for the discovery of laws.

Hence, if the world process as a whole represents a unique and unrepeatable development, it cannot be understood entirely as the instance of the application of a law. Furthermore, Pannenberg reasons: "Since each individual event shares in the uniqueness of the whole process, an event never repeats itself precisely as it occurred earlier; therefore, taken exactly, *an event is never exhaustively expressed by the law which it satisfies.*" [110] The conception of natural law requires the observer to disregard the particularity that constitutes the individuality of each event and distinguishes it from other similar events, and to concentrate instead upon the typical characteristics common to different occurrences. As in ordinary experience, where fine distinctions

[109] *Ibid.*, p. 65.
[110] *Ibid.*, p. 66. Italics added. This conclusion is essential to Pannenberg's entire conception of eschatological creation. Cf. "Theology and the Kingdom of God," *TaKoG*, p. 67, where he says: "The laws of causation have their own overwhelming significance, but do not plumb the depths of reality's foundation. Ideas of causality and the physical laws presuppose that something exists and that events do happen. Only the fact that each new event has to relate itself to the existing world makes it possible to describe phenomena in terms of causality."

in otherwise similar occasions are not noticed, the formulation of natural law depends upon such abstract concentration on typical aspects of events.

Not only does the perception of natural law occur from the observation of "When A, then B," but also the origin of the regular patterns in the events of nature which correspond to the law. If natural laws are related to the regularities in events, if they originate and change within the flow of material reality, then B must have succeeded A at some point for the first time. Some concrete connection between the two must have "interlocked." Such an interlocking of the unique succession from A to B would mean that the succession itself always tends to replace itself: As soon as A appears, B follows. Two conclusions emerge from these reflections: First, the regularities of nature described by natural laws originate as "patterns within the process" and, as with all such patterns, a certain but essentially limited stability corresponds to them; moreover, these forms tend to repeat themselves but are not simply unchangeable. Second, the origination of such process forms depends upon an initially contingent, but actual progression from A to B; furthermore, the interlocking occurs only after B is introduced. Ultimately, therefore, the relation between the two elements eventuates from B—retroactively. Such repetitive patterns do not represent unchangeable laws but originate within the process, within a concrete sphere of application. Thus natural laws were not really laws before the origin of their sphere of application but simply mathematical possibilities. Hence, Pannenberg concludes: "If the sphere of application of a natural law originates only in the flow of time in nature, the law itself as a law of *nature* cannot be independent of time." [111]

The analogy of the interlocking from A to B, the occurrence of a natural law within a specific sphere of application, is significant for understanding the principle of inertia that underlies all the events of nature. If the patterns described by natural law originated in and are subjected to time, inertia must also contain an element of contingency. Thus, the drive of bodies to continuation in their respective conditions loses its self-evident character upon the background of the contingent uniqueness of each natural event. Like other instances of uniformity in events of nature, the principle of inertia represents the faithfulness of God, whose identity does not consist in a natural unchangeableness but in the stability of his creative decisions. Therefore, Pannenberg

[111] "Kontingenz und Naturgesetz," p. 68.

refers the continuity of history and the regularity of nature to God's contingent but faithful activity:

> On the basis of the faithfulness of God—through his self-identification in the succession of his contingent works—it becomes understandable why contingent events do not simply accumulate unrelatedly but show the actual inclination to "interlock" in steady, regularly repeated patterns within the process.[112]

The continuity of the events of nature, which is continually established in the faithfulness of God, permits the possibilities of the computing of classifications and the formulation of natural laws.

3. The context of natural occurrences appears chiefly in the conception of natural law, which concentrates upon the typical characteristics of patterns within the uniqueness of the world process. This approach has been quite successful in comprehending the relation of the events of nature. However, if the whole of nature represents a unique process, the events of nature should reflect historical associations wherein specific events are joined to those which preceded them. While such historical unification would preserve the unique particularity of the preceding events (and not just their general structure), it is quite possible to neglect the uniqueness of the events of nature and to describe them as cases of general rules. If that happened, the unique development of the process of nature would not achieve historical continuity, only a regularity wherein the events of nature satisfy the uniform models of the process; correspondingly, the correlation of nonhuman occurrences of nature would be describable primarily through natural law.

Unlike human history, which has its continuity essentially in itself through man's historical consciousness, nonhuman nature lacks such a consciousness of time and the ability to correlate temporal events. Though the course of nonhuman nature is a unique and unrepeatable succession of contingent events (like human history), Pannenberg notes: "Non-human nature apparently does not have an ability comparable to the human consciousness to perceive the retroactive significance of the later for the earlier—apart from the 'interlocking' of the patterns of natural law within the process."[113] Indeed, there are

---

[112] Ibid., p. 69.
[113] Ibid., p. 70.

a number of intermediate stages between the occurrences of nonhuman nature on the one side and the historicity and individuality of man on the other. However, the experience of historical continuity and the appearance of historical forms of life are only possible on the level of human activity. Though that does not deny historicness to nonhuman nature, the world process acquired wholeness only with the origin of man and the appropriation of nature by man, that is, retroactively through human perception. Therefore, one cannot speak of a history of nature in itself but only of the history of nature in relation to man. The correlation of the successive forms of the world process retroactively, from man backwards, corresponds to the constitution of historical continuity generally—from the end. Nevertheless, the unity of the history of nature is not establishable in man but only in God. God allows each new event to illuminate the earlier and thereby establishes the historical continuity which man perceives even before he actively participates in it.

The Disclosure of Creation

Though the question of God cannot be answered conclusively from a knowledge of nature, Pannenberg contends that it is intelligible and meaningful "to conceive the whole of reality inclusive of nature as a process of God's history with his creation." [114] The contemporary knowledge of nature is entirely compatible with faith in God. The correlation of contingency and regularity coheres with the contingent activity of the Biblical God. The retroactive integration of the new into the old establishes the unity of history—human history as well as the history of nature and its forms. So Pannenberg reasons:

> The production of such continuity through a continual integration of the later into the earlier bears the mark of a personal power—not that of a mere law-structure—and so, perhaps only so, the unity of events becomes understandable under the standard of their contingency. [115]

Christian theology has historically affirmed that the origin and continuity of nature is an expression of the faithfulness and love of God. Affirming the interrelation of love, contingency, and futurity, Pannen-

[114] *Ibid.*, p. 72.
[115] *Ibid.*

berg interprets each event in history and nature as a creative work of love:

> First, it is a work of creative love simply in its being originated as a unique event. Second, it is a work of creative love in that it is held by creative love's ultimate intention to preserve the bond between itself and the creature. The creature-event has freedom in relation to the power of the creative love that does not let it go. . . . Thus the creative power proves itself to be also unifying power. The events in their relation to one another participate in the love that created them. Each preliminary integration among events and that from which they eventuated emerges as an anticipation of an ultimate unity.[116]

Therefore, the regularity within nature, which provides the basis for enduring existence, becomes the expression of God's creative love which sustains and liberates his creation. Yet the understanding of the origin of all reality in the love of God does not violate scientific descriptions of the processes of nature, for these two perspectives lie on different levels. However, these observations are based upon a reversal of the time sequence usually presupposed in the idea of causality. Creation must be conceived in reference to the *eschaton* instead of the primordial past. All events and beings eventuate contingently from the ultimate future, which means time flows creatively from the future through the present and into the past.

[116] "Theology and the Kingdom of God," *TaKoG*, p. 66.

VIII

THE GOD OF THE COMING KINGDOM

"IF THE KINGDOM OF GOD and the mode of his existence (power and being) belong together," Pannenberg reasons, "then [Jesus'] message of the coming Kingdom of God implies that God in his very being is the future of the world." [1] Thus the import of Jesus' eschatological message for the presence of God in the world means that "God himself is yet in the mode of coming and only as the coming One, as the future of the world, is already present in it." [2] God is not only transcendent beyond the world as the creative power of the future, he is also present in the world as the power of love. Pannenberg emphasizes the importance of the immanence of the transcendent God, affirming: "An exclusively transcendent God would actually be just a reflection of man or an illusion; only through his immanence is God [a] reality, for only through his entrance into the world can he become master of it—and divine reality measures itself according to its power." [3]

The transcendence and immanence of God belong together. Christian theology understands God's immanence as his devotion to the world, as his presence in the world through the power of love. As Pannenberg says, the immanence of God's transcendence is the inbreak of the future of God into the world. Whereas the transcendence of God creates the possibility of human freedom and preserves the secularity of the world, the gift of freedom itself represents God's

---

[1] "Theology and the Kingdom of God," *TaKoG*, p. 61.
[2] "Wie kann heute glaubwürdig von Gott geredet werden?" in *Gottesfrage heute*, ed. by Friedebert Lorenz (Stuttgart: Kreuz-Verlag, 1969), p. 57.
[3] *Ibid.*, p. 63.

231

gracious turning in love toward the world, a turning which seeks to grasp each man and to effect through him the wholeness of human relationships. The turning of God to the world, the immanence of God's transcendence, occurs as the presence of the future—decisively through the inbreak of God's future in the Christ event. Pannenberg interprets the coming of God's Kingdom in the following way:

> The Kingdom of God which Jesus proclaimed to come and which by his proclamation already invaded the present of his audience is God's own ultimate reality and brings with it the reconciliation of all men in a society of peace and justice which the Old Testament prophets announced in contrast to the social and political realities of their own times. Only that future can substantiate faith in a loving God when his love will attain satisfaction in reconciling all suffering and aberration of his creatures.[4]

THE ADVENT OF THE FUTURE IN JESUS CHRIST

Affirming futurity as the mode of God's being, Pannenberg explicates the essential presence of God's future in the Christ event through a philosophy of appearance. When something appears, it is actually present; consequently, appearance and existence are closely related. However, the concept of appearance also implies that something manifests itself which is more "in itself" than actually appears. The ambiguity of the concept of appearance, Pannenberg observes, roots in the relation of appearance to being: "On the one hand, appearing and existence mean the same thing. But on the other hand, appearance, taken literally, points to a being transcending it."[5]

Whereas the history of philosophy reflects a dominant tendency to separate appearance and being, Hegel formulated the relation of essence and appearance as one of reciprocity, which was a significant advance. Thus, appearance not only points back to the essence appearing in it as its truth, but essence which is not mere being *must* appear. Yet Hegel's insight was crippled by the ontological preference of essence over its appearance, which, in spite of his insight into the reciprocity of appearance and being, reduced appearances to illus-

---

[4] "Future and Unity," *Hope and the Future of Man*, ed. by Ewert H. Cousins (Fortress Press, 1972), p. 65.
[5] "Appearance as the Arrival of the Future," *TaKoG*, p. 128.

trations of a fixed logical structure. Thus the separation of being (or essence) and appearance requires one to begin with appearance even more decisively than Hegel. While Kant reflected impulses in this direction, Heinrich Barth offers a consistent systematic formulation of a "philosophy of appearance." Barth restricts being in the sense of substance only to appearance, and he rejects any reduction of appearance to nonappearing being-in-itself. Moreover, he understands the "something" that appears as the eidetic content in the act of appearing, which forms the theme of the interpretation of the appearance. Barth's contention that the meaning of the appearance is expressed in the *eidos* reverses the traditional interpretation of the relation of *eidos* and appearance, because the appearing as existence takes priority over all notions of essence; the appearing simultaneously comprehends the act of coming-into-appearance and the "something" that appears, the eidetic or essential element.

Heinrich Barth's conception of appearance permits a new interpretation of the contingency of events, the historicity of all experience, whose occurrence is presupposed in the interpretation of its content. The interpretation of contingent appearances is not limited to the sphere of events but transcends it; indeed, it must, for the "something" which appears is not totally exhausted in the act of appearing. Since interpretation surpasses the event of appearance, a difference between appearance and being (or essence) arises anew. The *eidos* which appears not only "here" but "elsewhere" transcends the individual appearance wherein it is encountered, and it exhausts itself in none of its appearances. So Pannenberg reasons: "The individual appearance always presents itself as only a partial realization of the possibilities of the *eidos* appearing in it." [6] Thus neither the separation of being and appearance nor the thesis of their identity can be maintained independently. The *separation* of essence and appearance illuminates their unity; correspondingly, the assertion of the *identity* of appearance and what appears indicates their difference (for interpretation transcends the individual appearance).

The relationship of the futurity and presence of the Kingdom of God in Jesus' proclamation illuminates the unity as well as the difference between the appearance and that which appears. Since the oldest New Testament traditions of Jesus' proclamation of the Kingdom of God contain both present and future sayings, Pannenberg

[6] *Ibid.*, p. 132.

does not eliminate one group in favor of the other but defines the uniqueness of Jesus' message in their juxtaposition: "In the ministry of Jesus the futurity of the Reign of God became a power determining the present." [7] The obedient turning to the future of the Kingdom of God actualized God's reign in the present, "and such presence of the Reign of God does not conflict with its futurity but is derived from it and is itself only the anticipatory glimmer of its coming." [8] Hence, the future reign of God has already appeared in Jesus' ministry without ceasing to be distinguished from the presentness of its appearance. God's confirmation of Jesus in the Easter event established the truth of the unique and definitive appearance of God in Jesus without dissolving the difference between God the Father and Jesus the Son, a distinction which corresponds to the difference between the futurity of God's Kingdom and the presence of his reign in Jesus' activity. Pannenberg cogently argues:

> The difference between Jesus' present and the Father's future was ever and again actualized in the surrender of the man Jesus to the coming Reign of God that he proclaimed, insofar as it was the future of another. Jesus pointed away from himself; therefore, the interpretation of *that which appeared in him* must go beyond the *appearance* of Jesus, to God, whom his message concerned. For this reason any mixture of the divine and human in the event of the appearance of God in this man is in error. And yet, precisely in Jesus' *pointing* away from himself to God's future did this future as such become present in and through him. The appearance of God in this man, which transcends his finite existence, means, just because of this, an existence of God in him, a oneness of God with him. [9]

Though a general concept of appearance may not be abstracted from God's appearance in Jesus of Nazareth, the theological paradigm is relevant to a consideration of the philosophical problem of appearance. Christian reflection upon the appearance of God in Jesus unites the two elements implied in appearance, namely, the actual presence of what appears in the appearance, and its transcendence

[7] *Ibid.*, p. 133.
[8] *Ibid.*
[9] *Ibid.*, p. 134. Italics added.

beyond the individual appearance. The conception of the revelation of God in Jesus of Nazareth unifies these elements. God is completely and conclusively present in this man, but he remains distinct from him; moreover, only as the One who is different from Jesus is God himself in him. Therefore, if one employs the theological paradigm of the futurity of God in the history of Jesus, the identity and the nonidentity of appearance and being are united in the temporality of the relationship—that which appears in the appearance presents itself in the mode of futurity.

The diverse understandings of the appearing reality as either the appearance of something which always is or as the arrival of what is future have their religio-historical background: The former originates from myth's orientation to primal time and the archetypical, the latter originates from being grasped by the eschatological future. Though there are advantages to the former conceptual framework, namely, the possibility of forming and applying general concepts, such a view inevitably underestimates the importance of the contingently new, the individual, and time. "Accordingly," Pannenberg reasons, "it seems more appropriate to consider the universal as a human construction, which indeed proves itself useful by its ability to grasp a reality that is probably of quite another character, since it is conditioned by contingency and time." [10] Therefore, the conception of true being, of eternal presence, would not refer to an unchanging structure but to the final future, the arrival of the ultimate future. Reflecting upon the theological model, upon the *definitive meaning* of the *appearance* of God's future in Jesus of Nazareth wherein God's love is revealed, Pannenberg concludes: "The future *wills* to become present; it tends toward its arrival in a permanent present." [11]

THE ACTUALIZATION OF THE FUTURE THROUGH THE SPIRIT

"In the New Testament," Pannenberg observes, "Spirit is the name for the actual presence of divine reality in Christian experience and in the Christian community." [12] Yet the Christian doctrine of the Holy Spirit is quite difficult to define, including the kind of reality which "Holy Spirit" represents. Though many would say that it is the

[10] *Ibid.*, p. 141.
[11] *Ibid.*, p. 143.
[12] "The Working of the Spirit in the Creation and in the People of God," in Pannenberg *et al.*, *Spirit, Faith, and Church* (The Westminster Press, 1970), p. 13.

Spirit of the Christian community or Christian experience, the reality of the Holy Spirit cannot be identified by distinguishing Christian experience and Christian community from all other human experience and community. Instead, the common elements between specifically Christian experience and generally human experience constitute a better starting point for defining the reality of the Spirit. The Biblical perspective identifies the Spirit as the origin of all life but especially the life of the Christian community. Thus Pannenberg eschews pneumatological statements of theology which do not relate the origin of all life to the Spirit.[13]

The Spirit and Creation

The anthropological dissolution of the concept of spirit apparently stems from the connotation of spirit as an immaterial substance. Since the term "spirit" suggested that the mind had to be conceived as an immaterial substance, the term was avoided and the idea suppressed. Unlike Edmund W. Sinnott, who describes the nonrational elements in human nature as "the human spirit," Pannenberg insists that spirit is not a function of the living organism; rather, life is a function of the spirit. Though the Biblical spirit gives life to the organism, it differs from the organic structure; consequently, the spirit is not just the human spirit but the divine power that gives man life. So Pannenberg reasons:

> [The Biblical] spirit is not identical with the idea of the soul as spiritual substance apart from the body. The spirit is not the individual man, but the divine power that makes the individual man alive. The human spirit is not an independent reality of its own, but a mere participation of the divine spirit, and a passing one.[14]

When the Biblical understanding of life dependent upon a reality that transcends the living organism is related to contemporary anthropology, ecstasy appears to be the essential element of life itself. Ecstasy or self-transcendence is a basic structural element of all life but especially of *human* life. Man not only lives beyond himself through environmental experience, but he also has the reflective ability to take

[13] *Ibid.*, p. 14. Cf. Pannenberg, "The Doctrine of the Spirit and the Task of a Theology of Nature," *Theology*, Vol. LXXV (1972), pp. 8–21.
[14] "The Working of the Spirit," p. 17.

his stance outside himself and to know himself as self-transcendent. Hence, Pannenberg observes:

> The human mind represents an intensified form of self-transcendence, i.e., of the ecstatic structure of life. The experience of freedom, the capability for abstract cognition, the particular ecstasy of imaginative inspiration—all this seems closely related to the distinctive structure of the mind, to his reflective nature, to his ability to look at himself from a distance and therefore to take the position of something else in distinction from himself. *This ecstatic element of the life of the mind I call "spirit."* It is at work in the ecstatic activity of all life, but only the human mind participates subjectively in the spirit since the mind is able to take his stand beyond himself, to have his center outside himself.[15]

One consequence of the reflective self-transcendence of man is quite important. As the human mind transcends itself, it does not produce the unity of its experience but seeks that unity beyond itself. Unity is experienced as anticipation, and the unity beyond the individual is concretized provisionally in the form of community. The spiritual unity which is beyond but constitutes individual existence is perhaps best explained by the idea of truth. Truth implies the unity of experience, .which excludes all contradiction. However, because man experiences truth and beauty and freedom only in self-transcending ecstasy, the spiritual dimension is not identical with human mind but gives creative life to it. Hence, spirit is both transcendent and immanent in man: Granting personal identity and fulfillment to life, spirit is immanent—the principle vitalizing human life; conversely, moving man beyond himself, the spirit is transcendent—the ecstatic unity which increasingly integrates life.

The element of transcendence in spirit prohibits a fundamental distinction between human spirit and divine spirit. The spirit does not belong to man strictly in his immanent nature, Pannenberg contends, but the creature participates in the divine spirit by transcending itself, namely, "by being elevated beyond itself in the ecstatic experience that illustrates the working of the spirit." [16] When a fundamental distinction between divine spirit and human spirit is not accepted,

[15] *Ibid.*, pp. 18–19. Italics added.
[16] *Ibid.*, p. 21.

the concept of spirit becomes a vehicle of clarity for the transcendence of God as well as for his immanence in creation. The distinctive ecstatic character of life, especially human life, reveals the working of God in the whole of creation. Correspondingly, the ecstatic events or spiritual experiences that integrate the differing aspects of life— an integration that occurs from beyond—reveals the transcendence of God. The presence of the spirit in the life of man occurs through participation in the unifying power of God, which continually antici- pates the unity of all the differing aspects of life; that is, it is the presence of a future that provisionally intimates the coming of God.

The Spirit and the Christian Community

To characterize the special form of spiritual presence in the Chris- tian community, Pannenberg says:

> While the spirit is working in all life as the vitalizing prin- ciple—[as] the lure to self-transcendence and as the inspira- tive power of ecstasy—the Christian community lives on the basis of the message of a new life, which is no longer separated from the spiritual origin of all life.[17]

The new life that appeared in the eschatological destiny of Jesus con- stituted the prolepsis of the End; consequently, the Spirit was an eschatological reality for primitive Christianity, corresponding to the end-time expectations of Israelite prophecy.

The Old Testament concept of the Spirit as the power of life clari- fies Paul's association of the Spirit with the reality of the resurrection appearing in Jesus and animating Christian hope. Since Jesus was raised through the Spirit (Rom. 1:4; 8:2, 11), resurrection life is pro- duced through the life-creating principle of the Spirit of God; more- over, the Spirit is one with that life in distinction from present, tem- poral life. Thus Paul describes the new life as a spiritual body and almost identifies the new life of the resurrected Christ with the reality of the divine Spirit. Correspondingly, whenever there is a reference to the reality of the risen Lord, one is already in the sphere of the Spirit's activity. Hence, Pannenberg comments: "Whoever believes the mes- sage of Jesus' resurrection has thereby already received the Spirit who guarantees to the believer the future resurrection from the dead be-

[17] Ibid., p. 23. Punctuation adapted.

cause he has already raised Jesus." [18] Ultimately, everything related
to the reality of the resurrected Lord is filled with the life-giving power
of the divine Spirit—from the apostolic message to the special tasks
and services of the individual members of the Christian community.

Since the Spirit unites the believer with God (I Cor. 2:10 ff.), Pannenberg judges: "If the Spirit who enters into the hearts of those who
hear and believe with the message of Jesus' resurrection were not the
Spirit of God himself, then the believer would have no true community with God through the message." [19] However, as Karl Barth
has emphasized, the divinity of the Spirit cannot be established
through an appeal to the experience of faith. Nevertheless, Barth's
argument that the reality of the Spirit is the supplementary power
that produces man's knowledge of Jesus' divinity is unconvincing.
Though knowledge of God's revelation is "not a human possibility,"
the power of the word of proclamation points back to the uniqueness
of Jesus' history, which penetrates into the understanding of men
through the word. Against a *supplementary* conception of the Spirit,
therefore, Pannenberg argues: "This word [of proclamation] brings
with it the Spirit, through whom we perceive God's revelation in the
history of Jesus recounted by the word." [20]

The ancient church did not consider the Spirit merely an impersonal working power but attributed the character of a working person
to him. That the Spirit does not extinguish the personal character of
human action through his activity but permits personal life to achieve
fulfillment through willing dedication indicates the personal reality
of the Spirit. Pannenberg observes:

> The confession that the Holy Spirit is "person" thus ex-
> presses primarily the experience that the Christian is not his
> own lord. Insofar as he lives out of faith in Christ, the center
> of his person that determines his behavior lies outside himself.
> The personal center of Christian action is the Holy Spirit.[21]

The description of the Spirit as the personal center of Christian action
transcending the believer illuminates the New Testament characterization of the Spirit: The Spirit is characterized as "person" distinguished
from Christians and as "power" they possess internally.

[18] *JGaM*, p. 172.
[19] *Ibid.*, p. 173.
[20] *Ibid.*, p. 174.
[21] *Ibid.*, p. 177.

Pannenberg approaches the most difficult problem of the personal
independence of the Holy Spirit within the Trinity from the perspective of the personal manner that characterizes the working of the
Spirit in believers. The patristic doctrine of the Trinity "apparently
sometimes all too rashly" inferred a personal uniqueness for the Spirit
comparable to that of the Son. Paul and John, while distinguishing
the Spirit from the Son, also identified the Spirit with the Son. So
Pannenberg indicates: "The question here is whether the personal
character of the Spirit who leads the believers is not perhaps identical
with that of the exalted Lord." [22] The most one finds in Paul are
"beginning points" for a distinction between the present reality of the
Spirit who dwells in the community and the Lord who will return.
Though a consciousness of the absence of Jesus from the community
begins to develop in Paul's debate with the Corinthians, that the
church has been given the Spirit in the interim between Easter and
the End *in the place of* the presence of Jesus only begins to emerge in
Luke and John. Hence, Pannenberg contends: "The independence of
the Spirit . . . can be taken as an indication that a third independent
moment in God's essence is to be assumed only when a personal
relation and thus also a difference of the Spirit from the Son can be
demonstrated." [23] The glorification of the Son as the work of the
Spirit might provide such legitimation from the history of Jesus, but
such a step exceeds the concepts expressed by John and Paul.

The New Testament portrays the dynamic presence of the Spirit
as faith, hope, and love. When faith is understood as the awakening of
freedom to a new vision of life in Christ, when hope opens up the
promise of life for all mankind, faith and hope converge into the
creativity of love, which elevates man beyond the narrowness of
self-interest to the universal intention of Christian love. Yet the most
pressing problem of the presence of the Spirit in the church is undoubtedly the weakness and inefficiency of Christian love. Pannenberg observes:

> [Christians] have their population centers in the richest
> countries of this world, but they don't manage to change the
> miserable living conditions of the majority of mankind, but
> rather to contribute to, continue, perpetuate, or even aggra-

---

[22] *Ibid.*, p. 178.
[23] *Ibid.*, p. 179.

vate the disastrous occurrences of hunger, war, and political or economical alienation.[24]

Obviously the present-day ecstatic power of the Spirit, especially its manifestation as creative love, does not fulfill the New Testament assurances concerning the presence of the Spirit in the Christian community. Yet the rule of God, the *eschatological* presence of the Spirit, does break into this world. Pannenberg affirms: "It breaks in where men are liberated to humanness, where they enjoy life in gratitude, and where they set over against their own suffering the 'nevertheless' of hope and [seek to] remedy the suffering and privations of others."[25] Since the inbreak of the future of God occurs among men, especially those who recognize the coming of the Kingdom of God upon the earth, humanity is the present "place" of God's reality. To be sure, God's deity is not dissolved into humanity; nevertheless, the spiritual presence of God in the world is either eclipsed or shines in man himself—all men generally, but especially those of the Christian church.

The Apocalypse of the Future at God's Coming

Though Pannenberg does not engage in eschatological speculation,[26] he does envision an end event which would include judgment, the resurrection of the dead, and the realization of the Kingdom of God. Such an event would mark the end of the world and of history as these have previously existed. Since the eschatological formulations only specify the conditions for the accomplishment of man's destiny in the Kingdom of God, Pannenberg reasons: "The eschatological statements concerning the future tell us nothing of the happenings by which, in the material course of events, this essential future of human nature is to be realized."[27] Instead, eschatological hope leaves these questions open. Yet faith in the incarnation means that the apocalypse of God, the coming of the ultimate future, will not just destroy the

---

[24] "The Working of the Spirit," p. 24.
[25] "Wie kann heute glaubwürdig von Gott geredet werden?" p. 64.
[26] Pannenberg is quite skeptical of a descriptive analysis of the End. He says: "Only the biblical promises have made the new thing of the future visible on the one hand and reliable on the other. . . . Thus they create courage for a future that is not yet visible" (*WIM*, p. 43). Instead of concentrating upon the characteristics of the *eschaton*, Pannenberg focuses upon the significance of the eschatological appearance of Jesus Christ for the realities and hopes of the existing world. Cf. "The Kingdom of God and the Church," *TaKoG*, pp. 72–101.
[27] "Eschatology and the Experience of Meaning," *IGaHF*, p. 199,

present and past. Rather, Pannenberg says: "The future of God will be in many ways an extrapolation of the message and history of Jesus of Nazareth, as much as this was based on the future of the kingdom invading the present." [28] The promissory history of the God of hope will ultimately find fulfillment in the coming of God himself. Reflecting upon the history of God's promises to Israel for the coming Kingdom—which has already appeared proleptically in the destiny of Jesus—Pannenberg perceives a correspondence between man's hope for God's reign and the God of hope himself:

> Then the author and the content of the promises are ultimately one, and the future to which they pointed was a form of manifestation of God's future itself, the future of his lordship, whose power over what was then present proclaimed itself in the realization of the promises.
>
> The unity of the promising God with his promise itself is consummated in the fulfillment of what was promised; for the fulfillment brings about the glorification of man and of the world, and thus their participation in the glory of God. The salvation that God promises is himself.[29]

Therefore, the promise of God's future—the ultimate coming of the Kingdom of God—is significant for the definition of man and of God, namely, the destiny of man to eternal community with God and the reality of God as self-differentiated unity.

The Destiny of Man

The Old Testament refers the essence of man to the divine sphere through the concept of the "image of God." Conversely, the New Testament declares that the essential humanity of man has been fully realized only in Jesus of Nazareth, the perfect image of God, the accomplishment of God's intention for man from the beginning of creation.

The meaning of the "image of God" in man derives from its function, namely, that man is to represent the rule of God in the creation. Through such representative lordship man is to achieve his destiny, which includes the humanization of nature through its responsible appropriation and the realization of human freedom through com-

[28] "Future and Unity," p. 62.
[29] "The God of Hope," *BQiT* II, p. 248.

munity. Hence, Pannenberg affirms a vital interrelationship between the image of God and the reign of God: "For the New Testament Jesus could be the image of God because he proclaimed the coming reign of God in the world and placed everything which exists under its rule." [30] Pannenberg's eschatological interpretation of Jesus as "the true man," the one in whom the image of God has appeared, implies a vital concept of salvation which comprehends "present reconciliation" and "future resurrection." Salvation is nothing less than the fulfillment of the ultimate destiny toward which man is aimed and for which he seeks. However, salvation occurs only when man is united in his present with his past and future, which is impossible without concurrence with the world and without community with other men. Pannenberg insists that only through the gift of eschatological salvation is the essence of man accomplished: "The essence of man is the destiny that still lies beyond the empirical content of man's present and that always lures man beyond everything at hand for man." [31] Since the individual never achieves such unity of life on this side of death, the wholeness of life sought by man—unity with himself, the world, his fellowman, and God—can only eventuate beyond death. Hence, the question of human destiny, which is never conclusively answered in life, continually drives man to hope for "life" beyond death.

While all imaginable conceptions of life after death are metaphors, the adequacy of the fundamental metaphors that have been employed to formulate the destiny of man require critical examination. The concept of the immortality of the soul proves untenable for several reasons: (1) The preservation of a kernel of present human existence as imperishable minimizes the radicality of death and circumscribes the hope for the newness of the future. (2) The distinction between body and soul as two completely different realms contradicts modern anthropology which understands man as a corporeal unity. (3) The emergence of man's inner world of self-transcendence cannot be isolated from but is stamped by man's corporeal involvement. Pannenberg judges the concept of an independent soul in a functioning body an abstraction: "The only reality is the unity of the living creature called man, which moves itself and relates itself to the world." [32]

[30] Pannenberg, "Was ist der Mensch?" in *Disputationen zwischen Christen und Marxisten*, ed. by Martin Stöhr (Munich: Chr. Kaiser Verlag, 1966), p. 190.
[31] *JGaM*, pp. 192–193.
[32] *WIM*, p. 48.

Unlike the immortality of the soul, the concept of a resurrection of the dead is compatible with modern anthropology. Not only does it affirm the unity of man and his openness to the future, *it also accepts the seriousness of death,* which means an end to everything. Pannenberg puts it plainly:

> The inner life of our consciousness is so tied to our corporeal functions that it is impossible for it to be able to continue by itself alone. This seriousness of death must be recognized by every conception of a life-beyond-death that is to be regarded as being meaningful for us today.[33]

The hope of resurrection acknowledges the inability of all elements of human existence to outlast death but posits the hope for a completely new existence, a radical transformation which is in some sense "bodily life." Pannenberg argues: "The fundamental relativity and mutual solidarity of all moments of human life make necessary a . . . conceiving the eternal destiny of man beyond death . . . as another mode of existence of the *whole* man." [34] The conception of the resurrection of the dead symbolically and mysteriously conveys such wholistic survival. Hence, the hope of resurrection coheres with the destiny man seeks and corresponds to the freedom of the Biblical God who contingently transforms the old into the new, who is defined by a love that is faithful to his creation.

Man's destiny to participate in God's eternal life is broken by the sinful self-centeredness of his temporality. As long as man is traveling in time, the judgment which eternity brings remains hidden. However, after the succession of events constituting life is terminated—after death—the whole of human existence is susceptible to judgment. If a man has not been faithful to his destiny of openness to the world, he will be destroyed in the judgment of God. Pannenberg poignantly says of the abortive destiny to a healed life: "This exclusion from God and from his own destiny is the pain of eternity." [35]

The wholeness of existence, which can only be represented as an event beyond death, involves resurrection and judgment. Eternity means judgment, for in the concurrence of eternity the contradictions of man's life are destroyed, especially the basic contradiction between

[33] *Ibid.,* pp. 49–50.
[34] *JGaM,* p. 87.
[35] *WIM,* p. 79.

the self and its infinite destiny. Yet Pannenberg also emphasizes the continuity between the life awakened in the resurrection and life lived historically. However, it is life seen from God's eternal present, which is completely different from man's ordinary, temporal experience. Hence, the resurrection of the dead actually discloses "that which already constitutes the depth of time now and which is already present for God's eyes." [36] Through the bridge of the eternal depth of life, a man is already identical in the present with the life to which he will be raised in the future; consequently, decay in the grave does not thwart resurrection, and the locus of the dead prior to resurrection proves an unnecessary inquiry.

Although Pannenberg affirms the importance of the destiny of the individual man, he does not ignore the unity of humanity in terms of the destiny of "man." The concept of the resurrection of the dead expresses the unity of mankind, for this event is expected as a universal destiny involving all men. Since the resurrection of the dead was an apocalyptic concept conceived as the destiny of righteous humanity, the single resurrection of Jesus was closely associated with the destiny of all mankind, that is, the general human destiny has occurred in Jesus. As in apocalypticism, moreover, the concept of the resurrection of the dead presupposes the end of the world, for a universal resurrection is not imaginable in the present world, and man cannot be understood without his world. Therefore, the picture of the resurrection happening to all men collectively instead of individually is appropriate, for the individual man has his human existence only in community with others in the world.

The content of eschatological hope is the essential future of mankind, the accomplishment of the destiny of man, for each individual and for all humanity. Pannenberg cogently reasons:

> The definitive removal of all alienation would require the accomplishment of the human destiny of the individual as well as of the society, and it would require that all human individuals should be granted a share in that perfect society. That is the meaning precisely of the Jewish and Christian eschatological imagery which is expressed by combining the Kingdom of God and the resurrection of the dead: the expectation of the Kingdom of God implies that only when God rules and no man possesses dominating political power any

[36] *Ibid.*, p. 80. Cf. *AC*, pp. 172 ff.

more, then the domination of people by other people and the injustice invariably connected with it will come to an end. . . . It takes a resurrection of the dead to have all human individuals of all times participate [according to their capacity] in the perfect society of the Kingdom of God. Only on this condition the destiny of mankind which comprises the total number of its individuals can be claimed to be accomplished. If the social and individual destinies of men condition each other so that they can only be realized together, then the totality of human individuals is required for the realization of the social destiny of man.[37]

Although these comments suggest universal salvation for all men, unlike Carl Braaten,[38] Pannenberg has consistently refused to espouse universalism unequivocally.[39] The apostle Paul does not speak in I Cor., ch. 15, of the general resurrection of all men, but he says in II Cor. 5:10 that all men must appear before Christ's judgment seat. Enoch 22:13 speaks of the end judgment upon sinners without their having been raised, which, as in Paul, issues from the identification of the resurrection from the dead as the blessing of salvation itself. Hence, when Paul says that in Christ all men are made alive (I Cor. 15:22; Rom. 5:18), the question arises whether or not Paul thought of a reconciliation of all things (Rom. 11:32).[40] Therefore, while Pannenberg has sought to maintain universal salvation as a theological option, he has affirmed the concept of the unity of mankind in the resurrection of the dead apart from universalism:

Even if the resurrection as a saving event does not happen to every individual, it is still related to the unity of humanity because it is connected with the idea of a universal judgment coming over all men at the end of history in which every man will be measured in terms of the destiny of man as such.[41]

[37] "Future and Unity," pp. 70–71.
[38] Carl E. Braaten, Christ and Counter-Christ: Apocalyptic Themes in Theology and Culture (Fortress Press, 1971), pp. 142–146.
[39] Cf. JGaM, pp. 271–272, pp. 76–80, esp. p. 76, n. 66; AC, pp. 92–95, esp. 95. Though Pannenberg's comments are considerably less qualified in "Future and Unity," p. 70, he has consistently interpreted the report in I Peter of Jesus' descent into hell to mean that "men outside the visible church are not automatically excluded from salvation" (JGaM, p. 272; cf. AC, pp. 92–95); but this does not denote universal salvation.
[40] JGaM, p. 76, n. 66.
[41] Ibid., p. 88.

The Deity of God

When Jesus described the coming Kingdom as the Kingdom of God which men should seek above all else, he affirmed the ontological primacy of the future of the Kingdom over everything present, including all that is spiritually present. Therefore, as already indicated, Pannenberg identifies the deity of God with the reign of God: "From the biblical standpoint the being of God and that of the kingdom are identical, since the being of God is his lordship," [42] "The deity of God is his rule." [43] "He is God only in the execution of his lordship, and this full accomplishment of his lordship is determined as something future." [44] Hence, the promise of the eschatological coming of God's Kingdom is the promise of the coming of God himself. The future of the reign of God is not unessential to his deity but intrinsic to it. The God of the Bible is God only in the accomplishment of his reign, only as he reveals himself as God. Ultimately, therefore, only the eschatological self-demonstration of God at the End of history will reveal unequivocally the deity of God, who has nonetheless already revealed himself proleptically in the history of Jesus. Until then, the deity of God remains wrapped in mystery and subject to doubt.

Reflecting upon the demonstration of God's deity as the creative power of love in the eschatological history of Jesus, Pannenberg observes:

> God is not an existing entity but is the future of his coming Kingdom. As this future, he was and is present through that man, Jesus, who testified to the coming Kingdom of God. Through this man God is present to the world as the spirit who gives freedom and life by creating faith. This faith is the quiet relatedness of everything to the origin of life.[45]

The reality of God reveals itself temporally as Trinity. The unity of God comprehends present and future—hence, the "persons" of the Trinity. The foundation for the Trinitarian conception of God roots in the event of revelation. The revelatory history of Jesus Christ contains within itself the Trinity of Father, Son, Spirit—three modes of God's being, which diverge in the divine self-disclosure. Pannen-

---

[42] "The God of Hope," *BQiT* II, p. 240.
[43] "Theology and the Kingdom of God," *TaKoG*, p. 55.
[44] "The God of Hope," *BQiT* II, p. 240.
[45] "Theology and the Kingdom of God," *TaKoG*, pp. 70–71.

berg contends: "If Father, Son, and Spirit are distinct but coordinate moments in the accomplishment of God's revelation, then they are so in God's eternal essence as well." [46] Yet the affirmation of God's threeness in oneness and oneness in threeness is problematic, as the history of the doctrine of the Trinity clearly shows. Three approaches to a solution of the problem are most important: (1) The doctrine of procession in the Eastern church envisions a unity of source, the Father, from whom the Son and Spirit proceed; however, the Platonic background of emanation and the subordinationist tendency of the Logos doctrine are evident weaknesses. (2) In the Western church Augustine's concept of the relational unity of the three "persons" has dominated Trinitarian formulations, despite the inclination to dissolve the personal character of Father, Son, and Spirit on the one side and the tendency to individualize the persons at the cost of the unity of the divine essence on the other. (3) Hegel understood the concept of "person" in such a way that God's unity becomes comprehensible precisely through the reciprocity of the divine Persons: Since the essence of the person is to exist in dedication to another person, the unity in the Trinity occurs through the process of reciprocal self-dedication. Pannenberg praises Hegel's interpretation as a conception of God's unity that attains an unparalleled vitality and intensity— precisely through the accentuation of the personality of Father, Son, Spirit.[47]

Though the Trinity roots in the historicality of God's revelation, Pannenberg does not distinguish sharply between a functional and an ontological Trinity, between the mode of God's revelation and the essence of God's being. Instead, he perceives a confluence of action and being in the historical revelation of the eternal God. However, he adamantly refuses to devaluate the mystery of God revealed as Trinity, observing: "The doctrine of the Trinity formulates the concept held by finite men of the God who is revealed in Jesus." [48] When taken for itself, the doctrine of the Trinity becomes contradictory, for the formulation does not involve finite objects that can be neatly defined over against one another and over against the one who describes them. The contradictory character of the Trinitarian formula refers to God's infinity, which remains mystery to finite understanding. Thus the concept of the Trinity, which intends to describe God's

[46] JGaM, p. 180.
[47] Ibid., p. 182.
[48] Ibid., p. 183.

eternal essence from God's acts in history, is doxological. As doxology, therefore, the Trinity anticipates God's future, which will first bring the full perception of his essence.

The unitary essence of God, however, should not be conceived as a tensionless uniformity. The Father is not displaced by the Son, because the consubstantiality of Jesus with God is established precisely in Jesus' directing mankind completely away from himself toward the coming reign of the Father. Hence, the oneness of the Son with the Father is mediated negatively, for Jesus served the coming reign of God and not himself. Similarly, Christians experience the active working of the Spirit of Christ. While they serve the future of God, the coming of his Kingdom among men, they participate already in the Sonship of Jesus. "Thus," Pannenberg reasons, "the *doctrine of the Trinity* is the seal of the pure futurity of God, which . . . draws [man's present] into itself and through enduring the pain of the negative reconciles it with itself." [49] With these comments Pannenberg disavows the reductionism of pantheism and projects an eschatological vision of a reconciled creation, namely, "panentheism." Affirming the integrity of the Christian doctrine of the Trinity, therefore, Pannenberg eloquently concludes:

> The trinitarian concept describes the particular unity of the living God, while philosophical monotheism conceived of the dead or static unity of a supreme being as an existing entity indistinguishable within itself. The trinitarian idea of God is congruous with historical process, while the notion of a supreme entity speaks of a "divine thing" outside man's history. The trinitarian doctrine describes the coming God as the God of love whose future has already arrived and who integrates the past and present world, accepting it to share in his own life forever. The trinitarian doctrine is, therefore, no mere Christian addition to the philosophical idea of God. Rather, the trinitarian doctrine is the ultimate expression for the one reality of the coming God whose Kingdom Jesus proclaimed.[50]

[49] "The God of Hope," *BQiT* II, p. 249.
[50] "Theology and the Kingdom of God," *TaKoG*, p. 71.

Part Three

PROBLEMS
AND PROSPECTS

IX

AN ASSESSMENT OF PANNENBERG'S THEOLOGICAL PROGRAM

GIVING TANGIBLE EXPRESSION to the new direction of theology, John Cobb says:

> The theology of Wolfhart Pannenberg has opened a quite new front in the theological scene on both sides of the Atlantic. A good many issues that theologians had widely assumed to be more or less settled have suddenly been brought vigorously to the fore. While much contemporary work continues to build upon the foundations established by the dialectical theology of the twenties, Pannenberg takes a critical look at those foundations and proposes a quite different direction for theological development.[1]

Since Pannenberg vigorously challenges many of the "settled" issues in modern theology, he has provoked a new, oftentimes vigorous debate in contemporary theology. Yet the discussion has been hampered by hasty attempts to categorize the new movement under the rubric of the past or by summary attack and dismissal from the lofty vantage point of some reigning theology of the present, an unwarranted response which reaches beyond the Continent[2] to include English and

---

[1] John B. Cobb, Jr., "Past, Present, and Future," *TaH*, p. 197.

[2] Cf. Lothar Steiger, "Revelation-History and Theological Reason: A Critique of the Theology of Wolfhart Pannenberg," in *History and Hermeneutic*, Vol. IV of Journal for Theology and the Church, ed. by Robert W. Funk (Harper & Row, Publishers, Inc., 1967), pp. 82–106. Pannenberg, "Nachwort zur zweiten Auflage" (1963), *OaG*, esp. pp. 134 ff., indicates that the review articles by Steiger and Günther Klein reflect a negative tone and caricatures, which makes an intelligent discussion of the issues difficult (cf. *ibid.*, pp. 134–135, n. 7).

American theologians.[3] Yet serious theologians have increasingly recognized that it is imperative to deal reflectively with the issues which
Pannenberg has raised.

If an issue-oriented dialogue is to proceed, however, there are definite pitfalls which the participants must avoid. First, Pannenberg's
summons to a post-Enlightenment theological perspective that acknowledges the positive role of reason in Christian theology cannot be
psychologically reduced to his experience of an initiatory, determinative "blik." Similarly, the structures of Pannenberg's theology cannot
be effectively defined by reference to his Lutheran identity, for he is
not an uncritical parrot either of Lutheran orthodoxy or of the
Reformation heritage.[4] Second, Pannenberg's admittedly ambitious
theological program must not be quickly dismissed as an overreaction
to dialectical theology, especially Bultmann's kerygmatic theology.
Whether or not Pannenberg has overreacted to Bultmann or Barth,
Heilsgeschichte theology or Lutheran orthodoxy, can be determined
only by serious debate on the issues. Third, Pannenberg cannot be
confuted by theological "sloganeering," such as "Faith is self-authenticating," for the legitimacy of a particular slogan finally depends upon
the adequacy of the theological position which it has come to represent.
Therefore, precisely because Pannenberg's theology aims toward a new
theological synthesis, the questions about his theological program
require critical theological dialogue where issues are defined and the
merits of specific conclusions carefully assessed.

Though it is not possible to present a thorough analysis of the

---

[3] Cf. Martin J. Buss, "The Meaning of History," *TaH*, pp. 135–154, Kendrick
Grobel, "Revelation and Resurrection," *TaH*, pp. 155–175, and esp. William Hamil-
ton, "The Character of Pannenberg's Theology," *TaH*, pp. 176–196; moreover, note
Pannenberg's initial remarks in response: "In any discussion which does not deal
directly with substantive problems, but with the conceptuality used in their description, the danger is especially great that the conceptuality will unintentionally
take on other nuances of meaning in the perspective of the critics than in that
held by the author who is being criticized" ("Response to the Discussion," *TaH*,
p. 221). However, such distortions continue. Cf. Robert T. Osborn, "Pannenberg's
Programme," *Canadian Journal of Theology*, Vol. XIII (1967), pp. 109–122, but
esp. pp. 117–122; and Hiroshi Obayashi, "Future and Responsibility: A Critique
of Pannenberg's Eschatology," *Studies in Religion/Sciences Religieuses*, Vol. I
(1971), pp. 191–203.

[4] Cf. Pannenberg, *Reformation zwischen gestern und morgen*, 1969; and "Luthers
Lehre von der zwei Reichen und ihre Stellung in der Geschichte der christlichen
Reichsidee," in *Gottesreich und Menschenreich* (Regensburg: Verlag Friedrich
Pustet, 1971), pp. 73–96. Indeed, William Nicholls, *Systematic and Philosophical
Theology*, The Pelican Guide to Modern Theology, Vol. I (Penguin Books Inc.,
1969), p. 339, suggests that Pannenberg calls Protestantism itself into question.

issues that have emerged in the last decade of theological debate, a representative treatment of crucial issues—especially those current in English-language theology—will be briefly summarized. The discussion will include a comparison of Pannenberg's theological program with other somewhat similar theologies, an evaluation of the key issues in the controversy over revelation, a sketch of the more important evaluations of Pannenberg's Christology, and a characterization of the direction that the dialogue is taking with reference to an eschatological understanding of God.

THE DISTINCTIVENESS OF PANNENBERG'S THEOLOGY

When a new theological movement appears on the stage of history, there are immediate attempts to classify it. Hence, efforts have been made to identify Pannenberg with different theological systems.[5] However, Carl Braaten pointedly suggests:

> Pannenberg's theology obviously escapes ready-made labels.
> . . . A synthetic thinker will construct his theological mosaics
> with many pieces of many shapes and colors. Of all the post–
> World War II theologians, Pannenberg has shown by far the
> widest scope and the greatest constructive power of thought.[6]

The originality and distinctiveness of Pannenberg's theology can best be highlighted by a comparative analysis of his approach with somewhat similar theological viewpoints.

Universal History and Salvation History

Some interpreters of Pannenberg categorize him rather quickly with some variation of salvation history, despite his strong criticism

[5] H. Paul Santmire, "Review: *Revelation as History* and *Theology as History*," *Dialog*, Vol. IX (1970), pp. 142–147, considers Pannenberg an extreme exaggeration of Barth, and suggests he may represent an "old frontier," regardless of the "sheen" of new vitality. Conversely, George H. Kehm, "Pannenberg's Theological Programme," *Perspective*, Vol. IX (1968), p. 261, suggests that Pannenberg's theology "seems more like a continuation of the work of Troeltsch and Tillich than it does of either Barth or Bultmann." Cf. "A Theological Conversation with Wolfhart Pannenberg," *Dialog*, Vol. XI (1972), pp. 294–295, where Pannenberg compares Barth and Troeltsch, indicating his empathy and admiration for Troeltsch's understanding of the problems of contemporary theology.

[6] Carl E. Braaten, "The Current Controversy on Revelation: Pannenberg and His Critics," *The Journal of Religion*, Vol. XLV (1965), p. 234.

of Hofmann and Kähler. Hence, James M. Robinson[7] and Ernst Fuchs[8] identify Pannenberg with the salvation history theology of Oscar Cullmann.[9] These observations are not entirely without foundation, for any constructive theological conception of history is oriented to *history*. However, there are significant differences between Pannenberg and the theologians of salvation history which should preclude a hasty attempt to identify these two movements as synonymous. Though there are variations within the salvation history school, the differences between Pannenberg's conception of universal history and the general orientation of salvation history are readily distinguishable.

Epistemology. In the salvation history schema, religious knowledge occurs within or follows the evangelical experience of faith: "Faith is a 'way of knowing.' " Conversely, Pannenberg's conception of universal history refers knowledge to the cognition of reason, which includes an imaginative and a critical dimension; and faith, which logically presupposes knowledge, is defined as trust: "Faith abandons self-reliance and depends upon God for the future."

Revelation. Salvation history understands revelation as the union of historical event in the past with a supplementary illumination by the Spirit in the present: Revelation is suprahistorical and supranatural. Pannenberg's universal history conceives revelation as Spirit-filled events defined within their original context of meaning but explicated continually in the history of the transmission of traditions. Thus revelation is historical and universal (requiring no *supplementary* illumination or interpretation).

Christology. The theology of salvation history presupposes (though not always explicitly) the incarnation as the historical and theological foundation of Jesus' unity with God; the resurrection, therefore, is the expected consequence of incarnation. The theology of universal history interprets Jesus' resurrection as the confirmation of his pre-Easter claim and the ground for his essential unity with God; hence, the incarnation is a historical and theological conclusion.

[7] James M. Robinson, "Revelation as Word and History," *TaH*, pp. 15 ff., lumps Pannenberg with Cullmann and Barth—an illegitimate attempt to reduce the field to two options, namely, Pannenberg or Bultmann.

[8] Cf. Ernst Fuchs, "Theologie oder Ideologie? Bemerkungen zu einem heilsgeschichtlichen Programme," *Theologische Literaturzeitung*, Vol. LXXXVIII (1963), cols. 257–260, a review article that contains more polemic than substance.

[9] Cf. Oscar Cullmann, *Salvation in History*, tr. by Sidney G. Sowers (Harper & Row, Publishers, Inc., 1967), pp. 57–58. Cf. also Pannenberg, "Response to the Discussion," *TaH*, pp. 247–248, n. 46, where he distinguishes himself from Cullmann.

The Kingdom of God. Salvation history interprets Jesus' proclamation of the Kingdom of God as essentially present, only to be consummated in the future: The image of the Kingdom is stamped by "prophetic forth-telling." Conversely, universal history conceives Jesus' announcement of the imminent Kingdom of God as the gracious pre-actualizing of the future in the present, but the Kingdom itself remains future which nonetheless impinges upon the present: The image of the Kingdom is stamped by (qualified) "apocalyptic expectation."

Soteriology. Salvation history identifies Jesus' mission in proclaiming the Kingdom of God as corresponding to his sacrificial death upon the cross: Jesus' mission and fate coincide (usually in Jesus' own consciousness). The conception of universal history recognizes an important break between Jesus' proclamation of the Kingdom and his execution, though the latter remains a consequence of the former: The unity of Jesus' history and the representative significance of the cross issue from the resurrection.

Eschatology. Salvation history interprets the End as "the final unveiling" of everything present in Jesus' life and destiny: The *eschaton* is essentially realization, for Christ is the "middle" of history. Universal history conceives the End as the arrival of the Kingdom of God, which Jesus' history only anticipates: The *eschaton* is finally the transformation of the whole of reality, but Christ is the prolepsis of the End of history.

Theology of Hope and Universal History

Though the theology of Jürgen Moltmann is occasionally set over against that of Pannenberg, there is also the tendency to identify these two as saying essentially the same thing. In *Theology of Hope,* Moltmann strained to distinguish himself from Pannenberg, for he not only emphasized actual points of disagreement but also constructed illusory differences between himself and Pannenberg. More recently, however, Moltmann and Pannenberg have acknowledged the agreement which exists between them. In his "Antwort auf die Kritik der Theologie der Hoffnung" (1967), Moltmann says: "Today I find more agreement than difference in the recent works of Pannenberg." [10] Similarly, in the "Vorwort" of his *Grundfragen systematischer Theo-*

---

[10] Jürgen Moltmann, "Antwort auf die Kritik der Theologie der Hoffnung," in *Diskussion über die "Theologie der Hoffnung" von Jürgen Moltmann,* ed. by Wolf-Dieter Marsch (Munich: Chr. Kaiser Verlag, 1967), p. 222, n. 19.

logie (1967) Pannenberg affirms: "Moltmann's striking renewal of the eschatological theme converges to a great extent with my thoughts." [11] These acknowledgments, *though qualified,* indicate that there are significant areas of agreement as well as disagreement between Moltmann and Pannenberg.

The common elements that Moltmann and Pannenberg share may be summarized as follows: Both recognize the inadequate appropriation of the apocalyptic eschatology of Jesus in twentieth-century theology; both affirm the ontological priority of the future; both define reality as history; both acknowledge the proleptic structure of language and events; both maintain the historicity of Jesus' resurrection; both seek a Biblical basis for revelation; both understand Jesus in relation to the Old Testament; both unite eschatological revelation with a universal mission; and both relate the church to a positive restructuring of the world.

Yet there are significant differences between Moltmann's "theology of hope" and Pannenberg's eschatological conception of universal history—differences that impinge upon the areas of agreement between them. First, whereas Pannenberg interprets apocalyptic eschatology as the first formal presentation of a universal conception of history, Moltmann uses apocalypticism to accentuate the *radical contradiction* between the historical and the eschatological, between the promise of hope and historical reality. Second, Pannenberg adopted but then relinquished the conception of a revelatory history of promise for the more comprehensive conception of "the history of the transmission of traditions"; conversely, Moltmann continues to conceive revelation on the horizon of promissory history. The difference is one of accent, but is of profound importance for Pannenberg's more positive evaluation of the traditions of the past. Third, although Pannenberg demonstrates lively concern for the pre-passion ministry of Jesus as the specific context for understanding Jesus' destiny, Moltmann shows a paucity of interest in the historical activity of Jesus and concentrates upon the dialectic of cross and resurrection—a sharp contrast to Pannenberg's Christology "from below." Fourth, whereas Pannenberg believes it crucial that the resurrection be subjected to historical investigation which inevitably *tends* toward a positive or negative historical judgment, Moltmann declares that the resurrection is beyond historical judgment as such, that it liberates from the "positivism"

---

[11] "Vorwort," *Grundfragen systematischer Theologie,* pp. 5–6, n. 2.

of history, and that it "balks at the category of 'having.' " [12] The distinction between Pannenberg and Moltmann at this juncture reflects Pannenberg's aversion to unfounded Biblical authoritarianism and Moltmann's dependence upon the authority of the Word of God interpreted as the word of promise. Moltmann does not break with dialectical theology on the issue of supernaturalism. Fifth, while Pannenberg always relates the resurrection to the pre-Easter path of Jesus— to the proclamation of the Kingdom and the tragedy of crucifixion— Moltmann speaks continually of the resurrection of the Crucified. The cross-resurrection dialectic, only loosely associated with the activity and preaching of Jesus, is another indication of the continuity of Moltmann with dialectical theology. Sixth, whereas Pannenberg has accentuated the arrival of the future in the history and destiny of Jesus—the incarnation is the prolepsis of the future—Moltmann speaks dialectically of the *anticipation* and *incarnation* of God in Christ, which corresponds to the dialectic of resurrection and cross, scorning the conception of the incarnation oriented to the prolepsis of the *eschaton* in the resurrection of Jesus.[13]

In addition to the actual differences between them, Moltmann has leveled several illegitimate criticisms at Pannenberg which have gained considerable popularity. First, Moltmann charged in 1964 that Pannenberg's conception of universal history intends to extend and to supersede the Greek cosmic theology: "The place of the cosmological proof of God . . . is taken by a theology of history which argues back in the same way from the unity of 'reality as history' to the one God of history." [14] Pannenberg, however, had rejected and criticized the "procedure of inference" of Greek natural theology and the doctrine of analogy between God and the world as early as 1959. Hence, he could respond: "I cannot repress a certain mild surprise when I see my own assertions interpreted, without close inspection, in this sense which I have rejected." [15] The cosmological proof is precluded in Pannenberg's emphasis upon the freedom of God which expresses itself in contingent events.

Second, since Pannenberg affirmed the verifiability of Jesus' resur-

[12] Jürgen Moltmann, *Religion, Revolution, and the Future,* tr. by M. Douglas Meeks (Charles Scribner's Sons, 1969), p. 54.
[13] *Ibid.,* pp. 212–215.
[14] Jürgen Moltmann, *Theology of Hope: On the Ground and Implications of a Christian Eschatology,* tr. by James W. Leitch (Harper & Row, Publishers, Inc., 1967), p. 77.
[15] "Response to the Discussion," *TaH,* pp. 254–255, n. 61.

rection, Moltmann accused him of presupposing "a concept of history dominated by the expectation of a general resurrection of the dead as the end and consummation of history." [16] Though Pannenberg has not responded directly to this accusation, it fails for two reasons: (a) When investigating Christian origins, Pannenberg has emphasized the necessity for the historian to be open in research to the question of God, who, if he is the Biblical "God," must be related to the consummation of the process of history. The conception of history which Pannenberg *presupposes* when approaching the problem of Jesus' resurrection is a conception *open to the question* of the Biblical God, not *dominated* [!] by the expectation of an eschatological resurrection. (b) Furthermore, Pannenberg has consistently argued at the level of probability when interrogating the Easter traditions. The problem of "verification" in history is never conclusive but always referred to "eschatological verification," though expectation for the latter is not unrelated to the results of the former.

Third, Moltmann inaccurately accused Pannenberg of conceiving the resurrection of Jesus "merely" as the first instance of the final resurrection of the dead, that the risen Christ himself did not have a future, "a universal future for all the nations." [17] Conversely, Pannenberg insists that the union of the church with Jesus' own eschatological life remains future for the resurrected One. The prolepsis of the End in the destiny of Jesus does not imply the "mere" anticipation of the general resurrection, for the eschatological tension between the prolepsis of the End and the *eschaton* itself has opened the path of a universal mission for the church. Yet Pannenberg does acknowledge:

> There may be a difference with Moltmann's conception in my conviction that the ultimate reality of eschatological life has appeared in Jesus himself in the *past* event of the resurrection, to which we can look back as in past time and thus as a historical event. For early Christianity the resurrection of Jesus was not only the "putting into force" of the promise . . . but the shift of aeons, in which the Old Testament promises have found their fulfillment, and not a "supposed fulfillment." . . . The happenedness of the ultimate, the perfect tense of the resurrection of Jesus—in the double sense of the word perfect—*became the basis of the Christian*

[16] Moltmann, *Theology of Hope*, p. 82.
[17] *Ibid.*, pp. 82–83.

doctrine of incarnation, which distinguishes Christianity from
the mere knowledge of hope of the Jewish faith.[18]

The Dynamic of Reason

Although his work on the "Theology of Reason" has not yet been
published, there is no doubt that the fundamental element in Pannenberg's epistemology is the dynamic of reason, or more precisely,
the dynamic of historical reason. Since historical reason must be
distinguished from the various forms of *a priori* reason which immediately set reason in conflict with revelation and from a receptive reason
oriented toward intuition and insight in contrast to imaginative constructions and projections, Pannenberg's understanding of reason
cannot be equated with or defined by any restrictive form of rationalism: neither the deductive reasoning of Protestant orthodoxy nor the
intuitive reason of theological supranaturalism, neither the speculative reason of idealism nor the reductive reason of logical positivism.
Instead, Pannenberg's conception of reason includes an awareness of
mystery, the critical function of judgment, the constructive creativity
of imagination, and the historicality of knowing. Pannenberg recognizes quite clearly that reason knows no absolute certainties, that it
is stamped by provisionality, that its perceptions and conclusions are
anticipatory and subject to the judgment of the future. Hence, the
reasoning of reason—provisional and anticipatory—is open to the
future for modification, invalidation, or confirmation. Since historical
reason is distinguished by openness entailing provisionality, it is
neither static nor restrictive but dynamic and expansive. Ultimately,
therefore, reason transcends criticism and analysis in order to gain
perspective on all the partial perspectives of life, that is, it seeks
the unity of truth.

At many points Pannenberg's conception of reason appears compatible with other interpretations of reason in modern theology. John
Macquarrie, for example, identifies reason as one of several "formative factors" in theology and maintains the ideal of a *reasonable*
religion.[19] Macquarrie actually distinguishes two dimensions of reason
which theology should employ in relation to revelation: the architectonic and the critical. He refers to the architectonic dimension as

---

[18] "Response to the Discussion," *TaH,* pp. 263–264, n. 74. Italics added.
[19] John Macquarrie, *Principles of Christian Theology* (Charles Scribner's Sons,
1966), pp. 13–16.

"a constructive use of reason in which we build up rational wholes, theories, or interlocking systems of ideas . . . by rational leaps which, so to speak, integrate the fragmentary elements in inclusive wholes." [20] Theology represents one such imaginative projection. However, the coherent revelatory whole grasped by architectonic reason requires immediate clarification and examination by the critical dimension of reason.

There are several similarities between Macquarrie and Pannenberg in the valuation of reason. Both affirm the creative function of the imagination in the construction of "wholes"; both strive to explicate the substance of revelation coherently and comprehensively; both exactingly define the content of revelation in the light of modern criticism. However, there is a fundamental difference between Macquarrie and Pannenberg at the point of history—history conceived eschatologically. Macquarrie's conception of reason would include historical criticism but it is not stamped by historicality; conversely, Pannenberg disavows any conception of reason that is not characterized by historicness and the historicness of truth which expresses itself in reason. Therefore, it is not insignificant that Macquarrie has so little to say about history and eschatology, that he concentrates instead upon "Being." Correspondingly, it is not accidental that Pannenberg's exercise of "imaginative reason" is most visible in his conception of universal history, that his most telling use of "critical reason" appears in his application of the historical-critical method to the Biblical traditions.

The Dispute Over Revelation

As an alternative to dialectical theology, Pannenberg poses a conception of "revelation as history." When he and "the working circle" published their symposium on revelation in 1961, a stormy debate erupted and innumerable rejoinders were directed against the "new" theology.[21] Many of the crucial issues continue to be debated, especially since the publication of the American symposium *Theology as History* (1967). In order to advance the dialogue, certain key issues will be delineated and responses summarized or anticipated.

---

[20] *Ibid.*, p. 15.

[21] Robinson, "Revelation as Word and History," *TaH*, pp. 1–100, summarizes the most important responses to Pannenberg and the circle.

Indirect Historical Revelation

Kendrick Grobel examined Pannenberg's conception of revelation as history and attempted to refute him through the category of "interpersonal analogy" found so frequently in the Bible.[22] Pannenberg answered Grobel by referring to the interpersonal analogy as an excellent description of indirect revelation. When theophanies of "God" in the Old Testament and elsewhere are represented as self-revelation, one fails to recognize that the deity *in its appearance* is not a self which is identical with its appearance. Furthermore, while the Old Testament reports various direct manifestations of God, Pannenberg thinks it questionable whether such self-manifestations qualify as self-*revelation*, "in the sense of the manifestation of the divinity of God as the power over everything in a way that is at least virtually universally valid." [23] Such a self-confirmation occurred, Pannenberg argues, in the eschatological destiny of Jesus. That which distinguishes Jesus' resurrection as the *final,* but *anticipatory* revelation over against the numerous *partial anticipations* of revelation is the eschatological demonstration of power in the Christ event; that is, the end of all things is anticipated by and thus united in the history and person of Jesus.

Similarly, the fundamental issue for Franz Hesse of Münster is the authenticity of the self-disclosure of God in the Old Testament.[24] Since he finds the self-disclosure of God in the divine manifestations to Israel, Hesse rejects Pannenberg's distinction between manifestations and revelation, which denotes the exclusion of partial self-disclosures from the category of revelation. Over against Pannenberg's thesis that revelation (unlike manifestations) occurs only at the End, Hesse declares: *"The revealing God is the presupposition, not the goal, of divine action in history."* [25] Hesse recognizes an eschatological dimension to God's revealing work, but, contrary to Pannenberg, he distinguishes between the "revelation of God" and the "unveiling of God's glory," between divine self-disclosure and divine self-demonstration. Since the self-confirmation of God is associated with God's glory and self-disclosure with revelation, Hesse asserts that Israel

---

[22] Grobel, "Revelation and Resurrection," *TaH*, pp. 163–166.
[23] "Response to the Discussion," *TaH*, p. 235.
[24] Franz Hesse, "Wolfhart Pannenberg und das Alte Testament," *Neue Zeitschrift für systematische Theologie und Philosophie,* Vol. VII (1965), pp. 174–199.
[25] *Ibid.*, p. 193.

originated and lived from revelatory disclosures but waited upon the promised unveiling of God's glory.

The validity of God's manifestations of himself to Israel seems to be the basic concern that permeates Hesse's critique of Pannenberg. However, as Pannenberg quickly indicates in his response, he too affirms that Israel continually lived from those events in which it experienced the self-manifestations of Yahweh. Yet these manifestations—authentic and valid—did not constitute an unveiling of the essence of Yahweh. Pannenberg cogently reasons:

> Unveiling of essence is something ultimate, and if one claims such an event of divine self-manifestation witnessed to in the Old Testament, it becomes impossible to understand the God of Jesus as identical with the God of Israel, at least in a Christian theology that first ascribes finality to Jesus' message of God and not already to the Old Testament.[26]

The real problem, which Pannenberg grasps but Hesse misses, is the *uniqueness* of revelation as self-revelation. If Pannenberg were to define revelation as an authentic manifestation of God's presence, Hesse would concur, at least at this point; conversely, if Hesse were to define revelation strictly as the eschatological demonstration of God's *doxa*, he would find himself in the company of Pannenberg. Hence, when Pannenberg restricts "revelation" to God's self-confirmation of his deity in and through Jesus of Nazareth, he is neither denying nor minimizing the manifestations of God reported in the Old Testament and in other religions. However, these anticipations of revelation are transformed in the light of God's eschatological self-revelation in the history of Jesus, the true revelatory perspective toward which all other partial perspectives must be oriented.[27]

Revelation and Faith

Paul Althaus views Pannenberg's theses on revelation, especially Thesis 3 (regarding the universal character of the historical revelation), as a legitimate reaction to existential theology, but he thinks "revela-

[26] "Response to the Discussion," *TaH*, p. 234, n. 12.

[27] Pannenberg, "The Question of God," *BQiT* II, p. 226, comments: "From the standpoint of the Christian faith, in any case, it can be said that the non-Christian religions are based on unclear provisional forms of the true answer to mankind that has happened in the history of Jesus." Cf. esp. Pannenberg, "Toward a Theology of the History of Religions," *BQiT* II, pp. 63–118.

tion as history" is itself an overreaction.[28] Though hope is essentially future-oriented, faith is primarily directed to the present; consequently, Althaus reasons, faith and knowledge are not to be fundamentally distinguished. Thus Althaus affirms two kinds of knowledge—the natural knowledge of reason and the knowledge perceived through faith. Correspondingly, the concept of revelation embraces unique revelatory events on the one side and illumination through inspired interpretation on the other. Hence, Althaus rejects the "universal openness" of God's revelation in the resurrection of Jesus, for only the Spirit-given interpretation of the kerygma transforms the "fact" into revelation. For Althaus, the knowledge of God's revelation through the kerygma can only occur through the work of the Holy Spirit, through "inner revelation." Since Pannenberg posits the openness of revelation to anyone who has eyes to see, Althaus charges that Pannenberg must therefore attribute nonrecognition of the revelatory event exclusively to man's sinfulness. Against Pannenberg's conceptualization, Althaus suggests that the inability to perceive the revelatory events involves the relative "hiddenness" of the revelation to human perceptivity, maintaining that "the possibility of unbelief is established in the manner of the revelation of God." [29] Therefore, Althaus thinks that the formula "revelation as history" should be modified to include the supplementary illumination of the Holy Spirit—"revelation as history and faith."

In a most significant reply Pannenberg emphasizes his agreement that faith is the gift of God.[30] The crucial issue is not faith as such but the mediation of faith, namely, the relationship of the knowledge of revelation to faith on the one side and to the Holy Spirit on the other. If faith is defined comprehensively so as to include *notitia, assensus,* and *fiducia,* Pannenberg argues, the knowledge of the content of faith remains the logical presupposition for trust; conversely, if faith is identified strictly as trust, faith must be grounded upon a presupposed knowledge. Hence, when Althaus says that the knowledge essential to faith discloses itself only in a believing reception of the message, he makes the *decision* of faith the basis for the certainty of faith's content—threatening the foundation of faith "outside my-

[28] Paul Althaus, "Offenbarung als Geschichte und Glaube," *Theologische Literaturzeitung,* Vol. LXXXVII (1962), col. 323. For Pannenberg's theses, see Chapter III, note 2, above.
[29] Althaus, "Offenbarung als Geschichte und Glaube," col. 328.
[30] "Insight and Faith," *BQiT* II, pp. 28–45.

self." The apostle Paul, however, did not found knowledge upon trust, but trust upon knowledge (Rom. 6:8 f.; II Cor. 4:13). To be sure, the logical priority of knowledge to faith does not mean that one could endlessly maintain such knowledge without faith, but the *logic* and the *psychology* of faith must be distinguished. Indeed, trust can originate in the expectation (logically already presupposed) that the knowledge will appear later—"a fore-conception of the result that is ordinarily characteristic not only of the attitude of faith but also of the cognitive process generally." [31] Pannenberg insists that the knowledge which trust presupposes must not be distinguished from natural knowledge. He says pointedly: "I admit that I cannot understand any knowledge as other than 'natural.' " [32] A special "knowledge of faith" distinguished from natural knowledge leads to the confirmation of faith in the "decision" of faith, which destroys the truth reference of faith outside the individual's subjectivity and distorts faith's essential dependence upon a truth outside itself.

In addition, Pannenberg argues, an appeal to the power of the Holy Spirit to authenticate an unconvincing message accomplishes nothing, for the Spirit is not the criterion for the truth of the message: "On the contrary, it is much more the assurance that one is speaking in the power of the Holy Spirit that is itself in need of a criterion for its credibility (I Cor. 12:1 f.), and this criterion is the testimony to the Lord Jesus Christ (I Cor. 12:3), thus, the content of the message." [33] Therefore, the power of the Holy Spirit issues *from the content* of the message, *not in addition to* or as a supplement of it. Pannenberg contends that the content of the message refers to the meaning inherent in the reported event, that is, to the knowledge which the Reformers called *notitia historica,* a knowledge that embraces an event's actuality and its significance. Nevertheless, the knowledge wherein faith believes does not replace the act of self-abandonment, for salvation only comes through trust. Yet the ground for trust remains the revelation of God in historical events. If an inspiration were to add something to the revelatory event which was not inherent in it, the affirmation of faith would become a *sacrificium intellectus* in response to the apostolic message.

To be sure, an illumination is necessary for men to see the truth. Men have difficulty acknowledging truth, for they are often gripped

[31] *Ibid.,* p. 33.
[32] *Ibid.*
[33] *Ibid.,* p. 35.

by prejudgments that hinder the perception of truth. Hence, man must be brought to reason in order to perceive the truth of the event revealing God's deity. However, the illumination that eliminates prejudgments adds nothing to the content of the event or the message reporting it; instead, it is a matter of the event becoming powerful through language. The illuminating Spirit leads to the truth of the kerygma and shows itself as the power of the word. Since the Spirit is intrinsic to the event that the word expresses, the word of proclamation is Spirit-filled and the hearers receive it powerfully into themselves. While such speaking of the Spirit is not overtly traditional, Pannenberg insists that it does not devaluate the Spirit's importance. The real problem is the tendency to identify the Spirit with pious subjectivity, an unaccountable *asylum ignorantiae*, a tendency that thwarts the life and power of the church. Instead of "revelation as history and faith," therefore, Pannenberg speaks of "revelation as history, anticipatorily summed up in Jesus Christ—but *for* faith, which lives between the prolepsis of the end in the Christ event and the universal onset of this end." [34]

Subsequent to Pannenberg's reply to Althaus, Helmut G. Harder and W. Taylor Stevenson thoughtfully took up the question of Pannenberg's understanding of the relationship of faith and revelatory history.[35] Analyzing Pannenberg's conception of history from the perspective of historical experience and its meaning structure, these authors find Pannenberg's theological program supportive of a hermeneutics which is also an "erotics" of history. However, they enunciate several criticisms against Pannenberg's conception of history, the most important being that Pannenberg's description of the movement from historical fact to faith is characterized by a fundamental ambiguity. He seems to say that knowledge of Jesus' history precedes faith, but he also speaks of "penetration," of being "drawn" into the meaning of Jesus' history. Harder and Stevenson interpret Pannenberg's latter

---

[34] *Ibid.*, p. 44. Daniel P. Fuller, "A New German Theological Movement," *Scottish Journal of Theology*, Vol. XIX (1966), pp. 160–175, urges a "slight" revision in Pannenberg's conception of history to permit a supernatural history running through and climaxing regular history, which would include a supernatural working of the Holy Spirit. Pannenberg's resistance to Fuller's suggestion indicates that such a revision would be far from "slight." Such a modification would require the *sacrificium intellectus* over against the kerygma and reduce the theology of universal history to another form of supernatural salvation history.

[35] Helmut G. Harder and W. Taylor Stevenson, "The Continuity of Faith and History in the Theology of Wolfhart Pannenberg: Toward an Erotics of History," *The Journal of Religion*, Vol. LI (1971), pp. 34–56.

affirmation to mean: "From the beginning, the perception of historical fact is inherently a perception of reality by means of faith." [36] Pannenberg's faith-assumption, which gives *logical* as well as psychological priority to faith, is "that God reveals himself in history." [37] The perception of the facts of Jesus' history is thus possible by means of the Holy Spirit.

As Pannenberg himself affirms in response to Harder and Stevenson,[38] the critical issue is "that the movement of faith is already operative in the very perception of historical fact." [39] Pannenberg expresses agreement that the particularities of experience must be interpreted within the more comprehensive framework of some totality of meaning; consequently, he judges the disagreement between them to be largely one of terminology. Yet Pannenberg continues to insist upon the logical priority of knowledge to faith, namely, that something different from faith is presupposed as its foundation. Thus he finds the Harder-Stevenson definition of history as perceived exclusively in terms of faith disturbing, because the question of the basis of faith remains unanswered, a basis that precedes and undergirds the subjective decision of faith. So Pannenberg says: "That basis, to be sure, is accessible only from within anticipated horizons of meaning, and so far as historical facts belong to that basis, it is accessible only through language, or by an act of experience which is always mediated through language." [40] The projection of these linguistic horizons of meaning is a function of reason—closely related to but not identical with faith. Likewise, the logical priority of knowledge to faith coheres with the primacy of dynamic reason in projecting different horizons of meaning. Therefore, when the distinction between the logical and psychological structure of faith is correlated with the wholistic projections of reason, the interpretation of the movement of faith as "penetration" is not in itself inconsistent with the affirmation of the logical priority of knowledge to faith.

History and Eschatology

Though Pannenberg claims the eschatological horizon of apocalyptic theology for the conceptual derivation of universal history, Hiroshi

---

[36] *Ibid.,* p. 53.
[37] *Ibid.,* p. 52.
[38] "A Theological Conversation with Wolfhart Pannenberg," p. 289.
[39] Harder and Stevenson, "The Continuity of Faith and History," p. 51.
[40] "A Theological Conversation with Wolfhart Pannenberg," p. 289.

Obayashi alleges that Pannenberg's concern for universal history covertly roots in the philosophical problem of ontology—an attempt to comprehend the whole of reality in order to establish a relationship of unity between existence and essence.[41] Conversely, aware of Pannenberg's initial dependence upon the dissertation of Dietrich Rössler, *Law and History: Investigations into the Theology of Jewish Apocalyptic and Pharisaic Orthodoxy*,[42] William R. Murdock and Hans-Dieter Betz attack Pannenberg's use of apocalyptic conceptions. Whereas Rössler and Pannenberg consider universal history a major concern of apocalypticism, Murdock argues that the intention of these writings concentrates upon the imminent expectation of the *eschaton* on the basis of a dualistic-eschatological understanding of history.[43] The relationship of history and the *eschaton* in apocalyptic thought was antithetical, for the *eschaton* only signified God's termination of the dualistic course of history. Again, while Pannenberg identifies the self-revelation of God with the end of history, Murdock argues that apocalypticism viewed history dualistically and hesitated to speak of revelation in history. Instead of historical revelation, the apocalyptists turned to literary revelations in order to maintain continuity between the present and the eschatological future. Thus Murdock charges that Pannenberg's understanding of history and of revelation actually contradicts apocalyptic conceptualization.

Similarly, Betz sharply criticizes Pannenberg's understanding and appropriation of apocalyptic concepts, especially the concepts of universal history and eschatological revelation.[44] Assuming Pannenberg's exclusive dependence upon Rössler's research, which he considers methodologically "ill-conceived," Betz levels several criticisms at Pannenberg and the conception of revelation as history: (1) It is completely uncertain that apocalypticism represents a development beyond Old Testament prophecy. (2) Universal history is not the central motif of apocalyptic thought; furthermore, the apocalyptist does not

[41] Hiroshi Obayashi, "Pannenberg and Troeltsch: History and Religion," *Journal of the American Academy of Religion*, Vol. XXXVIII (1970), pp. 401–403.
[42] Cf. Klaus Koch, *The Rediscovery of Apocalyptic*, Studies in Biblical Theology, 2d ser., No. 22, tr. by Margaret Kohl (Alec R. Allenson, Inc., 1972), p. 101. Cf. above, Chapter III, n. 33.
[43] William R. Murdock, "History and Revelation in Jewish Apocalypticism," *Interpretation*, Vol. XXI (1967), pp. 167–187.
[44] Hans-Dieter Betz, "The Concept of Apocalyptic in the Theology of the Pannenberg Group," in *Apocalypticism*, Vol. VI of Journal for Theology and the Church, ed. by Robert W. Funk (Herder and Herder, 1969), pp. 192–207.

anticipate the *eschaton* as the revelatory fulfillment but as the abolition of history. (3) While Jesus must be understood in the context of
an apocalyptic eschatology, Wilckens and Pannenberg err when they
say that he was an "apocalyptist"; in addition, the interpretation of
Jesus' resurrection as the proleptic fulfillment of his imminent expectation of the Kingdom of God lacks textual basis. Therefore, Betz
concludes, apocalypticism cannot provide the religio-historical basis
for Pannenberg's revelatory program.

Since Pannenberg has not replied to these particular criticisms of
his theology, only a tentative assessment of these arguments is possible.[45] First, while Obayashi is probably right when he identifies the
unity of existence and essence as one of Pannenberg's central concerns,
he wrongly infers that Pannenberg superimposes the concept of universal history upon the Biblical traditions. Indeed, as Klaus Koch
observes, only Pannenberg's extensive work within the theological
circle originally of Heidelberg accounts for the reevaluation and appropriation of apocalypticism into his theology, in itself "an extraordinary act of courage for a systematic theologian." [46] Again, Murdock's analysis of history and revelation in apocalypticism is not
without difficulties:[47] (1) The apocalyptic concern for the royal rule of
Israel precludes a simple antithetical relation of history to the *eschaton*,
as though the end marked only the destruction instead of the consummation of history. (2) The implication that the apocalyptists believed that God was just not active in history leaves the origin of
apocalyptic visions inexplicable. (3) Beyond the visions they experienced, the apocalyptists likely recognized important divine activity at
least in the external course of history. Furthermore, a close examination of Betz's critique indicates that he misconstrues fundamental
issues in the debate; most obviously, he mistakenly accuses Pannenberg and Wilckens of identifying Jesus as an "apocalyptist." [48] Of
course, the single most important issue in the critique of Betz and
Murdock against Rössler and Pannenberg involves the question of
universal history. Though several features of Rössler's analysis are
indeed questionable, Koch convincingly argues that his central point

---

[45] However, cf. Koch, *The Rediscovery of Apocalyptic*, esp. pp. 40–42, 86–93, 101–
106.
[46] *Ibid.*, p. 103.
[47] *Ibid.*, pp. 90–91.
[48] Betz, "The Concept of Apocalyptic in the Theology of the Pannenberg Group,"
p. 203.

remains valid: "That in the apocalypse history has entered the picture for the first time 'as a unit and as a whole,' with its 'basis in a pre-destined divine plan,' through which every event acquires 'its non-interchangeable place in the sequence of time,' has often been con-tested since [Rössler's dissertation], but never confuted." [49] Turning to the validity of the position of apocalypticism in Pannenberg's theol-ogy, which involves the crucial question of universal history, Koch concludes: "But these denials [of apocalptic interest in universal his-tory] are for their part so largely determined by dogmatic premises that Pannenberg's attitude (which more or less coincides with the views of Rössler and Rowley . . .) may be accounted the historically probable one, pending proof to the contrary." [50]

The crucial significance of apocalyptic for Pannenberg's theological program is unequivocal in the "Postscript" to *Revelation as History*, especially as the context for Jesus' resurrection:

> The proper meaning of the resurrection depends fundamen-tally on its connection with apocalyptic expectation of the resurrection, because only in relation to this context is the resurrection of Jesus already the inbreak of the expected end, which for the remainder of mankind is yet to come. And this eschatological character of the resurrection of Jesus as the prolepsis of the end event in Jesus establishes, within our sketch, its original significance as the revelation of God, be-cause . . . in the apocalyptic understanding of history the revelation of God's glory (and therefore of God himself) was expected in connection with the end event of the resurrection of the dead and the judgment.[51]

However, while Koch argues for the legitimacy of Pannenberg's ap-propriation of universal history from apocalypticism, he indicates serious reservations concerning Pannenberg's evaluation of Jesus' resur-rection. Indeed, the expectation of the resurrection of the dead is im-portant in apocalyptic drama, but Koch questions "whether, accord-ing to both apocalyptic and New Testament evidence, the resurrection of Jesus can sustain the weight which Pannenberg's conception lays on it." [52] Thus the problem of revelation converges with the problem

[49] Koch, *The Rediscovery of Apocalyptic*, p. 42.
[50] *Ibid.*, p. 105.
[51] "Nachwort zur zweiten Auflage," *OaG*, pp. 141–142.
[52] Koch, *The Rediscovery of Apocalyptic*, p. 106.

of Christology, the question of apocalyptic with the question of Jesus' resurrection.

THE DEBATE IN CHRISTOLOGY

Peter Hodgson says that Pannenberg's *Jesus—God and Man* "may prove to be the most important work in Christology since the great studies by Dorner and Ritschl in the nineteenth century." [53] Hodgson heaps an extraordinary amount of praise upon Pannenberg for his vast knowledge of the Christological tradition and for the ability to combine systematic concerns with studies of the history of traditions in the Gospels.

The Pre-Easter Path of Jesus

One of the most distinctive features of Pannenberg's Christology is his method of Christology "from below." Yet Hodgson indicates that Pannenberg gives the argument a decisive turn—moving directly from Jesus' pre-Easter claim to its confirmation in the resurrection. Since the activity and message of Jesus are not the medium of his divinity, but only anticipate it in a concealed and ambiguous fashion, Hodgson contends: "Thus Pannenberg only seems to take the historical life of Jesus (his words and deeds) with the same degree of radicalism as hermeneutical theology and the new quest." [54] Hence, Hodgson identifies Pannenberg's view with I. A. Dorner's theory of "progressive incarnation," which enables him to avoid taking the historical Jesus with "radical seriousness."

Hodgson understands Pannenberg to reject any effort to "existentialize" Jesus' concept of the Kingdom and to identify the Kingdom with God's universal rule, which Jesus announced as imminent. The proclamation of the near Kingdom orients man to the future, requiring of him an openness which will decide his destiny. However, because "nearness" refers to the quality of God's relationship to man instead of the time of his arrival, Hodgson perceives a tension between Pannenberg's emphasis upon the apocalyptic character of Jesus' preaching

---

[53] Peter C. Hodgson, "Pannenberg on Jesus," *Journal of the American Academy of Religion*, Vol. XXXVI (1968), p. 373. Yet cf. Hodgson, *Jesus—Word and Presence* (Fortress Press, 1971), a provocative but unconvincing alternative to Pannenberg's Christology "from below."

[54] Hodgson, "Pannenberg on Jesus," p. 376.

and the anthropological "openness to the future" which he associates with Jesus' concept of the Kingdom. In addition, he asks "whether the apocalyptic framework was not already shattered by the content of Jesus' teaching." [55] Pannenberg does not really examine this question, Hodgson argues, suggesting that Pannenberg's analysis of the teaching of Jesus lacks the "critical rigor" that characterizes his treatment of the resurrection.

John Cobb is not so negative in his evaluation of Pannenberg's approach to Christology "from below." He intimates that Pannenberg seeks to relate Jesus' destiny to the hopes of his contemporaries on the one side and to the message of the primitive church on the other. Since Jesus anticipated the imminent coming of the End and the general resurrection of the dead, Cobb interprets Pannenberg's approach to say: "The message of Jesus is to be understood in the light of his expectation, and the message of the early Church expressed the sense of living in the time when the end had already begun in the resurrection of Jesus." [56] Cobb recognizes that some scholars dispute this fact, e.g., Ernst Käsemann and Norman Perrin,[57] but, like Pannenberg, he believes that they tend to isolate Jesus from his environment, namely, Jewish apocalypticism. Yet Cobb finally questions Pannenberg's tendency to define not only the *context* but also the *content* of Jesus' message from apocalypticism: "[Pannenberg] seems to interpret the entire message [of Jesus] as determined by this expectation of the end in such a way that its validity in every respect hinges upon the fulfillment of that expectation." [58]

The different perspectives which Cobb and Hodgson reflect regarding Pannenberg's treatment of the pre-Easter path of Jesus is most revealing. Hodgson's reaction shows that to raise the question of Jesus' divinity immediately in terms of the resurrection gives the impression of devaluating the "radical seriousness" of Jesus' humanity. Conversely, Cobb's estimate of Pannenberg's application of Christology "from below" shows how important Jesus' cultural context was for his proclamation and accentuates the great historical distance between the contemporary world and the Galilee of Jesus—a question crucial to Jesus'

---

[55] *Ibid.*, p. 386.

[56] John B. Cobb, "Wolfhart Pannenberg's 'Jesus: God and Man,'" *The Journal of Religion*, Vol. XLIX (1969), p. 194.

[57] Cf. Norman Perrin, "Putting Back the Clock," *The Christian Century*, Vol. LXXXV (1968), pp. 1575–1576; but note Pannenberg's response, "A Theological Conversation with Wolfhart Pannenberg," p. 291, also pp. 292–293.

[58] Cobb, "Pannenberg's 'Jesus: God and Man,'" p. 195.

universality, his divinity. The disparity between Hodgson and Cobb at this point would be diminished considerably if Pannenberg discussed substantially Jesus' proclamation of the Kingdom of God in conjunction with the proleptic structure of Jesus' claim to authority. Precisely because in *Jesus—God and Man* Pannenberg's incisive, foundational discussion of Jesus' proclamation of the coming Kingdom of God tends to get lost behind the important, yet far-reaching theological discussion of Jesus' divinity, I restructured Pannenberg's Christology "from below" in Chapters V and VI. As I have attempted to show, such a procedure illuminates the radical seriousness of Jesus' humanity and clarifies the continuity of Jesus' ministry with the proclamation of the primitive church.

Pannenberg himself has recently responded to Hodgson's methodological criticism to the effect that he has based his Christology *de facto* on the resurrection instead of the historical Jesus, judging such criticism one-sided. Pannenberg perceives a correspondence between the Jesus traditions on the one side and the resurrection tradition on the other, concluding: "Neither of the two by itself could establish or explain the faith of Christians in Jesus, but only their interrelationship." [59] Again, while both Hodgson and Cobb fail to grasp Pannenberg's conception of Jesus' fundamental modification of apocalypticism, Hodgson particularly fails to recognize the character of that modification in its effect upon Pannenberg's understanding of the "nearness" of the Kingdom, namely, that the existential openness to the future that emerged in Jesus' message cannot be isolated from, but actually roots in, Jesus' temporal expectation of the near End.

The Problem of Jesus' Resurrection

The assessments of Pannenberg's Christology thus far have focused predominantly upon his theological method, especially on the problem of the meaning and facticity of Jesus' resurrection.[60] Since Pannen-

---

[59] "A Theological Conversation with Wolfhart Pannenberg," p. 291.

[60] So also Donald G. Dawe, "Christology in Contemporary Systematic Theology," *Interpretation*, Vol. XXVI (1972), pp. 269–272. Cf. Herbert Burhenn, "Pannenberg's Argument for the Historicity of the Resurrection," *Journal of the American Academy of Religion*, Vol. XL (1972), pp. 368–379. Contrary to Pannenberg, Burhenn puts the question of the historicity of Jesus' resurrection prior to a consideration of its significance; consequently, he not only accepts a rigidly agnostic definition of the historical method but also divorces the historian's work from any hermeneutical endeavor. Does the "common-sense knowledge" which constitutes the "picture of everyday experience" really exclude a historical affirmation of Jesus' resurrection? If the historian affirms the historicity of the resurrection, must he "present it

berg understands history as the history of the transmission of traditions, he contends that the meaning of Jesus' resurrection was immediately available to his contemporaries, insofar as they shared the apocalyptic expectation. Yet Frederick Herzog rejects Pannenberg's understanding of history as a unity of fact and meaning, arguing: "On purely historical grounds it is quite unintelligible why a resurrection should tell us more about God than a cross." [61] Hence, he protests Pannenberg's interpretation because the historical method cannot penetrate to "inner history." However, Herzog's contention that "a" resurrection as such does not say more about God than "a" crucifixion rests upon an abstraction. If one speaks of the Jesus who proclaimed the nearness of God's Kingdom but was accused of and subsequently executed for blasphemy, the resurrection of *this* Jesus, if acknowledged, does communicate its own meaning in the light of the prior expectation of the risen One.

Like Pannenberg, Klaus Koch thinks that the resurrection of Jesus is far more significant in the New Testament than present-day systematic theology allows, and that the New Testament statements about the resurrection presuppose their apocalyptic pre-history. However, he considers Pannenberg's conception of the confirmation of Jesus' claim in the resurrection rather dubious: "Is not the fulfillment of Jesus' prophecies (and hence the confirmation of his person and destiny) expected primarily through the coming of the Kingdom?" [62] As Koch himself realizes, Pannenberg answers this question through the con-

---

with the qualification that he has departed from his customary procedure as a historian at this point, even if the nature of the evidence [!] has helped to prompt this departure"? (p. 379). Pannenberg's redefinition of historical methodology receives considerable support from Richard R. Niebuhr, *Resurrection and Historical Reason: A Study of Theological Method* (Charles Scribner's Sons, 1957), but note Pannenberg's qualification, "The Revelation of God in Jesus," *TaH*, p. 114, n. 8. Though not directed toward him, the most formidable challenge to Pannenberg's position comes from Van A. Harvey, *The Historian and the Believer: The Morality of Historical Knowledge and Christian Belief* (The Macmillan Company, 1966). However, while the differences between Pannenberg and Van Harvey are enormous, there are some striking similarities between them: Both affirm the crucial problem of responsible belief and judgment with respect to historical claims involving Jesus of Nazareth, both recognize the epochal significance of the Enlightenment, both acknowledge the relevance of Troeltsch for defining contemporary theology. Cf. Van A. Harvey, "Secularism, Responsible Belief, and the 'Theology of Hope,'" in Jürgen Moltmann et al., *The Future of Hope*, ed. by Frederick Herzog (Herder and Herder, 1970), pp. 126–153, a devastating critique against Moltmann which, if I understand Pannenberg correctly, he could at least engage, perhaps effectively.

[61] Frederick Herzog, *Understanding God: The Key Issue in Present-Day Protestant Thought* (Charles Scribner's Sons, 1966), p. 63.

[62] Koch, *The Rediscovery of Apocalyptic*, p. 151, n. 19.

cept of the prolepsis of the End in Jesus' eschatological destiny (which confirmed the *presence* of the Kingdom in Jesus' ministry). Nonetheless, Koch does not perceive either the priority of prolepsis to exaltation or the convergence of prolepsis with an eschatological incarnation in Pannenberg's Christology "from below." Yet Pannenberg consistently affirms:

> The special character of the proleptic event of the resurrection of Jesus should then be sought in its *full* participation in the reality of eschatological life. The provisional aspect, by which even this event is still only prolepsis, consists simply in this—but what does *'simply'* mean here!—that here the eschatological reality of life appeared only in an individual, and not yet in all mankind and the world as a whole.[63]

Koch's criticism suggests the importance of correlating prolepsis with exaltation more rigorously than Pannenberg did in *Jesus—God and Man* and the necessity of referring the ultimate confirmation of Jesus' expectation to the *eschaton*.

Robert W. Jenson questions Pannenberg's conception of history and the hermeneutic that it implies. He says: "More radically than any other, Pannenberg develops a monistic view of history and proclamation: Distanced, objectivizing historical-critical research results in assertions that just *are* eschatological proclamation." [64] Jenson believes that Pannenberg's hermeneutic falls apart when applied to the question of Jesus' resurrection. Though the affirmation of Jesus' resurrection corresponds to the logic of the witness given by those who experienced Jesus' appearances, predictions about man's future historical experience cannot be derived from such an affirmation. Thus verification of the statement "Jesus rose from the dead" is impossible: (1) The witnesses speak of appearances, not of meetings; i.e., the tangibility of the risen Jesus coincides exactly with the experiences of the risen Jesus. (2) The witnesses claim that the Jesus experienced was living in the reality of life-beyond-death. Though historical research is not irrelevant to the resurrection, Jenson emphasizes the limitation of such research: "Reliable sources make it probable that certain persons experienced appearances of Jesus as risen, and there are no

[63] "Response to the Discussion," *TaH*, p. 263. Italics added.
[64] Robert Jenson, *The Knowledge of Things Hoped For: The Sense of Theological Discourse* (Oxford University Press, 1969), p. 227.

grounds for explaining these experiences in terms of delusion and the like." [65] Yet the statement *itself*, "Jesus is risen," can neither be affirmed nor denied in historical research; consequently, Pannenberg's hermeneutic fails at the crucial point. It cannot verify the resurrection itself, Jesus' *meaning* as God's revelation.

While Jenson contends that Pannenberg's conception of history and hermeneutic fails to confirm the affirmation of Jesus' resurrection, he does not recognize that Pannenberg's historical conclusion rests upon an inference from the appearances.[66] Pannenberg's positive judgment coheres with (1) Jesus' expectation of the End event, including the resurrection of the dead, (2) the authenticity of the report of the empty tomb of Jesus, and (3) the unprecedented designation of Jesus' singular destiny as resurrection. Jenson's dualism of historical research (law) and proclamation (gospel) prevents him from acknowledging that historical research is not finally neutral with respect to Jesus' resurrection; this dualism forces him to base the actuality of Jesus' resurrection-destiny upon the continuous tradition of proclamation and the hope for eschatological verification. To be sure, Pannenberg acknowledges much similarity between Jenson's analysis and his own. Since Jenson grants the probable authenticity of the appearances, which "indeed may be regarded as a certain historical confirmation of the Resurrection," [67] Pannenberg judges the difference between them less an evaluation of the resurrection tradition as a difference in their respective understandings of reality. Like Jenson, Pannenberg believes that language transcends given reality; however, because language cannot arbitrarily transcend reality and retain a cognitive claim, the assertion of resurrection simultaneously transcends its linguistic expression but alleges a happening in past history. So Pannenberg concludes:

Therefore there must be some relation to reality that enables us to distinguish between language that, although transcending the given, is still related to it, and language

---

[65] *Ibid.*, p. 229.

[66] Cf. above, Chapter V, under the heading "The Problem of the Historicity of Jesus' Resurrection." Reginald H. Fuller, *The Formation of the Resurrection Narratives* (The Macmillan Company, 1971), rejects Pannenberg's designation of Jesus' resurrection as "historical" and affirms its "meta-historical character" (pp. 22–23), but his analysis of the resurrection narratives is strikingly similar to Pannenberg's. However, see C. F. Evans, *Resurrection and the New Testament*, Studies in Biblical Theology, 2d ser., No. 12 (Alec R. Allenson, Inc., 1970), an especially cautious interpretation which offers little support to Pannenberg's Christological formulation.

[67] Jenson, *The Knowledge of Things Hoped For*, p. 229.

that arbitrarily differs from something given. Because Jenson does not offer such a distinction, I am rather uneasy with his shift from history to the idea of the word, which he justifies because even in historical experience the question of language is fundamental. He finally says that we have to rely on language, on word, and not on historical fact.[68]

Analyzing the treatment of the resurrection, Peter Hodgson regrets Pannenberg's distinction between resurrection-reality and the resurrection-event; the former refers to the reality of new life after death and the latter to transition from earthly to resurrection life.[69] Hodgson indicates problems with Pannenberg's use of the metaphor "resurrection," because it is inextricable from the horizon of Jewish apocalyptic expectation and seems to apply more to the "event" of resurrection than to the "reality." Furthermore, while Hodgson considers Pannenberg's historical analysis of the tradition of the appearances compelling, he questions (what he considers) Pannenberg's conclusions deduced from the analysis: Instead of interpreting the appearances as prototypical descriptions of the experience of the living Lord that is universal to the Christian faith, Pannenberg identifies the appearances with the past *event* of resurrection (the transition from death to new life), "which happened at a definite time and place," in order to establish the historicity of the resurrection-event as a basis for faith.[70] Hodgson rejects this conclusion: (1) "Appeared" is distinguished from "raised" in I Cor., ch. 15, referring thereby to a present experience; (2) the historian cannot critically apprehend the *reality* of the living Christ to which the appearances refer; (3) the probable certainty obtainable through historical research is qualitatively distinct from the certainty of faith and cannot serve as *legitimation* or corroboration of faith, though helpful to an understanding of faith; (4) the "event" of resurrection must remain a mystery of faith, "in principle" inaccessible to conceptual explication. In addition, Hodgson calls Pannenberg's attempted verification of the empty tomb "an instance of bad historical and theological judgment," [71] for the tradition of the empty tomb requires belief in the revivification of a corpse. Since Pannen-

[68] "A Theological Conversation with Wolfhart Pannenberg," p. 290.
[69] Hodgson, "Pannenberg on Jesus," p. 376. Cf. Pannenberg, "Response to the Discussion," *TaH*, pp. 265–266, n. 76.
[70] Hodgson, "Pannenberg on Jesus," p. 377.
[71] *Ibid.*, p. 378.

berg himself refers ultimate confirmation beyond the prolepsis of Jesus' resurrection to the *eschaton,* Hodgson argues that the attempt to confirm Jesus' pre-Easter claim and the Christian's present confession in terms of the resurrection should be abandoned, and that the resurrection should be interpreted as the present reality of the living Lord.

Though Hodgson raises several important issues, unfortunately he has not always accurately understood Pannenberg's treatment of Jesus' resurrection. While Hodgson thinks Pannenberg associates the metaphor of resurrection primarily with the event instead of the reality of Jesus' resurrection, the metaphor refers comprehensively to both aspects of Jesus' eschatological destiny;[72] consequently, Pannenberg speaks frequently of the facticity of Jesus' resurrection and the appearances of the resurrected One. Furthermore, Hodgson erroneously thinks that Pannenberg identifies the past *event* of the resurrection with the appearances, when in fact Pannenberg distinguishes sharply between the event of resurrection and the appearances of the risen One (resurrection-reality perceived in the form of apocalyptic visions). In addition, Hodgson faults Pannenberg's affirmation of the empty tomb, insisting that the traditions of the empty tomb *require* belief in the revivification of a corpse; conversely, Pannenberg considers the empty tomb confirmatory evidence of Jesus' transformation from earthly to resurrection life. The legitimate issue between Pannenberg and Hodgson involves the interpretation of the appearances of the living Christ. Whereas Pannenberg defines them as unique objective visions of the past, Hodgson interprets the appearances as descriptions of the living Lord, prototypical of the *universal* experience of Christian faith. However, without the witnesses to the appearances of the resurrected Jesus, the identification of the "presence of the living Lord" with Jesus the crucified remains unfounded speculation. Hence, the Biblical traditions of the appearances of the resurrected One are not only distinguished from the spiritual presence of the living Lord, they also provide the rationale for identifying the living One with the crucified Jesus. Pannenberg convincingly argues:

---

[72] Cf. Pannenberg, "Nachwort," in Ignace Berten, *Geschichte, Offenbarung, Glaube,* tr. by Sigrid Martin (Munich: Claudius Verlag, 1970), p. 138. Pannenberg indicates that "resurrection" is not just a metaphor; instead, he now perceives a tangible, analogous relationship between the phenomenon of life and the hope of resurrection, that is, resurrection represents the goal and fulfillment of the deeper meaning of life itself (cf. esp. p. 138, n. 2).

The Christian faith remains dependent upon the witness of those who not only have seen the Resurrected One but also have known the earthly Jesus and therefore could recognize this one in the appearances which happened to them. The primitive Christian tradition about the resurrection of Jesus and its examination, therefore, remains decisive for the acceptance or rejection of such an event, even if one hypothetically allows for the possibility of a present immediate self-manifestation of the Resurrected One.[73]

Focusing upon several important issues in Pannenberg's Christology, John Cobb questions whether or not the conception "resurrection of the dead" is necessary to locate the fulfillment of man's life in the future. Since Pannenberg rejects the non-bodily continuation of human experiences after death—for reality is bodily reality—Cobb asks Pannenberg what he considers to be an acute question, namely, where is the resurrected body of Jesus? Though the alternative would be to project the bodily reality of Jesus to the future, Cobb reasons: "But in that case the future must be posited as already extant or as an eternity alongside of time or abrogating the reality of time in a way that Pannenberg usually wishes to avoid." [74] Cobb does not intend to circumscribe Pannenberg's options, but he does insist upon "a conceivable doctrine" which is not unthinkable and achieves internal consistency. Hence, Cobb thinks the trivial question of the locus of Jesus' resurrected body "may prove a major issue requiring the modification of other aspects of [Pannenberg's] thought." [75] Cobb thinks that the primacy of the body is dubious and that Pannenberg has enmeshed himself in unnecessary difficulties in maintaining "bodily" resurrection.

In addition, Cobb contends: "Final judgment of the systematic value of [Jesus—God and Man] must rest on [one's] judgment of the adequacy of Pannenberg's case for the historicity of Jesus' rising from the dead." [76] When the historian approaches the report of Jesus' resurrection, Pannenberg, according to Cobb, insists that the historian ask whether or not the actual occurrence of the event is the best explanation for the belief of its happening as attested in the New Testa-

[73] "Dogmatische Erwägungen zur Auferstehung Jesu," Kerygma und Dogma, Vol. XIV (1968), p. 110.
[74] Cobb, "Pannenberg's 'Jesus: God and Man,'" p. 197.
[75] Ibid., p. 201.
[76] Ibid.

ment. When the question is so posed, Cobb thinks that Pannenberg can construct a weighty case for Jesus' resurrection. While sympathetic to Pannenberg's interpretation, Cobb asks whether reports of unique events in the past should not require considerably more evidence for their occurrence than is demanded of more ordinary events: "Would not an explanation of past belief in a unique event in terms of more ordinary occurrences have *some* preferability?" [77]

The ordinary phenomena that Cobb considers interpretive of Jesus' resurrection are "visionary appearances" of recently deceased persons to the living. Since Jesus' appearances occurred in the cultural context of resurrection in bodily form instead of individual life in spiritual form, they were interpreted as "resurrection" appearances. However Cobb argues that the appearances themselves militate against that interpretation: Since resurrection appearances preclude virtually all traits normally associated with a body—occupancy of space, visibility— the retention of the category "body" seems unjustified. Instead, referring to parapsychological analogies whereby one mind works on another mind and causes it to project appropriate visual images, Cobb argues "that the preference for the symbol 'resurrection of the body' depends in both primitive Christianity and in Pannenberg on prejudgments brought to the evidence rather than on the evidence itself." [78] Though the tradition of the empty tomb supports "bodily resurrection," Cobb believes this tradition most doubtful.

When Cobb's criticisms are analyzed, they seem to diverge into three distinct problems: the evidence for the resurrection, the feasibility of "bodily" resurrection, and the location of Jesus' risen body. (1) Though Cobb may be justified in insisting upon more evidence for the occurrence of unique events than for ordinary ones, the suggestion that the interpretation of past reports of a unique occurrence (Jesus' resurrection) in terms of more ordinary occurrences (visions of the recently departed) threatens to reduce Jesus' expectation and destiny to generalized anthropological experience. Not only does such a procedure minimize the contingency of history, it also destroys the *eschatological* character of Jesus' history which constitutes the foundation of his revelatory unity with God. Is not the uniqueness of Jesus' resurrection denied when it becomes one of many instances of the spirits of the dead appearing to those formerly known in mortal life?

---

[77] *Ibid.*, p. 199. Cf. Van A. Harvey, *The Historian and the Believer*, pp. 227 ff.
[78] Cobb, "Pannenberg's 'Jesus: God and Man,' " pp. 199–200.

Would not the individuated appearances of various spirits of the dead destroy the promise of the eschatological unity of mankind preserved in the concept of the resurrection of the dead? (2) Questioning the advisability of the category "bodily" resurrection to explain personal survival of death, Cobb argues that the removal of traits normally associated with a body makes it difficult to retain the term. However, he subsequently suggests a general conception of "spiritual" life after death which minimizes the psychosomatic unity of man, the utter seriousness of death, and, with specific reference to Jesus' resurrection, the historical kernel behind the tradition of the empty tomb. Though Pannenberg's use of the Biblical conception of a "transformed body" is not unproblematic, personal survival beyond death would require some continuity of form (implicit in the recognition of persons) and must account for the radicality of death—conditions more compatible with the concept of resurrection of the dead than with a notion of the survival of personal spirit.

(3)The problem of the location of the resurrected Jesus, which Cobb considers a major difficulty in Pannenberg's interpretation, has not escaped the latter's attention: Even prior to Cobb's discussion of the question, Pannenberg had acknowledged that the most difficult problem which the resurrection of Jesus implies involves the present reality of the resurrected One.[79] The problem of "where is the risen Jesus" did not exist for the primitive church, for they could answer clearly, "in heaven." However, the modern world picture will not permit such an answer, at least not in terms of "an ascension into heaven." The difficulty that threatens talk of the resurrection involves the apparent conclusion that the risen One has disappeared into nothing. Conversely, Pannenberg suggests that heaven is to be identified as the sphere wherein God lives; consequently, the ascension into heaven refers to union with God, i.e., an imperishable life, a spiritual body, a life eternally bound to the origin of all life. So Pannenberg says: "The life of the Risen One in heaven can only mean that he lives by God, that he shares the life of God." [80] When God is conceived as futurity, resurrection means to enter the future of God. Hence, as one with the life of God, the risen Christ is contemporaneous with all time through the power of God. The language problem encountered when resurrection is so described corresponds to the problem of God-language gener-

[79] "Dogmatische Erwägungen zur Auferstehung Jesu," p. 114.
[80] Ibid., p. 115.

ally. Ultimately, therefore, the possibility of conceiving the risen Christ in the future of God hinges upon the propriety of the future as the mode of God's being.

Aware of the diversity of conclusions among competent exegetes and theologians concerning Jesus' resurrection, Pannenberg has increasingly acknowledged a plurality of approaches and the provisionality of all approaches to the resurrection. Yet a plurality of approaches does not eliminate controversy or conflicting judgments, as an examination of Willi Marxsen's alternative to Pannenberg's understanding of Jesus' resurrection aptly illustrates. Marxsen accepts without hesitation that the witnesses saw Jesus who was crucified, but he states what he means rather precisely: "Witnesses claim, after the death of Jesus, to have seen *him*, and it is just this vision which they express in different ways, partly already with incipient interpretations of what they say." [81] On the basis of the vision they supposedly experienced, Marxsen maintains, the witnesses reasoned through a process of reflective interpretation and concluded, Jesus has been raised by God. Though the witnesses thought they were speaking of an event, the historian and the theologian can only be concerned with the interpretive statement, namely, the interpretation of their experience to mean that Jesus had been raised from the dead. Thus Marxsen does not understand the resurrection as an event but as an "interpretive category"—a category interchangeable with many others. Pannenberg accepts Marxsen's conception of "resurrection" as an interpretive category, because there were no witnesses to the event of Jesus' resurrection. The basic question, however, is whether or not the interpretive category "resurrection" is generally exchangeable for others. So Pannenberg asks:

> Were profound considerations about the relativity of the then-current ways of thinking really necessary to explain the early Christian talk about the resurrection on the basis of the appearances of Jesus? How should this "interpretive category" be avoided, once one reflects that he who appeared as living had previously died? [82]

When Marxsen asserts that relating the appearances to the fact of

[81] Willi Marxsen, "The Resurrection of Jesus as a Historical and Theological Problem," in C. F. D. Moule, ed., *The Significance of the Message of the Resurrection for Faith in Jesus Christ*, tr. by Dorothea M. Barton; Studies in Biblical Theology, 2d ser., No. 8 (Alec R. Allenson, Inc., 1968), p. 30.
[82] "Response to the Discussion," *TaH*, p. 266, n. 77.

Jesus' death was a reflection which the disciples could have evaded in understanding the appearances, Pannenberg charges that his argument becomes abstractly artificial. Such reflection was essential to the function of the apostolate. Reflection was not an unnecessary second stage, but was occasioned by the experience of those who witnessed the appearances, namely, those who knew of Jesus' death. With devastating sharpness, therefore, Pannenberg asks: "With Marxsen's method, could not the assertion that the appearances were appearances of *Jesus* also be easily proved to be a secondary 'interpretive category'?" [83]

Finally, accentuating the provisionality of all historical statements about Jesus' resurrection, Pannenberg says plainly: "I attach absolutely no conclusive power for historical judgment to the arguments for the historicity of the resurrection of Jesus." [84] The assertion of the resurrection of Jesus as a historical event is nothing other than the affirmation that Jesus has been raised from the dead. Such an affirmation includes the claim to historicity, because the clarification of the statement itself requires historical examination. As soon as it is asserted that Jesus has been resurrected, a historical claim is made whether such a claim is desired or not; otherwise, the claim itself is forfeited. Although the results remain disputed, there are valid reasons which substantiate the facticity of Jesus' resurrection. However, it is crucial that the concept of historicity not be redefined outside the sphere of historical research. Pannenberg carefully explains:

> The accent of my assertion of the historicity of the resurrection of Jesus means primarily that an event which is asserted to have happened in the past is also thereby affirmed as historical—thus the historical character of this event. On the other hand, I think it quite difficult to affirm this event as a fact in the same sense as other facts. . . . For me, therefore, the eventness does not lie in the homogeneity of the resurrection of Jesus as an event comparable to other events; but only that this event, insofar as it is an event, must also be designated historical. Therein I presuppose that historicity does not require the homogeneity of all events which are designated as historical. The limitation which you encounter here, it seems to me, is not only a limitation of the historical method but also a limitation of our justification of describing the resur-

---

[83] *Ibid.*
[84] "Nachwort," in Berten, *Geschichte, Offenbarung, Glaube*, p. 135.

rection of Jesus as an event. It is probably not coincidental that at this point the problem of the appropriateness of our language proves to be similar to the problem of speaking about God.[85]

THE DISAGREEMENTS ABOUT GOD

Perhaps the truly novel, radical dimension of Pannenberg's theology is his doctrine of God. Though he has not published a *theology*, he has written several essays on the Christian understanding of God; moreover, Pannenberg is the first of the eschatological theologians to conceive God as "the power of the future." So Pannenberg affirms: "This priority of the eschatological future which determines our present demands a reversal also in our ontological conceptions." [86] The adequacy of the eschatological model hings upon its capacity to comprehend in a more convincing way the deity of the Biblical God, the power over everything.

Prominent Models for Understanding God

As contemporary theology seeks to understand God anew, three models for conceiving God evoke frequent attention. First, John Macquarrie offers a dynamic model for God as Being, which expresses itself as Trinity.[87] The Father refers to "primordial" Being, which points to the ultimate act of energy, of letting-be. The Son, designated "expressive" Being, is the agent of the Father in creation. The unity of God through the Holy Spirit is called "unitive" Being, who maintains, strengthens, and restores the unity of Being with beings. Second, Schubert Ogden formulates a new conception of theism on the basis of "the reformed subjectivist principle," which requires an experiential basis of all fundamental concepts in the primal phenomenon

---

[85] *Ibid.*, p. 137, note. Therefore, while Pannenberg eschews the categories of the supranatural (above history) and the metahistorical (other than history) to describe Jesus' resurrection, he does mean something more than historical event. Perhaps it would be appropriate to categorize Pannenberg's interpretation as "trans-historical" —historical because it really occurred as an event *within* history, trans-historical because it finally lies *beyond* the specificity of history (though it remains a historical event). Thus Jesus' resurrection is subject to but not *comprehended* by historical research.

[86] "Theology and the Kingdom of God," *TaKoG*, p. 54.

[87] Macquarrie, *Principles of Christian Theology*, pp. 180–185.

of existence as an experiencing self.[88] By utilizing this particular "analogy of being," Ogden conceives God "as a genuinely temporal and social reality," a living and growing God who is related to the universe somewhat like the human self is related to the body. Third, Wolfhart Pannenberg poses the conception of God as the power of the future. When God is conceived as the absolute future, he does not destroy the freedom of man nor the openness of history; on the contrary, he is the source of freedom's fulfillment and the End who brings history to perfection. Yet it is not easy to think of God as futurity, for that makes the future prior to the past and the present.[89] Instead of time flowing from the past toward the future, time flows from the future through the present and into the past; correspondingly, creation does not occur from the beginning as such, but from the End. Hence, Pannenberg's eschatological model for God is radical and novel, but, he contends, it roots in revelation instead of anthropological or philosophical projection: While the future is a fundamental aspect of man's subjective awareness, Pannenberg attributes ontological priority to futurity *on the basis* of Jesus' proclamation of the imminence of God's Kingdom and its unique prolepsis in Jesus' own resurrection.

The Priority of the Eschatological Future

One of the central features of Pannenberg's attempt to reformulate the Christian understanding of God is his overt rejection of traditional theism. Pannenberg, much like Tillich, understands theism as the affirmation of a supreme Being alongside all other beings. Such a God precludes the freedom of man and often appears unwilling to eliminate the pain and suffering in the world. Pannenberg, however, says that God in some sense does not yet exist; instead, God is the power of the future, the God of the coming Kingdom. Yet Philip Hefner looks to the reverse side of Pannenberg's conception, reasoning: "[The future] is, *in a sense,* really 'out there,' and its presence is indicated by

---

[88] Schubert Ogden, *The Reality of God, and Other Essays* (Harper & Row, Publishers, Inc., 1966), pp. 57–60.

[89] However, futurity is not simply set over against the past and the present, but *futurity* embraces past, present, and future. Recently Pannenberg has responded to the charge that the priority of the eschatological future minimizes the importance of the present: "I would say that all my discussion of past and future is meant to rehumanize the present. . . . The depths of the present are opened up only in view of future possibilities, that is, through an awareness of the novelty that the future may bring. . . . There is a pressure of the future on the present" ("A Theological Conversation with Wolfhart Pannenberg," p. 288).

correlating it to some very concrete empirical manifestations in the world." [90]

The eschatological model for God which Pannenberg champions has emerged only recently as a viable option in Christian theology; consequently, evaluations and judgments concerning its adequacy are quite tentative. However, the model of futurity already offers compelling reasons for its consideration. First, against the theology of Being, the conception of God as the power of future—as the God of the coming Kingdom—claims the historical dynamic of Hebraic thought as the overarching framework of conceptuality. Though the Greek conception of "that-which-is is," even dynamic "is-ness," is not discarded (but affirmed), Hebraic conceptuality and the historical revelation of God retain priority over Greek conceptuality and its philosophical conception of God. Second, against process theology, Pannenberg's eschatological model consciously avoids an analogy of being between God and man (or the world), emphasizing instead the mystery of the infinite God of Christian revelation. Indeed, anthropomorphic characterizations of God are recognized and acquire validity within the context of revelation; nevertheless, the difference between God and the world, the infinite and the finite, is tenaciously preserved.[91] Finally, the eschatological conception of God which Pannenberg espouses does not exclude a teleological *dimension* from its interpretation of the world process.[92] Affirming a "retroactive

[90] Philip Hefner, "Questions for Moltmann and Pannenberg," *Una Sancta,* Vol. XXV, No. 3 (1968), p. 38. Italics added.

[91] Cf. "A Theological Conversation with Wolfhart Pannenberg," p. 294. Pannenberg questions whether Whitehead's doctrine of God is actually compatible with the Biblical affirmation of God as the infinite, all-determining reality, whether Whitehead "has really spoken of God at all." God must not be conceived like finite creatures but as infinite. Pannenberg continues: "In some way, according to our experience, the reality of God is still in process for every finite point of view. This does not mean that it is in the same way a process on its own terms." However, as frequently noted, anthropology is of crucial significance in Pannenberg's understanding of revelation and God. Responding to Wilhelm Weischedel's discussion of the problem of God, Pannenberg acknowledges the role of one's life experience in the affirmation of God's reality: "You are absolutely right that my argument [in "The Question of God"] depends upon the meaningfulness of human existence, which is accepted as self-evident." (Pannenberg, letter of clarification, in *Philosophische Theologie im Schatten des Nihilismus,* ed. by Jörg Salaquarda [Berlin: Walter de Gruyter & Co., 1971], p. 177).

[92] Cf. Sigurd Martin Daecke, *Teilhard de Chardin und die evangelische Theologie* (Göttingen: Vandenhoeck & Ruprecht, 1967), pp. 166–179. Though Daecke is not so positive as I am at this point, he insists that Pannenberg is the closest German Protestant theologian to the thought of Teilhard de Chardin (p. 166). However, note Daecke's reservation, *ibid.,* pp. 390 ff., esp. p. 392.

continuity" of history and nature, Pannenberg correlates the categories of eschatology and teleology (though eschatology remains definitive).

Aware of Pannenberg's concern for the whole of history, Robert Jenson questions whether Pannenberg anticipates an end event which terminates history or whether the process of new interpretations of the whole of history will continue indefinitely. Jenson considers either conception of *completed* history a fundamental problem for an eschatological theology: "But if God is God in that history stops and becomes a completed entity, this God is the God of *past* history after all; and what we are bidden to await is the transformation of the God who is the power of the future into the God who *was* the power of the future." [93] Though such a conclusion is not necessary to Pannenberg's theological program, Jenson asks how the anticipated end will not preclude the continuing openness of reality.

Pannenberg believes Jenson's criticism important and valid, "because an eschatological theology that would envision the end just as a stop of the process would have extreme difficulties in understanding that end as eternal life rather than eternal death." [94] On the one side, Pannenberg indicates that Christian eschatology specifies the conditions for the fulfillment of human destiny but not what events will actually effect the essential future of man; consequently, the ongoing process of events will not necessarily stop at a given point, the end. On the other side, Pannenberg suggests the possibility of a contortion of time, wherein eschatological statements about the end would not exclude an entirely different process beyond an end event.

> In some ways, of course, we have indications in the biblical writings, of a process which would be different from the one we experience—a "process of glorification," as it is expressed in several instances—which would proceed from "glory to glory." But this would be different in some way from the forces of time which we experience at present. It would rather be a process into the depths of our present lives concerning the direction of the relation to God, participation in God's glory.[95]

Though not unappreciative of Pannenberg's theologizing, Daniel Day Williams has directed several criticisms against his eschatological

---

[93] Robert W. Jenson, *God After God: The God of the Past and of the Future as Seen in the Work of Karl Barth* (The Bobbs Merrill Company, 1969), p. 178.
[94] "A Theological Conversation with Wolfhart Pannenberg," p. 288.
[95] *Ibid.*, pp. 287–288.

theology. First, he accuses Pannenberg of positing "an absolutely universal consummation which is the essence of every event, no matter what relation to good and evil it may sustain." [96] However, as noted earlier, if Pannenberg has not eliminated the qualifiers in his vision of the future, the unity of mankind presupposed in the resurrection of the dead includes the risk of lostness and does not require an unqualified universalism. In addition, Williams charges that Pannenberg is a Neo-Platonist who demands that the essence of things be identical with the transcendent One, that the temporal process contributes nothing to Ultimate Reality.[97] Yet Pannenberg's conception of eschatological identity between existence and essence does not preclude community. Consequently, defending himself against Williams' charge of Neo-Platonism, Pannenberg maintains that all will not finally be absorbed into the One, but that a plurality of essences will indeed remain.[98]

Furthermore, reviewing Pannenberg's *What Is Man?* (first German ed., 1962), Williams judges Pannenberg's conception of temporal openness to the future and an eternal present contradictory. He describes the "concurrence of all events in an eternal present" as "sheer incoherence for a doctrine of God." [99] Pannenberg acknowledges that he did not conceptualize the grounding of eternity in the future of God until his essay "The God of Hope" (1964), so Williams' criticism is somewhat understandable. However, Williams does neglect in Pannenberg's earlier formulation the affirmation of the irreversibility of the flow of time as well as the conception of eternity as the unity instead of the opposite of time. "Nevertheless," Pannenberg writes, "I would not speak today as I did then of a standpoint outside the flow of time but rather of the absolute future of God." [100] Precisely because Pannenberg attempts to reformulate the concepts of time and eternity eschatologically, the conception of the contemporaneity of all time in the final future of God must not be judged by traditional concepts of time and eternity.

[96] Daniel Day Williams, "Response to Wolfhart Pannenberg," in *Hope and the Future of Man*, ed. by Ewert H. Cousins (Fortress Press, 1972), p. 87.
[97] *Ibid.*, p. 88.
[98] So reports Ewert H. Cousins, "Introduction," in Cousins, ed., *Hope and Future of Man*, p. xi.
[99] Daniel Day Williams, "Review: *What Is Man?*" *Theology Today*, Vol. XXVIII (1971), p. 108. Similarly, Norbert J. Rigali, "Anthropology from Above," *Interpretation*, Vol. XXV (1971), pp. 504–505.
[100] Wolfhart Pannenberg, July 26, 1971: personal communication.

X

AN APPRAISAL OF PANNENBERG'S
THEOLOGICAL PERSPECTIVE

THE ENDEAVOR to survey the several theoretical dimensions of Pannenberg's theology provides the basis for a "wholistic" appraisal of his theological program and thus of the perspective that defines it. Philip Hefner has aptly characterized Pannenberg's approach to theology: "The intellectual task that Pannenberg seems to have set for himself is a monumental one, namely, to construct a fundamental system of thought in which the ontological principle is futurity." [1]

Wolfhart Pannenberg is preeminently an "eschatological theologian." He maintains nonetheless an open theological stance within the contemporary Christian church. Thus Pannenberg articulates a theological perspective that comprehends the rich heritage of the Christian tradition on the one side yet redefines it through the critical spirit of the Enlightenment on the other. While appreciative of the classical concerns of the church's tradition, Pannenberg assumes a modern critical stance in relation to the traditions of the past and tenaciously affirms the horizon of the open future. Perhaps the following appraisal of Pannenberg's theological program and the perspective that shapes it will elucidate the neoclassical and the post-Enlightenment dimensions of his theology. The appraisal focuses upon the advantages that Pannenberg's theological program convincingly establishes and the problems that demand additional clarification or concrete solution.

[1] Philip Hefner, "Questions for Moltmann and Pannenberg," *Una Sancta*, Vol. XXV, No. 3 (1968), p. 43.

POSITIVE ACHIEVEMENTS

An appraisal of Pannenberg's theological program must begin with his approach to the contemporary theological enterprise—an approach that reflects a brilliant, comprehensive grasp of the issues which confront theology and the church today. Pannenberg's most tangible methodological achievements reflect *the synthesis of classical theological concerns with a modern critical posture.* (1) Unlike neo-Reformation theology, which appeals to the "authority" of the Word of God, Pannenberg's theology is stamped by the non-authoritarian climate of the Enlightenment—an atmosphere of reasonableness and freedom. Pannenberg's post-Enlightenment posture compels him to oppose authoritarianism in every form, especially the authoritarianism of the "self-authenticating" Word as well as the authoritarianism that masquerades under the guise of the "Spirit." (2) Pannenberg's theology disavows the isolation of systematic theology from the critical conclusions of Biblical and historical studies or from the contemporary insights of philosophical and nontheological thought. Since the task of theology is to speak responsibly of God to critical understanding, he recognizes that theology must represent the integration of the insights of the theological and nontheological disciplines. (3) Pannenberg espouses the logical priority of theology to ethics without asserting the primacy of theology over ethics, that is, of thinking over doing.

(4) Instead of securing faith in the fortress of subjectivity, Pannenberg restores the crucial significance of history for the integrity of Christian faith and the definition of the church's theology. Over against positivism, existentialism, and supranaturalism, he affirms the genuine historicality of the Christian religion and projects its historical claims into open, public debate. (5) Pannenberg thrusts apocalypticism and eschatology into the center of contemporary theological discussion. Accordingly, he poses a comprehensive conception of reality as history moving toward the goal of eschatological fulfillment (universal history) and interprets the significance of Jesus' activity and destiny on the horizon of Jewish apocalyptic. (6) Pannenberg reflects an enormous appreciation for the Biblical traditions, but eschews every form of Biblicism: He demonstrates that the integrity of the Biblical witness does not hinge upon the "doctrine of inspiration," but upon the historicality of the acts of God which the traditions report. (7) Unlike

Cullmann and Barth, Pannenberg is openly committed to rigorous historical-critical research and to its consequences for the integrity of Christian faith. Acknowledging the legitimacy and the importance of tendency criticism, Pannenberg displays no conservative timidity in analyzing and evaluating the Biblical traditions, especially the Gospel traditions.

(8) Demonstrating the historicality of faith and reason (through precise conceptualization uncommon to recent theology), Pannenberg rejects an antithetical relationship between them but does not collapse their distinctiveness. Furthermore, he construes reason as imaginative and critical, which effectively transcends any restrictive form of rationalism and every untested claim of intuition. (9) Instead of obscuring the issues, Pannenberg frequently drafts pregnant, penetrating theses that clearly define his understanding of theological issues—a procedure typical of his openness to truth as well as to the perspective on truth espoused by others. Indeed, Pannenberg considers such constructive sketching of hypotheses fundamental to systematic theology; however, while some sketches are more convincing than others, he contends that none correspond to the finality of the truth of God.

Pannenberg self-consciously constructs *a theology of revelation,* for he recognizes that the question of God thrusts the issue of revelation to the forefront of theological discussion. (1) Instead of the direct revelation of God within history, i.e., through the revelatory word, Pannenberg postulates the indirect revelation of God through the whole of history—an eschatological conception of historical revelation corresponding to the universality of the Biblical God. (2) Pannenberg defines self-revelation as the final disclosure of God's essence—a disclosure that includes by definition the demonstration of the deity of God as the all-determining reality. Thus, the question of God's identity proves inseparable from the question of his reality (his power). (3) Pannenberg's solution to the crisis of religions and revelation preserves the authenticity of numerous divine manifestations and the uniqueness of God's singular self-revelation. As manifestations of God to different men at different times in different ways, the theophanies that undergird the religions of man (insofar as they are consistent with the one revelation of God to man) communicate partial but redemptive knowledge of God. Conversely, as the proclaimer and the prolepsis of the *eschaton* itself, Jesus the Christ constitutes the final revelation of God: The God of the coming Kingdom is the creative power of love who has power over everything.

(4) Against the subjectivity of existentialism and the supranaturalism of salvation history, Pannenberg affirms the objectivity and universality of historical revelation, which confronts and illuminates human understanding. (5) Pannenberg redefines the historical-critical method in openness to the question of God without introducing supernatural hypotheses; that is, he affirms the principle of universal correlation but disavows the dogmatic tutelage of known analogies. Hence, he eschews the supranaturalism of salvation history on the one side and the agnosticism of a doctrinaire historiography on the other. (6) Pannenberg recognizes the importance of hermeneutic for modern theology and specifies two foci to the hermeneutical problem: (a) the gulf between the interpreter and the text, and (b) the gap between the text and that which it attests. Since the hermeneutical problem converges with the problem of history, he shows that universal history is the necessary solution. (7) Unlike Hegel, Pannenberg preserves the eschatological horizon in his conception of universal history, affirming: The End has dawned in the history of Jesus, but the meaning of its mode of appearance, Jesus' resurrection, remains beyond and resists human comprehension.

(8) Pannenberg poses a conception of universal history that accentuates the provisionality of knowledge and reality on the one side but the prolepsis of ultimate reality and its perception on the other.[2] Hence, he acknowledges the relativity of the historical, but he also affirms the anticipatory appearance of final reality within history. (9) Against Immanuel Kant (philosophically) and Martin Kähler (theologically), Pannenberg affirms the intrinsic unity of event and interpretation, fact and meaning; furthermore, such dynamic unity discloses the ongoing significance of an event along the expanding horizon of universal history. (10) Pannenberg's conception of "the history of the transmission of traditions" comprehends the origin, the transmission, and the criticism of tradition; therefore, he defines history with a clear consciousness of the importance of the past, the difficulty in reconstructing the occurrences of the past, and the necessity to criticize the forms of traditions which purport to tell the story of the past. (11) Grounding faith in the actuality of revelatory history, Pannenberg reasserts the logical priority of knowledge (faith's ground) to faith

---

[2] Pannenberg, "Nachwort zur zweiten Auflage," *OaG*, p. 139, affirms the validity of his conception of universal history but acknowledges its historical-conditionedness, which indicates "the provisionality of all sketches, their distance from the finality of the eschaton."

(understood as trust). He candidly acknowledges that the public assessment of the knowledge of revelation can be an obstacle to faith and threaten the believer with the loss of faith's foundation.

Affirming the centrality of the Christ event for Christian faith—an event that embraces the particularity and the universality of Jesus' history—Pannenberg presents *an incisive analysis and assessment of the entire Christological tradition.* Several insights are especially significant: (1) In order to ground the church's confession in Jesus as the Christ of God, Pannenberg posits the necessity of a Christology "from below," which eventuates from the actuality of the history of Jesus. Similarly, he insists that Christology logically precedes and establishes soteriology (though soteriology constitutes the motivation for interest in Christology itself). (2) Since Jesus' proclamation included the announcement of the presence of the Kingdom of God and also the imminent future of God's reign, Pannenberg does not reject the authenticity of either the presence or the future of God's Kingdom; however, he coordinates present and future through Jesus' eschatological proclamation wherein the future becomes present—a coordination that reveals the priority of the future. (3) Unlike many theologians of salvation history, Pannenberg does not harmonize the mission of Jesus to announce the imminence of God's Kingdom with the execution of Jesus as traitor and blasphemer; instead, he candidly acknowledges the eschatological unification of the elements of Jesus' history in the resurrection—which retroactively establishes the unity of Jesus' earthly pilgrimage.

(4) While affirming the universality of Jesus the Christ, Pannenberg accepts the historical conditionedness of Jesus' activity and refuses to absolutize the historical particularity of Jesus' pre-Easter path for the whole of humanity. Thus he affirms the unrepeatability of Jesus' history and frees the church to interpret the relationship of the Kingdom of God to the world in the light of Jesus' humanity and eschatological destiny. (5) Pannenberg reasserts the centrality of the resurrection of Jesus of Nazareth for the whole of Christian faith. However, he neither isolates Jesus' resurrection from the crucifixion nor from the announcement of God's coming reign; instead, the resurrection and subsequently the crucifixion are interpreted in the light of Jesus' gracious proclamation of the imminent Kingdom of God. (6) Interpreting the significance of Jesus' crucifixion as representation, Pannenberg sketches a conception of reconciliation that maintains objective and subjective elements. Thus, when understood in the light

of Jesus' resurrection, the cross is simultaneously the revelation of God's redemptive love and the solution to man's experience of Godforsakenness. (7) Pannenberg perceives that the assertion of the actuality of Jesus' resurrection contains a historical claim, whether such a claim is intended or not; consequently, he does not opt for the neutrality of historical research but for the ability of historical investigation to render a tentative judgment for the probability of Jesus' resurrection.

(8) Without *presupposing* the reality of the incarnation, Pannenberg projects a creative understanding of the uniqueness of Jesus Christ that does not disparage the Christological tradition of the Bible and the church. Moving from Jesus' activity and destiny to the affirmation of his deity and Sonship, Pannenberg maintains the unity of history and eschatology, or, in Christological categories, of "adoption" and "incarnation." (9) Suggesting an eschatological Christology "from before," Pannenberg grounds the incarnation in the prolepsis of the *eschaton* in the activity and destiny of Jesus. (10) Pannenberg poses an innovative conception of Jesus' revelatory unity with God as unity of essence, but he avoids presupposing the principle of incarnation and its corollary of descent-ascent. Hence, Pannenberg establishes Jesus' identity as the Son in his relational unity with God as Father (instead of a direct relation to the Logos). The revelatory unity of Jesus with God, therefore, coheres with the indirect identity of Jesus as the Son. (11) Pannenberg affirms the deity of Jesus but does not damage the authenticity of his humanity. While maintaining the sinlessness and freedom of Jesus, he does not reflect the docetic or Nestorian tendencies of traditional "orthodox" Christologies oriented to the history of Jesus.

As the first contemporary exponent of an eschatological conception of God, Pannenberg presents with increasing clarity *a cogent and coherent vision of the Biblical God as "the power of the future."* Several features of his developing conception of God are noteworthy: (1) On the basis of Jesus' proclamation of the coming Kingdom of God, Pannenberg affirms the ontological priority of the future and thus the futurity of God; however, he does not disparage the past or the present but perceives God's presence in the whole of creation through the animation of the Spirit and the unique arrival of the futurity of God in the Christ event. Thus futurity is not just set over against the past and present, but embraces past, present, and future. (2) Analyzing the structures of human existence, Pannenberg interprets man's "openness to the world" as the question of God. Consequently, while rejecting the theory of a religious *a priori*, he correlates the questionableness of human existence with the revelatory answer of God. (3) Pannenberg acknowledges the ability of atheism to assist Christian theology in the formulation of the question of God. Though the precise formulation of the question emerges from the revelatory answer, the challenge of atheism frees Christian theology to see the revelatory answer anew apart from the limitations of the historical forms of Christian theology.

(4) While affirming the necessity for an analogy of language in speaking of the Biblical God, Pannenberg rejects any form of an analogy of being; consequently, he preserves the mystery or incomprehensibleness of God to man. However, he anchors speech about God in divine revelation, which legitimates the anthropomorphic character inherent in all human God-talk. Pannenberg's doxological conception of theological language actually moves the debate of God-talk beyond theism as such to the revelatory action of the Biblical God. (5) Pannenberg rejects an antithetical interpretation of the relationship of Greek and Hebraic thought; however, he maintains the priority of the dynamic of Hebraic conceptual thought in the correlation of these modes of thinking. (6) Pannenberg acknowledges the radical freedom of God over against the world, without, however, isolating the being of God from the occurrences in the world. Thus he does not speak of God's unchangeability but of divine faithfulness; correspondingly, he does not consider eternity beyond the dynamics of historical time. (7) So long as Christian theology speaks of the Biblical God whom Jesus proclaimed as "coming," Pannenberg concedes that the reality of God will remain debatable. Yet the prolepsis of the *eschaton* in the resurrection of Jesus from the dead remains the single most important element in determining *if* and *who* God really is. Though the question of God is not reduced to the revelation in Christ, God's eschatological self-revelation in the confirmation and exaltation of Jesus remains definitive for God's identity and decisive for God's reality.

(8) Pannenberg coordinates the unity of futurity, contingency, and love in God's creative activity with a depth that surpasses all other attempts to attain such theological wholeness. (9) Though the affirmation of the ontological priority of the future issues from the proclamation and destiny of Jesus, Pannenberg demonstrates that an eschatological ontology is compatible with the scientific picture of the world and the theological conception of creation. Instead of implying an absurd reversal of causality, eschatological creation attains cogency through

the appearance of contingent newness on the one side and "retroactive continuity" on the other. (10) Whereas Moltmann accentuates the radical discontinuity of the future with present and past, Pannenberg affirms that historical time not only flows from the future into the present toward the past, but also tends (subsequently) toward the future through recurring patterns and heightened integration. Hence, Pannenberg's eschatological theology remains distinctive from but compatible with the insights of teleological and process thought. (11) Pannenberg relates revelation and God to wholeness and unity, which points beyond every provisional form of life in the world to eschatological life in God. Hence, he proposes a *promissory* conception of *panentheism* which roots in the creative, integrative love of God. (12) Not only does Pannenberg's conception of the eschatological destiny of man reflect anthropological realism, it also coheres with the affirmation of the futurity of God. The hope for resurrection neither minimizes nor finalizes the seriousness of death; moreover, it thrusts the entirety of human hope for eternal life upon the termination of history and the transformation of the whole of reality through the creative power of God.

POINTS REQUIRING CLARIFICATION

While Pannenberg has achieved a strikingly new theological thrust which reflects careful and thoughtful work, several features of his theological program require additional clarification and/or substantiation. Such a situation is not uncommon in a developing theological program.

First, Pannenberg needs to present a systematic, critical evaluation of the role of apocalyptic in his theology. Since apocalyptic is of central importance to his entire program, a responsible assessment of his theology requires a better understanding of his (critical) appropriation and modification of fundamental issues that characterize the debate over apocalypticism. (1) Though not unaware of the apocalyptic tendency toward historical determinism[3] and the accent upon eschatology instead of history, Pannenberg has yet to explain the precise rationale for and the modification in apocalypticism that he discerns in the Christ event and to explain how such modification preserves the con-

---

[3] Cf. Pannenberg, "Kontingenz und Naturgesetz," *Erwägungen zu einer Theologie der Natur* (Gütersloh: Gütersloher Verlagshaus Gerd Mohn, 1970), p. 43.

tingency of history and coheres with the affirmation of the incarnation of the *eschaton* within history. (2) The question of apocalyptic influences upon Jesus' understanding of the Kingdom of God requires additional substantiation, particularly in view of the prominence of the so-called "prophetic" conception of the Kingdom which Norman Perrin describes and which salvation history generally shares.[4] The fundamental issue is the correctness of the correlation of cosmic hope and future expectation in Jesus' conception of the Kingdom of God. (3) Finally, the relationship of the Kingdom of God to the expectation of a future resurrection needs to be established more convincingly —an issue of special importance in view of Pannenberg's interpretation of Jesus' resurrection as the confirmation of his pre-Easter claim[5] (which came to expression through the announcement of the nearness of God's Kingdom).

Second, the universality and objectivity of revelation to human understanding, which Pannenberg initially articulated in *Revelation as History* (Thesis 3), needs to be reexamined and clarified. Pannenberg has progressively explained (or qualified) his original intention: The events of revelation are Spirit-filled; the objectivity of revelation does not constitute a claim to the rational knowledge of everything; the facticity of revelatory events is not beyond legitimate, intelligent debate. However, a fundamental ambiguity exists regarding the primary locus of the claim of revelation's objectivity and universality; hence the question: Does such objectivity depend essentially upon the historical-critical verification of the events which the Biblical traditions report (especially Jesus' resurrection), or primarily upon the coherence for understanding the whole of reality which the universal-historical scheme (based upon the report of Jesus' resurrection) positively provides? If the case for the resurrection and thereby for revelation hinges more upon the coherence and comprehensiveness of the scheme of universal history than upon the direct results of historical research confirming that conception, the interpretation of the objectivity and universality of revelation would be qualified considerably.

---

[4] Cf. Norman Perrin, *The Kingdom of God in the Teaching of Jesus* (The Westminster Press, 1963), pp. 160–185, esp. pp. 177–178. Perrin argues that Jesus rejected the apocalyptic understanding of history and returned to the prophetic, emphasizing thereby God's kingly rule breaking into history rather than the End of history itself.

[5] Cf. Koch, *The Rediscovery of Apocalyptic*, p. 151, n. 19. Also, C. F. Evans, *Resurrection and the New Testament*, Studies in Biblical Theology, 2d ser., No. 12, pp. 11–40 and pp. 177 ff., esp. p. 180.

Third, Pannenberg's predominant emphasis on historical verification and its concomitant of eschatological verification tends to eclipse the role he allows for the existential dimension of the verification of the truth of Christian faith. On the one hand Pannenberg refuses to grant the immediacy of religious experience an autonomous, self-authenticating status ("Immediate religious experience cannot *by itself alone* establish the certainty of the truth of its content" [6]). On the other hand there is considerable ambiguity concerning the significance he grants personal religious experience as corroboration of (not a substitute for) historical confirmation of the events of revelation. What value, if any, does religious experience have for establishing the truth of the claims of faith?

Fourth, several aspects of Pannenberg's eschatological conception of God provoke intriguing questions: Is an eschatological ontology really a viable option? Does the priority of eschatology preclude the determinism of predestination? Can Jesus be described as the "eternal" Son of God? What is the relationship of the prolepsis of God in the Christ event to the fullness of God's being in the *eschaton?* What does the bodily resurrection of Jesus and subsequent "disappearance" into God's futurity imply about the "existence" of the eschatological future of God? These several questions converge in a fundamental issue which Pannenberg considers quite significant, namely, the relationship of historical time to the eternity of God. Pannenberg's conception of eternity as "the concurrence of all events in a single present" is attractive, but its embryonic development denies it convincing power.

PROBLEM AREAS

Beyond these problematic issues, there are several areas of Pannenberg's program which, because of inattention or inadequacy, represent basic problems for his overall theological perspective. Though these problems may not be judged fatal flaws, they must not be minimized nor their solution evaded.

First, a fundamental problem appears in Pannenberg's theology concerning the relation of the cross to the Kingdom of God. Though the interpretation of Jesus' resurrection as the surprising fulfillment of his eschatological expectation and the interpretation of the significance

---

[6] "Response to the Discussion," *TaH*, p. 239.

of the cross in the light of the resurrection command historical and theological cogency, the interpretation of the crucifixion as a consequence of Jesus' mission, while attaining descriptive historical value, fails to clarify the material relationship of the cross to God's coming Kingdom. If the relationship of the cross to the Kingdom were clarified, perhaps the interpretative significance of the cross for the resurrection itself would emerge—without making the cross the central interpretative category for Jesus' mission on the one side or for the resurrection on the other.[7] To be sure, Pannenberg's interpretation of the cross is of considerable soteriological significance; however, the theological rationale for the "must" of the cross between Jesus' proclamation of the Kingdom and its anticipatory arrival in the resurrection is lacking. Why did God allow Jesus to endure the Godforsakenness of the cross prior to the eschatological fulfillment of Jesus' expectation of God's coming Kingdom? Was the cross prerequisite to the eschatological appearance of God's Kingdom? Pannenberg fails to answer these crucial questions.

Second, though Pannenberg acknowledges the radicality of evil and suffering in the world, the problem of theodicy remains a peripheral issue in his theological program. Pannenberg's arguments against the atheism of freedom and the reduction of God to an illusory projection of man are forceful and penetrating, while his examination of the moral argument against the existence of God is at best sketchy. But is not the moral argument against the existence of God at least as crucial as the atheism of freedom in the contemporary debate about God? If the Anglo-Saxon debate about God accurately portrays the central issues in the problem of God for the English-speaking world, the atheism of freedom is not any more significant than the theodicy problem (which reinforces the suggestion that God is an illusion of man). Since Pannenberg describes the God of the coming Kingdom as the creative power of love, the problem of theodicy acquires even greater urgency: Why does the God who comes yet linger in his eschatological glory, *waiting* to heal the brokenness and pain of mankind? Though Christian theology cannot offer a conclusive answer to

---

[7] Cf. Walter Kreck, "The Word of the Cross," *Interpretation*, Vol. XXIV (1970), pp. 220–242, esp. pp. 223–227. However, unlike Kreck, I do not reject Pannenberg's Christology as one "in which the cross as saving event seems to play no decisive role" (p. 227). Nor do I agree that Pannenberg's emphasis upon the historicality of Jesus' resurrection precludes combination "with a theology of the cross as presented by Paul" (p. 225). The "scandal" of the cross cannot be isolated from the resurrection of the Crucified.

such a question, it must take account of it more seriously than Pannenberg has done thus far.

Third, a basic problem emerges from Pannenberg's tendency to interpret history primarily from the standpoint of God. Hence, contrary to Pannenberg's intention, two problematic impulses continually appear. (1) There is the tendency to minimize the role of man as a creative participant in the making of history. (2) Correspondingly, there is the inclination to understate (or ignore) the radicality of the destruction and brokenness within history as expressions of the sinfulness of man. Thus Pannenberg's theology all too frequently reflects an unqualified optimism that lends credibility to the charges of Christianized idealism or historical monism. If Pannenberg's theology is to reflect more accurately the perspective of Biblical realism, history must be interpreted candidly from the human perspective of brokenness as well as hopefully from the eschatological perspective of wholeness.

Although these problems are formidable, quite formidable, they are not essentially insurmountable. Pannenberg's theology actually contains impulses toward their solution, but these impulses require substantial elaboration and consistent development. In 1959 Pannenberg noted the centrality of the cross for a Christian eschatological theology, observing: "Also our participation in [Christ's resurrection], the hope of our own resurrection, is still hidden under the experience of the cross. . . . We know that everything earthly must pass through the cross." [8] In addition, as early as 1956, Pannenberg indicated the necessity of a redemptive instead of a rational solution to the problem of theodicy: "The Christian answer to the problem of evil is solely the event of the divine victory over evil through the cross and resurrection of Christ." [9] Furthermore, in 1969 Pannenberg frankly acknowledged the radical power of evil which continually threatens man's life in the world and his experience of God: "A world which is overcrowded with horror and hunger and satiated self-satisfaction, a world which again and again deteriorates into the madness of war and seldom truly seeks justice, a world which instead verbalizes the great slogans of humanity in order to disguise its selfishness and evil —such a world is not the Kingdom of God." [10] Finally, Pannenberg

---

[8] "Redemptive Event and History," *BQiT* I, p. 37.
[9] "Das Böse," *Evangelisches Kirchenlexikon*, ed. by Heinz Brunotte and Otto Weber (Göttingen: Vandenhoeck & Ruprecht, 1956), Vol. I, p. 561.
[10] "Wie kann heute glaubwürdig von Gott geredet werden?" in *Gottesfrage heute*, ed. by Friedebert Lorenz (Stuttgart: Kreuz-Verlag, 1969), p. 63.

has eloquently articulated the responsibility of the church for constructive Christian action in the world as the reconciling people of God:

> The inbreak of the future of God happens with us, in the neighborly relations of our lives, in the struggle for a humane form of society . . . and for the peace of mankind. We ourselves are the present place of the reality of God. . . . The men who are living today and especially the Christians of our time among them are the place of the reality of God. Whether the reality of God is eclipsed or illuminated in the present world depends upon us.[11]

Ultimately, therefore, Pannenberg's innovative theological program represents more than a new and invigorating theological synthesis cast in the form of eschatological theology. Pannenberg presents a contemporary Christian theology significant for the life of the church as it strives to actualize in today's world the future Kingdom of God which appeared proleptically in the eschatological history of Jesus Christ.

[11] *Ibid.*, p. 64.

Postscript
BY WOLFHART PANNENBERG

DR. TUPPER'S BOOK presents the most comprehensive report that has been published so far on my theology. His careful interpretation and balanced discussion of the numerous controversies surrounding it and the clarity of his presentation of the issues at stake will prove helpful, I hope, in urging substantial theological discussion dealing with the epochal problems of theology rather than providing an occasion for empathetic or depreciative evaluation of personalities.

As Dr. Tupper himself emphasizes, his systematic presentation communicates an interim balance of a process of thought that is still in development. I did not start to design a system, although I always thought it a prerequisite of disciplined thinking to care for the systematic implications and consequences of one's observations. I am often surprised and pleased, therefore, to discover the convergence of initially distinct findings. But again and again there has been the experience that the implications of a particular conclusion lead to new problems. Therefore, systematization is but a provisional summary of the special research that has been done and of the problematic itself as it appears at a given point in the process of one's thought. Thus, it might be possible that a final systematization of my ideas could look different from what either Dr. Tupper or myself would expect at present.

The same provisionality in the situation of my thought makes me receptive to Dr. Tupper's concluding enumeration of a number of important questions that I have not yet adequately dealt with. It is correct to say that the role played by sin, evil, suffering, destruction, and brokenness in human history has not received very extensive treatment in my writings. Such a treatment should correspond to the vast importance of these phenomena for human experience in both individual and political life. But I have not yet published a detailed theology of history, which will have to deal to a great extent with the sin of man and with the judgment of God. Nor have I submitted to the public a full-scale anthropology which deals with the peculiarity and radical character of sin and evil in human nature and behavior. However, in my radio lectures on anthropology dating back to 1962 (*What Is Man?*), I identified sin as a basic component in the structure of the human organism and behavior, having the character of self-centeredness which is inescapable though supersedable in human life. I was prepared for somebody to charge me with Flacianism, i.e., for identifying sin with the nature of man, but fortunately nobody seems to have meditated on the consequences of that statement for the evaluation of the empirical situation of man. It could sound more negative than many people would like. Closely connected also is my view that freedom does not belong to the natural (i.e., empirical) status of man, but is to be received again and again as an experience of liberation. And I would not blame people who would attribute my reservations over against the anthropological optimism of a certain brand of political theology precisely to this estimation of the radical character of sin in human nature.

As to the problem of theodicy I do not think it the task of theology to exculpate God theoretically for the evil in the world. In the face of the horrors of evil every theoretical theodicy would function as an ideological device. There can be only one valid answer to the reality of evil: the eschatological reconciliation of God with his world by that glorification of his suffering creatures which alone will finally prove his true divinity.

That I concentrated my attention hitherto on the positive structure of human destiny, history, and salvation is largely due to the fact that the positive nature of things is to be presupposed in order to describe their perversion. And since there is so much uncertainty in our day concerning the positive foundation of the Christian faith, I thought it the main task of theology at present to reestablish confidence in the positive foundations of faith rather than to follow the pessimistic mood in so much of modern culture. But I basically agree that a convincing interpretation of the human situation has to take into account also the negative aspects of human experience and behavior. Otherwise no balanced evaluation of the reality of man would be achieved.

Another important criticism of Dr. Tupper's refers to my interpretation of the cross of Jesus. When a revised version of my Christology (*Jesus—God and Man*) is undertaken, I will supplement the interpretation given in the chapter on the crucifixion by a discussion of the action of God in the cross of Jesus. That seems to be precisely what Dr. Tupper is asking for. Because of my approach from the anthropological-historical perspective ("from below"), I concentrated my attention on the inherent meaning of the events rather than on a divine intention attributed to them, although I did relate the historical events to the activity of God. Only after the Christology was published was I able to clarify certain aspects in the doctrine of God to my own satisfaction so that I could dare now to speak of a divine intention in historical events. As a consequence, in relation to the crucifixion, as in other respects, the self-explication of God in the history of Jesus will get closer attention when I am able someday to revise the text of that book.

There are a number of further points in my writings that are in need of clarification and further development. Dr. Tupper mentions a few of them. They may indicate to the reader that theology is not something like a closed system, but an open and accumulative process of research!

A BIBLIOGRAPHY OF THE WRITINGS OF WOLFHART PANNENBERG

The bibliography includes almost all of Pannenberg's writings through 1972, with the exception of a few articles and most of his book reviews. Each English translation is listed according to the most accessible source, and the subsequent German reference is to the original date and place of publication.

"Abendmahl II. Dogmengeschichtlich-dogmatisch," *Evangelisches Kirchenlexikon,* I, 6–11. Ed. by Heinz Brunotte and Otto Weber. Göttingen: Vandenhoeck & Ruprecht, 1956.

"Akt und Sein im Mittelalter," *Kerygma und Dogma,* VII (1961), 197–220.

"Das Amt in der Kirche," *Una Sancta,* XXV (1970), 106–116.

"Analogie," *Evangelisches Kirchenlexikon,* I, 113–114. Ed. by Heinz Brunotte and Otto Weber. Göttingen: Vandenhoeck & Ruprecht, 1956.

"Analogie," *Die Religion in Geschichte und Gegenwart,* I, 350–353. Dritte Auflage. Ed. by Kurt Galling *et al.* Tübingen: J. C. B. Mohr (Paul Siebeck), 1957.

"Analogie und Offenbarung: Eine kritische Untersuchung der Geschichte des Analogiebegriffs in der Gotteserkenntnis." Unpublished *Habilitationsschrift,* University of Heidelberg, 1955.

"Analogy and Doxology," *Basic Questions in Theology,* Vol. I. Tr. by George H. Kehm. Fortress Press, 1971. Pp. 211–238. A translation of "Analogie und Doxologie," *Dogma und Denkstrukturen: Festschrift für Edmund Schlink.* Ed. by Wilfried Joest and Wolfhart Pannenberg. Göttingen: Vandenhoeck & Ruprecht, 1963. Pp. 96–115.

"Anthropology and the Question of God," *The Idea of God and Human Freedom*. Tr. by R. A. Wilson. The Westminster Press, 1973. Pp. 80–98. A translation of "Anthropologie und Gottesfrage," *Kerk en Theologie*, XXII (1971), 1–14.

The Apostles' Creed: In the Light of Today's Questions. Tr. by Margaret Kohl. The Westminster Press, 1972. A translation of *Das Glaubensbekenntnis, ausgelegt und verantwortet vor der Fragen der Gegenwart*. Hamburg: Siebenstern Taschenbuch Verlag, 1972.

"Apostolizität und Katholizität der Kirche in der Perspektive der Eschatologie," *Theologische Literaturzeitung*, XCIV (1969), 97–112.

"Appearance as the Arrival of the Future," *Theology and the Kingdom of God*. The Westminster Press, 1969. Pp. 102–143. A translation of "Erscheinung als Ankunft des Zukünftigen," *Studia Philosophica* (Basel), XXVI (1966), 192–207.

"The Appropriation of the Philosophical Concept of God as a Dogmatic Problem of Early Christian Theology," *Basic Questions in Theology*, Vol. II. Tr. by George A. Kehm. Fortress Press, 1971. Pp. 119–183. A translation of "Die Aufnahme des philosophischen Gottesbegriffs als dogmatisches Problem der frühchristlichen Theologie," *Zeitschrift für Kirchengeschichte*, LXX (1959), 1–45.

Basic Questions in Theology: Collected Essays. Tr. by George H. Kehm. Fortress Press, Vol. I, 1970; Vol. II, 1971. A translation of *Grundfragen systematischer Theologie: Gesammelte Aufsätze*. Göttingen: Vandenhoeck & Ruprecht, 1967.

"Das Böse," *Evangelisches Kirchenlexikon*, I, 559–561. Ed. by Heinz Brunotte and Otto Weber. Göttingen: Vandenhoeck & Ruprecht, 1956.

"Christianity as the Legitimacy of the Modern Age," *The Idea of God and Human Freedom*. Tr. by R. A. Wilson. The Westminster Press, 1973. Pp. 178–191. A translation of "Die christliche Legitimität der Neuzeit," *Radius*, 1968, No. 3, pp. 40–42.

"Christian Theology and Philosophical Criticism," *The Idea of God and Human Freedom*. Tr. by R. A. Wilson. The Westminster Press, 1973. Pp. 99–115. A translation of "Christliche Theologie und philosophische Kritik," *Revue de Theologie et de Philosophie*, XVIII (1968), 349–371.

"Christlicher Glaube und menschliche Freiheit," *Kerygma und Dogma*, IV (1958), 251–280.

"Christologie II. Dogmengeschichtlich," *Die Religion in Geschichte und Gegenwart,* I, 1762–1777. Dritte Auflage. Ed. by Kurt Galling *et al.* Tübingen: J. C. B. Mohr (Paul Siebeck), 1957.

"The Church and the Eschatological Kingdom," *Spirit, Faith, and Church.* The Westminster Press, 1970. Pp. 108–123.

"The Crisis of the Scripture Principle," *Basic Questions in Theology,* Vol. I. Tr. by George H. Kehm. Fortress Press, 1970. Pp. 1–14. A translation of "Die Krise des Schriftprinzips," *Grundfragen systematischer Theologie.* Göttingen: Vandenhoeck & Ruprecht, 1967. Pp. 11–21. Cf. the earlier essay, "Die Grundlagenkrise der evangelischen Theologie," *Radius,* 1962, No. 4, pp. 7–14.

"Dialektische Theologie," *Die Religion in Geschichte und Gegenwart,* II, 168–174. Dritte Auflage. Ed. by Kurt Galling *et al.* Tübingen: J. C. B. Mohr (Paul Siebeck), 1958.

"Did Jesus Really Rise from the Dead?" *Dialog,* IV (1965), 128–135. A translation of "Ist Jesus wirklich auferstanden?" *Geistliche Woche für Südwest-Deutschland der Evangelischen Akademie Mannheim,* February 16–23, 1964, pp. 22–33.

"The Doctrine of the Spirit and the Task of a Theology of Nature," *Theology,* XXV (1972), 8–21.

"Dogmatische Erwägungen zur Auferstehung Jesu," *Kerygma und Dogma,* XIV (1968), 105–118.

"Dogmatische Thesen zur Lehre von der Offenbarung," *Offenbarung als Geschichte.* Beiheft 1 zu *Kerygma und Dogma.* (Dritte Auflage, 1965). Göttingen: Vandenhoeck & Ruprecht, 1961. Pp. 91–114.

"Duns Scotus, Johannes," *Evangelisches Kirchenlexikon,* I, 980–982. Ed. by Heinz Brunotte and Otto Weber. Göttingen: Vandenhoeck & Ruprecht, 1956.

"Der Einfluss der Anfechtungserfahrung auf den Prädestinationsbegriff Luthers," *Kerygma und Dogma,* III (1957), 109–139.

"Einführung," *Offenbarung als Geschichte.* Beiheft 1 zu *Kerygma und Dogma.* (Dritte Auflage, 1965.) Göttingen: Vandenhoeck & Ruprecht, 1961. Pp. 7–20.

"Erfahrung der Wirklichkeit: Fragen an Carl Friedrich von Weizsäcker," *Evangelische Kommentare,* IV (1971), 468–470.

"Erwählung III. Dogmatisch," *Die Religion in Geschichte und Gegenwart,* II, 614–621. Dritte Auflage. Ed. by Kurt Galling *et al.* Tübingen: J. C. B. Mohr (Paul Siebeck), 1958.

"Er wird unser Gott sein," *Radius,* 1961, No. 4, pp. 3–10.

"Eschatology and the Experience of Meaning," *The Idea of God and*

Human Freedom. Tr. by R. A. Wilson. The Westminster Press, 1973. Pp. 192–210. A translation of "Eschatologie und Sinnerfahrung," *Toekomst van de Religie: Religie van de Toekomst?* Uitgeverij Emmaus (N. V. Desclée de Brouwer), 1972. Pp. 134–148.

"Facts of History and Christian Ethics," *Dialog,* VIII (1969), 287–296. A translation of "Geschichtstatsachen und christliche Ethik," *Evangelische Kommentare,* I (1968), 688–694.

"Faith and Reason," *Basic Questions in Theology,* Vol. II. Tr. by George H. Kehm. Fortress Press, 1971. Pp. 46–64. A translation of "Glaube und Vernunft," *Grundfragen systematischer Theologie.* Göttingen: Vandenhoeck & Ruprecht, 1967. Pp. 237–251.

"Die Fragwürdigkeit der klassischen Universalswissenschaften," *Die Krise des Zeitalters der Wissenschaften.* Frankfurt: Hirschgraben-Verlag, 1963. Pp. 173–188. The original version of "Die Grundlagenkrise der evangelischen Theologie," *Radius,* 1962, No. 4, pp. 7–14.

"Der Friede Gottes und der Weltfriede," *Frieden.* Vorlesungen auf dem 13. Deutschen Evangelischen Kirchentag Hannover 1967. Stuttgart: Kreuz-Verlag, 1967. Pp. 45–62.

"Future and Unity," *Hope and the Future of Man.* Ed. by Ewert H. Cousins. Fortress Press, 1972. Pp. 60–78.

"Glaube IV. Im prot. Glaubensverständnis," *Lexikon für Theologie und Kirche,* IV, 925–928. Zweite Auflage. Ed. by Josef Höfer and Karl Rahner. Freiburg: Verlag Herder, 1960.

"Glaube und Wirklichkeit im Denken Gerhard von Rads," in *Gerhard von Rad: Seine Bedeutung für die Theologie.* Ed. by Hans Walter Wolff. Munich: Chr. Kaiser Verlag, 1973.

"Gnade III. Dogmengeschichtlich IV. Dogmatisch," *Evangelisches Kirchenlexikon,* I, 1607–1614. Ed. by Heinz Brunotte and Otto Weber. Göttingen: Vandenhoeck & Ruprecht, 1956.

"Gnadenmittel," *Evangelisches Kirchenlexikon,* I, 1615–1617. Ed. by Heinz Brunotte and Otto Weber. Göttingen: Vandenhoeck & Ruprecht, 1956.

"The God of Hope," *Basic Questions in Theology,* Vol. II. Tr. by George H. Kehm. Fortress Press, 1971. Pp. 234–249. A translation of "Der Gott der Hoffnung," *Ernst Bloch zu ehren.* Ed. by Siegfried Unseld. Frankfurt: Suhrkamp Verlag, 1965. Pp. 209–225.

"Die Gottesidee des hohen Mittelalters," *Der Gottesgedanke im Abendland.* Ed. by Albert Schaefer. Urban-Bücher, 79. Stuttgart: W. Kohlhammer Verlag, 1964. Pp. 21–34.

"Gott V. Theologiegeschichtlich," *Die Religion in Geschichte und*

Gegenwart, II, 1717–1732. Dritte Auflage. Ed. by Kurt Galling *et al.* Tübingen: J. C. B. Mohr (Paul Siebeck), 1958.

"Hermeneutic and Universal History," *Basic Questions in Theology,* Vol. I. Tr. by Paul J. Achtemeier and George H. Kehm. Fortress Press, 1970. Pp. 96–136. A translation of "Hermeneutik und Universalgeschichte," *Zeitschrift für Theologie und Kirche,* LX (1963), 90–121.

"I Believe in God the Father Almighty," *A New Look at the Apostles' Creed.* Ed. by Gerhard Rein. Tr. by David LeFort. Augsburg Publishing House, 1969. Pp. 14–19. A translation of "Ich glaube an Gott, den allmächtigen Vater," *Das Glaugensbekenntnis: Aspekte für ein neues Verständnis.* Stuttgart: Kreuz-Verlag, 1967. Pp. 11–15.

The Idea of God and Human Freedom. Tr. by R. A. Wilson. The Westminster Press, 1973. A translation of several works: "Späthorizonte des Mythos in biblischer und christlicher Überlieferung," *Terror und Spiel: Probleme der Mythenrezeption.* Munich: Wilhelm Fink Verlag, 1971. Pp. 473–525. In addition: *Gottesgedanke und menschliche Freiheit.* Göttingen: Vandenhoeck & Ruprecht, 1972. And finally: "Eschatologie und Sinnerfahrung," *Toekomst van de Religie: Religie van de Toekomst?* Uitgeverij Emmaus (N. V. Desclée de Brouwer), 1972. Pp. 134–148.

"Insight and Faith," *Basic Questions in Theology,* Vol. II. Tr. by George H. Kehm. Fortress Press, 1971. Pp. 28–45. A translation of "Einsicht und Glaube. Antwort an Paul Althaus," *Theologische Literaturzeitung,* LXXXVIII (1963), 81–92.

"Jesus Christus III C. Die protestantische Christologie," *Lexikon für Theologie und Kirche,* V, 961–964. Zweite Auflage. Ed. by Josef Höfer and Karl Rahner. Freiburg: Verlag Herder, 1960.

"Jesus Geschichte und unsere Geschichte," *Radius,* 1960, No. 1, pp. 18–27.

Jesus—God and Man. Tr. by Lewis L. Wilkins and Duane A. Priebe. The Westminster Press, 1968. A translation of *Grundzüge der Christologie.* Gütersloh: Gütersloher Verlagshaus Gerd Mohn, 1964.

"Kerygma and History," *Basic Questions in Theology,* Vol. I. Tr. by George H. Kehm. Fortress Press, 1970. Pp. 81–95. A translation of "Kerygma und Geschichte," *Studien zur Theologie der alttestamentlichen Überlieferungen: Festschrift für Gerhard von Rad.* Ed. by Rolf Rendtorff and Klaus Koch. Neukirchen: Neukirchener Verlag, 1961. Pp. 129–140.

"The Kingdom of God and the Church," *Theology and the Kingdom of God.* The Westminster Press, 1969. Pp. 72–101. A reprint from *Una Sancta,* Vol. XXIV, No. 4 (1967), pp. 3–27.

"The Kingdom of God and the Foundation of Ethics," *Theology and the Kingdom of God.* The Westminster Press, 1969. Pp. 102–126. A reprint from *Una Sancta,* Vol. XXV, No. 2 (1968), pp. 6–26.

"Kontingenz und Naturgesetz," *Erwägungen zu einer Theologie der Natur.* Gütersloh: Gütersloher Verlagshaus Gerd Mohn, 1970. Pp. 33–80.

"Die Krise des Ethischen und die Theologie," *Theologische Literaturzeitung,* LXXXVII (1962), 7–16.

"The Later Dimensions of Myth in Biblical and Christian Tradition," *The Idea of God and Human Freedom.* Tr. by R. A. Wilson. The Westminster Press, 1973. Pp. 1–79. A translation of "Späthorizonte des Mythos in biblischer und christlicher Überlieferung," *Terror und Spiel: Probleme der Mythenrezeption.* Ed. by Manfred Fuhrmann. Munich: Wilhelm Fink Verlag, 1971. Pp. 473–525.

Letter of Clarification to Wilhelm Weischedel in *Philosophische Theologie im Schatten des Nihilismus.* Ed. by Jörg Salaquarda. Berlin: Walter de Gruyter und Co., 1971. Pp. 176–181.

"Live Parables," *Master Sermon Series,* I, 6 (1970), 329–335.

"Luthers Lehre von den zwei Reichen und ihre Stellung in der Geschichte der christlichen Reichsidee," *Gottesreich und Menschenreich.* Regensburg: Verlag Friedrich Pustet, 1971. Pp. 73–96.

"Der Mensch—ein Ebenbild Gottes?" *Was ist das—der Mensch? Beitrag zu einer modernen Anthropologie.* Munich: R. Piper und Co. Verlag, 1968. Pp. 27–41.

"Möglichkeiten und Grenzen der Anwendung des Analogieprinzips in der evangelischen Theologie, *Theologische Literaturzeitung,* LXXXV (1960), 225–228.

"Mythus und Wort: Theologische Überlegungen zu Karl Jaspers Mythusbegriffe," *Zeitschrift für Theologie und Kirche,* LI (1954), 167–185.

"Nachwort," *Geschichte, Offenbarung, Glaube,* by Ignace Berten. Tr. by Sigrid Martin. Munich: Claudius Verlag, 1970. Pp. 129–141. A translation of "Postface," *Historie, Révélation et Foi: Dialogue avec Wolfhart Pannenberg.* Brussels: Les Éditions du CEP, 1969. Pp. 105–115.

"Nachwort zur zweiten Auflage," *Offenbarung als Geschichte.* Beiheft 1 zu *Kerygma und Dogma.* (Zweite Auflage, 1963.) Göttingen: Vandenhoeck & Ruprecht, 1961. Pp. 132–148.

"Nation und Menschheit," *Monatsschrift für Pastoraltheologie*, LIV (1965), 333–347. Cf. "Reich Gottes und Nationalismus: Vom politischen Sinn der christlichen Hoffnung," *Kontexte*, Band 1. Ed. by H. J. Schultz. Stuttgart: Kreuz-Verlag, 1965. Pp. 41–48.

"Natürliche Theologie II. Im evangelischen Verständnis," *Lexikon für Theologie und Kirche*, VII, 816–817. Zweite Auflage. Ed. by Josef Höfer and Karl Rahner. Freiburg: Verlag Herder, 1962.

"Neue Wege katholischer Christologie," *Theologische Literaturzeitung*, LXXXII (1957), 95–100.

"Nikolaus von Kues," *Deutsches Pfarrerblatt*, LXIV (1964), 577–579.

"Die Offenbarung Gottes und die Geschichte der Neuzeit," *Das unveränderte Evangelium in einer veränderlichen Welt*. 4. Deutscher Evangelischer Akademikertag, 4.–7. Oktober 1962 in Marburg/Lahn. *Der Kreis*, Sonderreihe, No. 3. Stuttgart–Bad Cannstatt: Radius-Verlag, 1962. Pp. 7–21.

"On Historical and Theological Hermeneutic," *Basic Questions in Theology*, Vol. I. Tr. by George H. Kehm. Fortress Press, 1970. Pp. 137–181. A translation of "Über historische und theologische Hermeneutik," *Grundfragen systematischer Theologie*. Göttingen: Vandenhoeck & Ruprecht, 1967. Pp. 123–158.

"Ontologie," *Evangelisches Kirchenlexikon*, II, 1689–1691. Ed. by Heinz Brunotte and Otto Weber. Göttingen: Vandenhoeck & Ruprecht, 1958.

"Person," *Die Religion in Geschichte und Gegenwart*, V, 230–235. Dritte Auflage. Ed. by Kurt Galling et al. Tübingen: J. C. B. Mohr (Paul Siebeck), 1961.

"Die politische Dimension des Evangeliums," *Die Politik und das Heil*. Ed. by Reinfried Hörl. Mainz: Matthias-Grünewald-Verlag, 1968. Pp. 16–20.

"Prädestination IV. Dogmatisch," *Die Religion in Geschichte und Gegenwart*, V, 487–489. Dritte Auflage. Ed. by Kurt Galling et al. Tübingen: J. C. B. Mohr (Paul Siebeck), 1961.

Die Prädestinationslehre des Duns Skotus. "Forschungen zur Kirchen- und Dogmengeschichte," Band 4. Göttingen: Vandenhoeck & Ruprecht, 1954.

"The Question of God," *Basic Questions in Theology*, Vol. II. Tr. by George H. Kehm. Fortress Press, 1971. Pp. 201–233. A translation of "Die Frage nach Gott," *Evangelische Theologie*, XXV (1965), 238–262.

"Redemptive Event and History," *Basic Questions in Theology*, Vol.

I. Tr. by Shirley Guthrie and George H. Kehm. Fortress Press, 1970. Pp. 15–80. A slightly abbreviated translation of "Heilsgeschehen und Geschichte," *Kerygma und Dogma*, V (1959), 218–237 and 259–288.

Reformation zwischen gestern und morgen. Gütersloh: Gütersloher Verlagshaus Gerd Mohn, 1969.

"Response to Dr. J. N. D. Anderson," *Christianity Today*, XII (1968), 681–683.

"Response to the Discussion," *Theology as History*. Ed. by James M. Robinson and John B. Cobb, Jr. Vol. III of New Frontiers in Theology. Harper & Row, Publishers, Inc., 1967. Pp. 221–276.

"The Revelation of God in Jesus of Nazareth," *Theology as History*. Ed. by James M. Robinson and John B. Cobb, Jr. Vol. III of New Frontiers in Theology. Harper & Row, Publishers, Inc., 1967. Pp. 101–133.

"Review: Leff, Gordon, *Bradwardine and the Pelagians*," *Zeitschrift für Kirchengeschichte*, LXIX (1958), 355–361.

"Review: Lyttkens, Hampus, *The Analogy Between God and the World*," *Verkündigung und Forschung*, II (1956/1957), 136–142.

"Schriftautorität und Lehrautorität," *Autorität als Gegenstand und Element wissenschaftlichen Denkens*. Ed. by Erhard Denninger and Günter Eifler. Mainzer Universitätsgespräche. Sommersemester, 1962. Pp. 5–10.

"Speaking About God in the Face of Atheist Criticism," *The Idea of God and Human Freedom*. Tr. by R. A. Wilson. The Westminster Press, 1973. Pp. 99–115. A translation of "Reden von Gott angesichts atheistischer Kritik," *Evangelische Kommentare*, II (1969), 442–446.

"A Theological Conversation with Wolfhart Pannenberg," *Dialog*, XI (1972), 286–295.

"Theologische Motive im Denken Immanuel Kants," *Theologische Literaturzeitung*, LXXXIX (1964), 897–906.

"Theology and the Kingdom of God," *Theology and the Kingdom of God*. The Westminster Press, 1969. A reprint from *Una Sancta*, Vol. XXIV, No. 2 (1967), pp. 3–19.

Theology and the Kingdom of God. Ed. by Richard John Neuhaus. The Westminster Press, 1969.

Thesen zur Theologie der Kirche. Munich: Claudius Verlag, 1970.

"Thomas von Aquino," *Die Religion in Geschichte und Gegenwart*, VI, 856–863. Dritte Auflage. Ed. by Kurt Galling *et al.* Tübingen: J. C. B. Mohr (Paul Siebeck), 1962.

"Toward a Theology of the History of Religions," *Basic Questions in*

Theology, Vol. II. Tr. by George H. Kehm. Fortress Press, 1971. Pp. 65–118. A translation of "Erwägungen zu einer Theologie der Religionsgeschichte," *Grundfragen systematischer Theologie.* Göttingen: Vandenhoeck & Ruprecht, 1967. Pp. 252–295.

"Types of Atheism and Their Theological Significance," *Basic Questions in Theology,* Vol. II. Tr. by George H. Kehm. Fortress Press, 1970. Pp. 184–200. A translation of "Typen des Atheismus and ihre theologische Bedeutung," *Zeitwende,* XXXIV (1963), 597–608.

"Unser Leben, Unsere Geschichte—In Gottes Hand?" *Dialog mit dem Zweifel.* Ed. by Gerhard Rein. Stuttgart: Kreuz-Verlag, 1969. Pp. 78–83.

"Was ist der Mensch?" *Disputation zwischen Christen und Marxisten.* Ed. by Martin Stöhr. Munich: Chr. Kaiser Verlag, 1966. Pp. 179–194.

"Weltgeschichte und Heilsgeschichte," *Probleme biblischer Theologie: Festschrift für Gerhard von Rad.* Ed. by Hans Walter Wolff. Munich: Chr. Kaiser Verlag, 1971. Pp. 349–366.

"What Is a Dogmatic Statement?" *Basic Questions in Theology,* Vol. I. Tr. by George H. Kehm. Fortress Press, 1970. Pp. 182–210. A translation of "Was ist eine dogmatische Aussage?" *Kerygma und Dogma,* VIII (1962), 81–99.

What Is Man? Contemporary Anthropology in Theological Perspective. Tr. by Duane A. Priebe. Fortress Press, 1970. A translation of *Was ist der Mensch? Die Anthropologie der Gegenwart im Lichte der Theologie.* Göttingen: Vandenhoeck & Ruprecht, 1962.

"What Is Truth?" *Basic Questions in Theology,* Vol. II. Tr. by George H. Kehm. Fortress Press, 1971. Pp. 1–27. A translation of "Was ist Wahrheit?" *Vom Herrengeheimnis der Wahrheit: Festschrift für Heinrich Vogel.* Ed. by Kurt Scharf. Berlin: Lettner-Verlag, 1922. Pp. 214–239.

"Wie kann heute glaubwürdig von Gott geredet werden?" *Gottesfrage heute.* Vorträge und Bibelarbeit in der Arbeitsgruppe "Gottesfrage" des 14. Deutschen Evangelischen Kirchentages Stuttgart 1969. Stuttgart: Kreuz-Verlag, 1969. Pp. 51–64.

"Wie wahr ist das Reden von Gott?" *Evangelische Kommentare,* IV (1971), 629–633.

"Wie wird Gott uns offenbar?" *Radius,* 1960, No. 4, pp. 3–10.

"Wird Gott uns so offenbar? Diskussion," *Radius,* 1961, No. 1, pp. 47–49.

"Wirkungen biblischer Gotteserkenntnis auf das abendländische Menschenbild," *Studium Generale,* XV (1962), 586–593.

"The Working of the Spirit in Creation and in the People of God," *Spirit, Faith, and Church.* The Westminster Press, 1970. Pp. 13–31.

"Wort," *Theologie für Nichttheologen.* Ed. by Hans Jürgen Schultz. Stuttgart: Kreuz-Verlag, 1965.

"Zur Bedeutung des Analogiegedankens bei Karl Barth: Eine Auseinandersetzung mit Urs von Balthasar," *Theologische Literaturzeitung,* LXXVIII (1953), 17–24.

"Zur Theologie des Rechts," *Zeitschrift für evangelische Ethik,* VII (1963), 1–23.

"Zur theologischen Auseinandersetzung mit Karl Jaspers," *Theologische Literaturzeitung,* LXXXIII (1958), 321–330.

Pannenberg, Wolfhart, and Sauter, Gerhard, "Im Fegefeuer der Methode: Wolfhart Pannenberg und Gerhard Sauter im Gespräch über Theologie als Wissenschaft," *Evangelische Kommentare,* VI (1973), 4–10.

────── and Joest, Wilfried (eds.), *Dogma und Denkstrukturen: Festschrift für Edmund Schlink.* Göttingen: Vandenhoeck & Ruprecht, 1963.

────── and Müller, A. M. Klaus, *Erwägungen zu einer Theologie der Natur.* Gütersloh: Gütersloher Verlagshaus Gerd Mohn. 1970.

────── et al., *Evangelisch-katholische Abendmahlsgemeinschaft?* Göttingen: Vandenhoeck & Ruprecht, 1973.

────── et al., *Offenbarung als Geschichte.* Beiheft 1 zu *Kerygma und Dogma.* (Dritte Auflage, 1965.) Göttingen: Vandenhoeck & Ruprecht, 1961.

────── et al., *Revelation as History.* Tr. by David Granskou. The Macmillan Company, 1968. A translation of *Offenbarung als Geschichte.* Beiheft 1 zu *Kerygma und Dogma.* Göttingen: Vandenhoeck & Ruprecht, 1961.

────── et al., *Spirit, Faith, and Church.* The Westminster Press, 1970.

INDEXES

INDEX OF NAMES

317

INDEX OF SUBJECTS